ISBN:9781795269872

ACKNOWLEGEMENTS

Larousse Gastronomique, Woman's Day Encyclopedia of American Cookery 1974, Reader's Digest, Della Taylor Johnson Jenkins, (Maternal Grandmother) Mary Jones Taylor (Maternal Great-Grandmother)

A lot of talk goes around now and then to the effect that American cooks are way behind cooks of other lands when it comes to producing a first rate meal, and that American food in general lacks the elegant subtlety of foreign dishes. I don't know who started this nonsense, but nonsense it is, and it should be labeled so in large black letters. Actually, there is a great tradition in American cooking, and thousands of women have come to respect and perpetuate it.

To be sure, American cooking has had its ups and downs - but they were mostly ups.

More and more cookbooks were - and are - printed and, what is better, were sold and used; schools and colleges added classes in cooking and domestic economy; metropolitan dailies saw the trend and promoted it by publishing market news, recipes, specialized household information; radio supplemented the press; and television the internet has entered the field in a big way.

Larousse Gastronomique, first published in 1938, is an encyclopedia of gastronomy. The majority of the book is about French cuisine, and contains recipes for French dishes and cooking techniques; Escoffier's "The Complete Guide to the Art of Modern Cooking" is used along with Larousse's Gastronomique by most culinary institutes and professional chefs.

Whether you are a beginner or a seasoned home cook, I hope that you will find this book that uses basic text, techniques, and useful tips helpful.

CARE OF FOOD IN THE HOME

Carelessness in caring for and storing foods after they are brought into the home may result in various forms of deterioration and spoilage such as withering, discoloration, molding and decay. This brings about marked loss of natural flavor, attractive appearance, and vitamin content, and sometimes the complete loss of the food itself.

In the majority of cases, only enough of the perishable foods should be brought into the home for one or two days' supply and they should be stored carefully until used. The kind of storage space a family needs for foods depends on the source of supply. A farm family with a garden planted to provide a succession of fresh vegetables all summer, and which has a large, unheated storage cellar for winter vegetables, can get along with a medium size refrigerator for daily produces and the most perishable foods. The suburban homemaker has a different problem in obtaining and caring for foods. Her grocer buys fresh vegetables and fruits daily, and if they have adequate refrigeration facilities for storing them to preserve their freshness, it is to your advantage to purchase these foods shortly before you need them, so as not to burden your refrigerator with them. If you live in a house rather than an apartment, it may be possible and practical for you, too, to have an unheated storage space as well as an efficient refrigerator. But you are more likely to be entirely dependent on your refrigerator for food storage than is the farm homemaker. Many foods keep best in the refrigerator, as the low temperature slows down the action of organisms and enzymes which cause spoilage. Some food do not require refrigeration but need a cool dry place; others require a cool moist place, still others keep well at room temperature. Usually it is advisable to clean the foods before storing and to remove soft or damaged specimens; but sometimes washing is not recommended, as for berries or grapes, until just before serving.

FRESH VEGETABLES

Salad greens. Salad greens include not only lettuce, endive, watercress, escarole, romaine, cabbage, parsley and mint, but also any green or leafy vegetable such as spinach, celery and green onions which may be eaten raw as well as cooked. When any of these leafy vegetables are brought into the kitchen they should be trimmed immediately to remove bruised or soiled leaves. IF they are in tight heads, like cabbage, head lettuce, celery or French endive, washing is not necessary, but store in than enamel or glass container of a size and shape to hold them and a variety of other fresh foods without crushing.

Plastic bag or other waterproof material is a good container for bulky fruits or vegetables to be placed in; the ends should be folded together tightly to exclude air. Lacking a hydrator or plastic bag, the trimmed vegetables may be wrapped in cheesecloth wrung out in cold water and then in wax paper. Just before serving, the whole heads may be washed in cold water, and any discoloration of the stem end may be cut off.

Greens which grow in loose heads, like leaf lettuce and curly endive, should be washed carefully to remove any sand or dirt, drained well and the excess water removed by shaking them loosely in a towel. Then the head should be put way just like tight heads greens. Parsley, although it does not grow in heads, should be treated in the same way. *Spinach* requires special care in washing; the roots should be trimmed off and each leaf washed separately to avoid any grittiness in the cooked or raw vegetable. *Watercress* – is best to use the day purchased; however, to keep it a few hours; untie the string and swish cress gently through cold water, then shake off excess. Now stand watercress up in bowl or wide-mouth jar that has several folds of wet paper towels in the bottom. Cover watercress with a piece of wet paper towel or the jar lid and place in refrigerator. Light and air wilt and yellow the leaves. *Mint* keeps several days if, after it is washed and the excess water shaken off, it is place in a tall screw-top glass jar, tightly covered and stored in the refrigerator. *Green onions* may be kept in the same way as mint, but not longer than a few hours. *Chives*, which are usually purchased growing in little pots may be kept in a cool corner of the kitchen or in a window. They should never be watered from the top, as this causes the spears to turn yellow. To water them, set the pot in a shallow dish of cold water for a few minutes each morning.

Greens should never be allowed to freeze, for freezing make the leaves limp and watery. When trimming head lettuce, save 2 or 3 good outer leaves – do not wash; wrap them snugly around whole or cut head to impede "pink color."

Cucumber and radishes, though not belonging to the family of greens, are favorite salad materials. Cucumbers should be washed, dried, and placed in the refrigerator, and should not be peeled, if peeling is desired, until time of use. Any portion of the cucumber which is not required for that meal should be cut off and not peeled; a piece of wax paper may be fastened over the cut end with a rubber band. Radishes should be washed an most all leaves removed before placing in the refrigerator. The outer fresh leaves of radishes may be added to spinach to give a delicious new flavor; the heart leaves may be left attached to radishes when they are served, for they are attractive in appearance and have an appealing peppery flavor. Just before serving, cut off the tap root and elaborate, if desired, by cutting into petals. Left over radish roses have no food value and the flavor rapidly deteriorates because of the many cuts in their surface.

Other green vegetables. All green vegetables should be cooked the same day they are bought, if possible, to avoid vitamin loss. Green beans should not be washed before storing in the refrigerator, but should be washed, trimmed and broken just before cooking time. Peas should be left in their pods if they must be stored for a few hours; if the pods are very soiled they may be washed and dried before putting them in the refrigerator. After shelling, peas quickly lose freshness and vitamin content, so they should be shelled just before cooking time. Each spear of asparagus should be swished gently through cold water and all the scales along the stalk removed if any sand seems to be cause under them. If the spears are not crisp, the ends may be placed in cold water for a few minutes after trimming with a sharp knife; then they may be drained and placed in the refrigerator. To be at its best, asparagus should be kept more than a few hours after gathering or purchasing.

Root vegetables such a potatoes, carrots, turnips, parsnips and beets, require only to be kept in a cool place where the air is not too dry. In cold weather storing them is not a problem but in hot weather refrigeration is desirable for carrots and beats, so it is wise to buy them in small quantities, unless you have a cellar or a large refrigerator. When cool storage space is available outside the refrigerator, root vegetables should not be washed until just before paring; and they should never be pared until just before cooking time. When carrots and beets are stored in the refrigerator, carrot tops should be cut off close to the shoulder, and beet tops about 2½-inches from the beet. Young, tender beet tops may be washed, stored and cooked like spinach. Carrots may be washed but not scraped before storing; beets should be washed carefully, to avoid breaking the skin or tap root.

FRUITS

Apples are considered to be semi-perishable fruit. Due to their waxy, air-tight covering, they keep well out of the refrigerator in a cool not too dry place, so long as skins are not bruised or broken. In winter, both cooking and eating apples will keep for weeks in a cool place, and even in warm weather cooking apples may be kept in such a place for a week or more. They should never be allowed to freeze. Eating apples keep in the best condition in the refrigerator if the weather is warm, and most people prefer them chilled. They may be washed and dried, and placed in a hydrator.

Bananas should never be kept in the refrigerator as the cold darkens them. If several days' supply of bananas is purchased at one time, a good plan is to buy fully ripe ones to be eaten immediately, yellow-ripe ones for the next day or two, and green-tipped ones to be kept the longest. They ripen quite rapidly in a warm room; ripening may be slowed down by keeping them in a cooler place, but not in the refrigerator.

Berries of all kinds are quite perishable. One or two soft or moldy berries in a basket will spoil others, so it is always best to turn them out of the basket and pick them over as soon as they are brought home. Discard all soft ones and put the rest, without washing, into a clean bowl; cover and place in the refrigerator. They should not be washed until just before serving. **Raspberries and blackberries** need no other preparation for serving then looking over for hull and damaged fruit, than washing and draining. **Strawberries and dewberries** may be sandy, so before hulling, they should be washed as follows: *Place the berries in a large bowl and run cold water gently over them; swish them gently through the water and lift them out with outspread fingers to drain in a colander.* Badly soiled berries may need several washings, but this should not be done until just before serving time. If the berries have blemishes, these should be cut out when the berries are hulled. Some people prefer strawberries left whole, sprinkled with sugar, and served almost immediately; some like them sugared and left to stand until the juice begins to be drawn out; other want their berries sliced for crushed with sugar, to make them very juicy. Berries have a more intense flavor at room temperature, but some prefer them chilled. Their flavor deteriorates if they are allowed to stand more than half an hour after preparing.

Grapes should be picked over to discard any damaged ones, and then stored in the refrigerator without washing, in a covered bowl or hydrator. When ready to serve, wash by holding the bunch under the cold water faucet, and shake dry in a clean dry towel. Most people like them chilled in warm weather or warmed to room temperature when the day is cold.

Melons, if fully ripe, should be kept in the refrigerator, but if they seem hard, they will ripen slowly outside the refrigerator. Since they absorb both flavors and odors from other food and given off their own odor, it is desirable to keep them in a plastic bag if possible. After cutting, a piece of wax paper may be spread over the cut surface before returning the melon to the bag. For the best flavor and appearance, a melon should be cut just before serving, and most people like melon cold.

Peaches should never be washed or rubbed before storing, as the removal of the bloom or fuzz hastens spoiling. Perfectly sound peaches may be kept in the refrigerator for a day or two, but if they show any fresh bruises, they should be consumed the same day. Wash, pare and slice them just before serving; or if they are to be sugared, let them stand half an hour with the sugar on them after slicing, either in or our of the refrigerator, depending on the temperature preferred. Peaches are very perishable and need special care to avoid waste. **Apricots, nectarines and plums** require similar care, but are less perishable.

Oranges, grapefruit, lemons and limes may be kept either in or out of the refrigerator. It is preferable not to cut or squeeze them until just before they are to be served, because the "edge" of their fine flavor as well as some vitamin content may be lost when the juice or cut fruit stands a few hours.

Dried fruits have such low moisture content that they keep well at room temperature. If the room is fairly cool and dry so much the better. If not packaged, they should be wrapped tightly in wax paper or moisture-proof cellophane to preserve the moisture they have.

Canned fruits. Commercially canned fruits will keep for months in any cool dry place. The same applies to home-canned fruit put up in tin, but home-canned foods in glass require slightly different storage conditions. They should be stored in a place that is not only cool, but dark and slightly damp. If the air is too dry, the rubber rings may dry out and crack, permitting organisms to enter. Light bleaches the color of the food. Therefore, glass jars or canned food which must be stored in a light place either should be wrapped in tan colored heavy wrapping paper or should be shielded from the light by hanging a tan or cream-colored window shade over the front of the storage shelves.

MEAT

Fresh Meat. All fresh meat should be refrigerated, and since under average home refrigeration it loses its fine flavor if kept too long, it is never wise to buy more meat than is needed for two or three days, with the idea of keeping it in the uncooked state. Meat should go into the coldest spot in the refrigerator, under the freezing compartment. It is not harmed by freezing. Meats bought in the frozen state, such as chops and steaks, should be kept frozen until ready to use. It is best not to refreeze after thawing.

The small the proportion of cut surfaces exposed on a piece of meat, the better it keeps. Thus meat in one large piece, like a standing rib roast, will keep in good condition in the refrigerator for a longer time than meat cut in small pieces for stewing. *Ground meat*, which has a very high proportion of cut surface, loses flavor and juiciness rapidly, and should be used as soon as possible after purchasing.

As soon as fresh meat is brought into the home, it should be unwrapped and wiped off with a damp cloth-never washed in water. Then it may be placed on a clean dry plate or shallow refrigerator dish, and covered lightly or not at all; a piece of wax paper laid over the meat is sufficient, or a loosely fitting refrigerator-dish cover may be used. Meat should never be closely covered or tightly wrapped in wax paper, because a little drying of the surface retards bacterial growth and is therefore to be desired. If the meat is left wrapped in the butcher's original paper, cold penetration is slowed up and the paper will absorb some of the meat juices.

Cured meats. Old-fashioned country style ham and similar products (smoked picnics and smoked butts) may be kept out of the refrigerator in any dark, cold place, except in hot weather, when refrigeration is desirable. But most all hams have a mild cure and require about the same care as fresh meat before cooking, especially after they have been cut. *Sliced bacon* should be left in its original wrapping, or wrapped in clean wax paper and kept in the refrigerator in the coldest place. Only the amount to be used for the meal should be removed from the refrigerator. If the whole package is taken out and allowed to warm up, moisture will condense on the bacon and lessen its keeping qualities. It is not advisable to keep bacon, even in the refrigerator, longer than a week or two, as the fat tends to become hard and easily broken, and both appearance and flavor deteriorate. Corned beef should be treated just like fresh meat. **Sliced cold cuts** such as salami and bologna, should be stacked compactly, wrapped in wax paper and kept in the coldest part of the refrigerator.

Cooked meat. After cooking, any kind of meat should be made into the most compact parcel possible, and wrapped tightly or placed in a dish with a tight-fitting cover. Because the surface has already been dried out by cooking, no further drying is desirable, and there may be not only loss of flavor but absorption of other flavors if the meat is left uncovered in the refrigerator.

POULTRY

Like fresh meat, poultry should go immediately into the coldest available space in the refrigerator. Before storing, it should be drawn, cleaned, washed and thoroughly drained, then covered lightly with wax paper. If the bird is to be stuffed for roasting, do this the day it is to be cooked. In recent years experiment work has proven that it is unsafe to stuff the bird the day before it is cooked, even though the stuffed, trussed bird is kept in the refrigerator. If the bird is cut up for frying, stewing, or broiling, cover lightly with wax paper and store in refrigerator until cooking time.

DAIRY PRODUCTS AND EGGS

Fresh milk and cream should always be stored in the original containers, since the bottles or cartons are sterilized before being filled and the inside is therefore as clean as possible. If the outside of the container is soiled, it should be thoroughly washed with cold water, and dried, before placing in the refrigerator. Milk and cream belong in the coldest place in the refrigerator, and the manufacturer usually indicates where this place is by making it tall enough to accommodate bottles.

Evaporated and sweetened condensed milk should be kept in the can after opening, but the can should be well cleaned on the top and outside before it is opened, and any drip should be wiped off before the opened can is put away. Cover the opening with a hood of wax paper and fastened on with a rubber band. Condensed milk keeps almost indefinitely even when open if it is well cared for. Evaporated milk, however, should be used within a few days, for once opened it spoils almost as quickly as fresh milk.

Butter should have a special container with a close-fitting cover, because it absorbs food odors readily. Margarine should be given care similar to butter, but it is not so perishable.

Cheese, whether natural or packaged, requires refrigeration as soon as it is cut. Processed packaged cheeses are pasteurized and change very little, either in aroma or in texture when kept unopened without refrigeration for several months, but as soon as they are exposed to the air, organisms can enter and the cheese should thereafter be refrigerated.

All cut natural cheese, whether packaged or not, requires refrigeration because they are not pasteurized. Natural cheese such as Camembert, Brie, Roquefort and Liederkranz, which are cut and then packaged, are quite perishable and should be kept in the refrigerator even before opening, when kept cold, they hold their natural flavor well without giving off much aroma. The soft types, like Camembert and Brie, should be allowed to warm up to room temperature before serving, since this semi-liquid softens characteristic of such cheese when well ripened, and its flavor is best in this soft state. One way to keep cheese like the cheddar type is in the refrigerator. That old-time way of wrapping it in a cloth dipped in vinegar helps retard the development of mold which often appears in cheese, but it changes the appetizing aroma and flavor. A better way of retarding mold formation is to keep the cheese in a plastic bag.

Eggs should always be refrigerated, this not only prolongs their freshness, it also helps keep the yolk in the center of the egg. If eggs are to be separated they should be separated as soon as removed from the refrigerator as they separate more easily while cold. The yolks may be used at once or covered and returned to the refrigerator; but the whites should be allowed to warm up to room temperature before beating in order to get the greatest possible volume.

COOKED FOODS

Some cooked foods are much more perishable than others. It is not advisable to keep purchase foods containing custard more than a few hours, as the combination of eggs, milk and sugar is irresistible to bacteria; however, there is no danger from homemade custards, custard pies and cream puffs which are kept overnight in the refrigerator. Baked custards should be removed from the pan of hot water in which they are baked and placed on a rack to cool completely; then covered and kept in the refrigerator until they are served. Soft custards may be rapidly cooled by setting the top of the double boiler in a pan of cold water; when cool, pour the custard into a clean sterile jar, cover tightly with a screw-top lid and place in the refrigerator until serving time. Custard is best both in flavor and in texture if served the say day it is made.

White sauce may often be made conveniently ahead of time and stored until just before use. The sauce should be cooled thoroughly, stirring frequently as it cools to prevent skin from forming on top. Then it may be poured into a sterile glass jar and stored like soft custard. When ready to use, reheat it over boiling water, adding a little milk if needed to bring it to the desired consistency.

Gelatin desserts of the plain fruit variety keep better than those made with whipped cream or whipped evaporated milk; but it is best not to keep even these longer than a day or two. They should be kept constantly in the refrigerator, and if possible should be covered to prevent absorption of foreign odors and flavors, and frying out of the surface.

Leftover cooked foods should be placed in clean, covered containers and kept in the refrigerator. If small quantities of several vegetables or cooked or canned fruits are left, they may be combined in one container and used for soup or salad. Leftovers should always be used as soon as possible for the sake of flavor, appearance and nutritive value.

BAKED GOODS

Homemade *cake* keeps best if it is transferred from the baking pan to cake racks soon after removal from the oven, then frosted as soon as it is barely cooled. Frosting helps to keep cake fresh and moist. Of the various types of icings, a cooked fudge or panocha icing will keep in good condition longest; butter icing is next best; and seven-minute frosting is most perishable – it is at its best for only a few hours. Whether iced or not, the cake itself will keep in best condition if covered so as to be virtually air tight. Cake stands and covers do the job very satisfactorily. But it should be remembered that cake is at its very best when perfectly fresh, as soon as it has lost the oven heat. Bought cake should be kept the same way; if possible, it should be left or replaced in its original wrapper.

Cookies should be stored in a cookie jar or covered tin container. This helps to keep crisp cookies crisp and soft ones soft. Only one kind of cookie should be put into a cookie jar at one time, or there will be an interchange of flavors between different kinds which makes all of them taste nondescript. The cookie jar should be thoroughly cleaned, scalded and carefully dried between batches.

To have the best quality, *pie* should be made in a sufficient quantity for just one meal, for no pie can be stored with very satisfactory results. The crust becomes soaked on standing, and the filling, whether it is a fruit or custard type, becomes unattractive in appearance and loses the fine edge of its flavor. Mince, pumpkin and chiffon pies may if necessary be kept overnight; but they are at their best within a few hours after preparation. Of course they should be stored in the refrigerator and should be covered.

Bread keeps best if left in its original wrapping, or if wrapped snugly in wax paper. Then it should be stored either in a clean dry bread box or, if none is available, in a closed container in the refrigerator. Bread that is kept in the refrigerator shows less tendency to become moldy. If the bread is always kept wrapped, the bread box is much easier to care for than if the unwrapped loaf is placed in it; in the latter case, the box will require frequent washing with hot, soapy water, rinsing in scalding water and thoroughly dried to keep it sweet and fresh from mold spores.

MISCELLANEOUS FOODS

Coffee should preferably be kept in the home no longer than a week, so a family of five should not purchase more than a week's supply at a time. If the coffee is purchased in a paper bag, transfer it immediately to a clean dry glass or tin container. Cover it tightly, and never leave the cover off for a minute longer than necessary when measuring coffee into the coffee maker. The volatile substances which give coffee its pleasing flavor and aroma escape very quickly when exposed to air. Keep the tightly closed coffee container in the refrigerator, or other cool dark place. A good plan is to let stand upside down, so the rising aroma cannot escape through the crack around the lid but will be frapped in the upturned bottom of the container.

Syrups, such a molasses, honey, maple syrup and corn syrup, and also jellies, jams preserves and pickles, need no refrigeration so long as they are unopened, though they keep best in a cool, fairly dry place. After opening, the jars or bottles should be thoroughly cleaned on the outside to remove any sticky smears where bacterial growth might star, and the tops should be cover with a layer or two of strong wax paper, secured with a rubber band or a piece of string. If convenient, they should be stored in the refrigerator; but if the remainder is to be consumed within a few days, this is not necessary, provided a cool place is available outside the refrigerator. Honey should never be kept cold unless you particularly like the very thick; if refrigerated over a long period, it is liable to crystallize. Crystallized honey can be restored to its liquid state by setting the jar in a pan of hot water for a few minutes to melt.

Mayonnaise and various types of cooked salad dressing (either purchased or homemade), should be stored in the refrigerator, but not in the coldest spot. Keep them tightly covered and the outside container clean. Homemade dressings should be take out before using and allowed to warm up enough so that it can be mixed well by shaking before adding to the salad.

Shortening and oils. Hydrogenated shortenings, especially those made from vegetable oils, are very stable and need no refrigeration to keep them in good condition. These shortenings should be kept tightly covered, for if exposed to the air they will collect dust and will eventually contract and crack on the surface, they may not become rancid. If their storage place is so hot that they melt at any time, their texture will be changed. After these shortenings have once been melted and used for deep fat frying, they should be carefully strained into the original container, cared for in the same way as before using, and not used for any other purpose than frying.

Lard should be stored in the refrigerator, if possible. It is softer than the hydrogenated vegetable fats, and is relatively easy to handle even when chilled.

Cooking and salad oils (olive, cottonseed and corn oils) may be kept in the refrigerator to prevent rancidity, though if they are used within a few weeks, there is little danger of their becoming rancid in any cool place.

Spices and extracts should always be kept tightly covered, in a cool dark, dry place. Both light and heat affect the volatile substances which give them flavor and aroma, and some manufacturers are now putting out their flavoring extracts in dark bottles to exclude a maximum of light. It is not advisable to buy spices in large quantities, because even under the best storage conditions they lose their potency in time. They should be replaced every six months if possible.

Nuts contain a rather high percentage of oil, and if stored in a warm place they soon become rancid and discolored. Shelled nuts should be place in a clean dry glass jar, covered tightly, and stored in the refrigerator. Nuts in the shell may be kept in any cool, dry place. Neither should be expected to keep indefinitely.

Dry breadcrumbs are a great convenience to have on hand. They can readily be made from any stale mold-free bread by drying it out thoroughly in a very slow oven and then rolling it into fine crumbs with a rolling pin or putting it through a food mill or rubbing it over a coarse grater to obtain crumbs. When rolling the bread, crumbs will be prevented from flying if the dry bread is placed in plastic bag and rolled. Put the crumbs immediately into a clean dry glass jar and cover with a screw-top lid in which several holes have been punched, or with 2 or 3 thickness of cheesecloth tied on with string or fastened securely with a rubber band. Keep in a cool dry place. Crumbs should not be stored in an air-tight container, or they will become sale and musty in flavor. Stored as directed they will keep several weeks without deteriorating.

FREEZING FOODS

Freeze only the best in the best way

Freezing is a quick and easy method of preserving food because it retains much of the fresh flavor and texture of the fresh product. Remember, though, that freezing will not improve an under-ripe berry, over-ripe fruit or a poor pie or cake. Correct freezing methods require a considerable amount of money, time and labor, so it is poor economy to use anything but the best quality fresh foods. Besides, you will not want to give freezer space to sub-standard products.

Having chosen top-quality foods for freezing make sure you plan, pack and freeze so as to preserve all their quality. It is impossible to tell you all about freezing; I can only hit the high spots.

Wise planning is essential to get maximum value from your freezer. On the basis of your family's size and its tastes, the number of guest meals you are likely to serve, and the size of your freezer, decide what foods and how much of each you want to preserve for weeks or immediate needs. Freeze foods when seasonal supplies are high and prices low.

Package Foods Carefully

Choose the right type of container or wrap for the food you are freezing, on the basis of specific directions. The idea is always to eliminate as much air as possible, since air causes frozen food to deteriorate. Fill containers compactly, allowing only enough head space for expansion. Wrap meats or irregularly shaped foods snugly; tap cartons of dry foods such as peas and limas sharply against the table to settle them completely; dry-packed foods will expand into space between pieces, so ¾-inch of head space is enough. Pureed fruits and fruits in syrup need about ¼-inch of head space for a pint size carton, ½-inch for a quart.

Some head space is important lest expansion in freezing cracks the wax on the carton and breaks the seal. A tight seal is necessary too, to avoid loss of moisture and entrance of air.

If possible, pack all foods cold Foods deteriorate less if chilled before packing, and freeze more quickly. The more quickly food chills in the freezer to a safe 20°F, the less the loss of quality.

Select containers according to family needs. A pint cart of fruit or vegetables serves 3; quarts are better for larger families or for guest meals. Pack chops, steaks and roasts in meal-sized amounts (for 2 or 3 a family, or guest meals, etc.). Separate pieces of meat, fish, etc. with double thickness of freezer plastic wrap so they can be easily separated before thawing. Ground meat can be tamped into layers right in the carton, separating layers with wax paper.

Label Packages Plainly

So as to be able to find quickly the food you want, and to judge the success of method of preparation used, mark or tag each package with this information:

1. Kind of fruit, vegetable or meat, with weight, number of pieces or servings;
2. Date of freezing, to avoid holding too long;
3. Quality and variety of food (to judge which varieties freeze most successfully);
4. Method of preparation;

As to gain experience, you may need only the first two items.

Arrange Properly in Freezer

In a chest-type freezer, store in heavy, bulky packages on the bottom so as not to shift them each time smaller packages are removed. Place newly packaged food on bottom and along walls for fast freezing; shift longest-frozen ones toward top. Keep labeled sides up. Baskets at top should hold often-used foods.

In an upright freezer, ground foods of a kind together; meat on one shelf, vegetables on another, etc. Put frequently used foods in the door or on the most convenient shelf, with labels facing out. Little packages that might "get lost" can be collected in a freezer or mesh bag.

SAFE STORAGE TIMES

Frozen Food		Storage Time
Meats		
Ground meats		3 to 4 months
Fresh beef, lamb, pork, veal	(steaks)	6 to 12 months
	(chops)	4 to 6 months
	(roasts)	4 to 12 months
Meat Leftovers		2 to 3 months
Poultry		
Whole chicken, turkey		1 year
Raw pieces		9 months
Leftover pieces, plain		4 months
Fish		6 months
Shellfish		3 months

Fresh Food	Storage Time (40°F)
Meats	
Uncooked beef, lamb, pork, veal	3 to 5 days
Ground meat	1 to 2 days
Bacon	1 week
Raw Sausage	1 to 2 days
Smoked Sausage	1 week
Leftover meat dishes	2 to 4 days
Leftover gravy, broth	1 to 2 days
Hot dogs, opened	1 week
Hot dogs, unopened	2 weeks
Ham slices, pre-cooked	2 to 5 days
Ham, whole, fully cooked	2 weeks
Poultry	
Chicken or turkey, uncooked	1 to 2 days
Leftover poultry dishes, or plain pieces	3 to 5 days
Leftover poultry in gravy, broth	1 to 2 days
Fish and Shellfish	
Fresh	1 to 2 days
Leftovers	3 to 4 days

MEAT COOKING CHART for ROASTING

Roasting	Weight	Minutes per Pound	Oven Temperature	Internal Temperature
FRESH PORK				
Ribs and Loin	3 to 7 pounds	30 to 40	325°F	175°F
Leg	5 pounds	25 to 30	325°F	170°F
Picnic Shoulder	5 to 10 pounds	40	325°F	175°F
Shoulder, butt	3 to 10 pounds	40 to 50	325°F	170°F
Boned and Rolled				
Shoulder	3 to 6 pounds	60	325°F	170°F
BEEF				
Standing ribs - rare	3 to 7 pounds	25	325°F	135°F
-medium	3 to 7 pounds	30	325°F	165°F
-well done	3 to 7 pounds	35	325°F	170°F
For rolled and boned roasts, increase cooking time 5 to 12 minutes.				
LAMB				
Shoulder - well done	4 to 10 pounds	40	325°F	190°F
Shoulder-boned and rolled	3 to 6 pounds	40	325°F	182°F
Leg-medium	5 to 10 pounds	40	325°F	175°F
-well done	3 to 6 pounds	40 to 50	325°F	182°F
Crown-well done	3 to 6 pounds	40 to 50	325°F	182°F
VEAL				
Loin	4 to 6 pounds	35	325°F	175°F
Leg	5 to 10 pounds	35	325°F	175°F
Boneless Shoulder	4 to 10 pounds	45	325°F	175°F
POULTRY				
Chicken	3 to 5 pounds	40	325°F	170°F
Stuffed	Over 5 pounds	30	325°F	170°F
Turkey	8 to 10 pounds	20	325°F	175°F
	18 to 20 pounds	14	325°F	175°F
Duck	5 to 10 pounds	30	325°F	175°F
SMOKED PORK				
Shoulder and picnic hams	5 pounds	30 to 40	325°F	170°F
	8 pounds	30 to 40	325°F	175°F
Boneless butt	2 pounds	40	325°F	180°F
	4 pounds	25	325°F	170°F
Ham	12 to 20 pounds	16 to18	325°F	170°F
	Under 10	20	325°F	175°F
	pounds	25	325°F	170°F
	Half hams			

MEAT COOKING CHART for BRAISING

Braising	Weight or Thickness	Minutes per Pound
FRESH PORK		
Chops	¾ to 1½ inches	45 to 60 minutes
Spareribs	2 to 3 pounds	1½ hrs.
Tenderloin		
Whole	¾ to 1 pound	45 to 60 minutes
Fillets	½ inch	30 minutes
Shoulder Steak	¾ inch	45 to 60 minutes
BEEF		
Pot Roast	3 to 5 pounds	3 to 4 hours
Swiss Steak	1½ to 2½ inch	2 to 3 hours
Beef Ribs	½ inch	1½ to 2½ hours
Short Ribs	½ inch	1½ to 2½ hours
Round Steak	¾ inch	45 to 60 minutes
Stuffed Steak	½ to ¾ inch	1½ hours
LAMB		
Breast – stuffed	2 to 3 pounds	1½ to 2 hours
Breast – rolled	1½ to 2 pounds	1½ to 2 hours
Neck Slices	¾ inch	1 hour
Shanks	½ pound, each	1 to 1½ hours
VEAL		
Breast - stuffed	3 to 4 pounds	1½ to 2 hours
Breast - rolled	2 to 3 pounds	1½ to 2 hours
Chops	½ to ¾ inch	45 to 60 minutes
Chops – breaded	½ to ¾ inch	45 to 60 minutes
Steaks or cutlets	½ to ¾ inch	45 to 60 minutes
Shoulder chops	½ to ¾ inch	45 to 60 minutes

PREPPING AND COOKING FRESH VEGETABLES

Vegetable	Preparation	Cooking Technique	Time
Artichoke (French, Globe)	Cut off 1-inch of the top with sharp knife. Trim stems leaving ½-inch stub. Remove outside lower leaves and thorny leaf tips. Tie leaves to keep its shape. After cooking, cut off stub	Boil in 1-inch salted water, add a few lemon slices. Then cover and cook until leaf pulls away easily.	30 to 45 min.
Artichoke, Jerusalem	Scrub with vegetable brush in cold water. Do not peel.	In saucepan over medium heat, in 1 inch salted water, cook until fork tender, peel	Boil: 20 to 25 min.
Asparagus	Wash; gently scrub with vegetable brush. Break the stalk; they will snap where tender part starts	Cook covered in small amount of boiling salted water Cut up Whole	 8 to 10 min. 10 to 15 min.
Beans, green or wax	Wash, remove ends and strings. Cut in 1-inch pieces, leave whole or split lengthwise.	Cook covered in small amount of boiling salted water.	20 to 30 min.
Navy Beans, dried	Rinse. Soak overnight in 3 times as much water as beans; or bring to boil; simmer several minutes and let stand 1 hour or more.	Cover and simmer in water used for soaking. Add salt.	1 hour, 30 min.
Beets	Cut off all but 1 inch of stems and root; wash and scrub thoroughly. Do not pare.	Cook covered in boiling salted water, peel once cooked.	35 to 60 mins
Broccoli	Remove tough part of stalks and outer leaves. Split rest of stalk almost to flowerets; or cut in 1-inch pieces; separate stalk from flowerets.	Tie stalks in bundles using folded strips of foil. Cover, cook standing up in boiling, salted water. Cook pieces covered in boiling salted water to cover .	15 to 20 min. 10 to 15 min.
Brussels Sprouts	Wash thoroughly; cut off wilted leaves. If large, cut in half lengthwise.	Cook covered in small amount of boiling salted water.	10 to 15 min.
Cabbage, green	Wash, remove wilted outer leaves. Cut in 6 to 8 wedges or shred.	Cook covered in small amount of boiling salted water.	10 to 12 min.
Carrots	Wash, scrape or pare. Slice, cut up in quarters or strips, or leave whole.	Cook covered in small amount of boiling salted water or in consommé.	20 to 25 minutes (Whole)
Cauliflower	Remove leaves and some of the woody stem. Leave whole or	Cook covered in small amount of boiling	20 to 25 min. (Whole)

	separate into flowerets.	salted water.	15 to 20 min. (Flowerets)
Celery	Scrub thoroughly. Cut off leaves and trim roots. Slice into desired lengths.	Cook covered in small amount of boiling salted water or in consommé.	10 to 15 min.
Corn	Remove husks and silks from fresh corn. Rinse and cook whole.	Cook covered in small amount of boiling salted water; or cook uncovered in enough boiling salted water to cover ears.	10 to 15 mins.
Eggplant	Wash. If skin is tough, pare. Cut in ½ inch slices.	Dip in beaten egg, then in fine dry breadcrumbs. Brown slowly on both sides in hot oil. Season.	Approx. 4 min.
Endive, French or Belgian	Rinse. Trim any bruised leaves.	Heat in ½ inch boiling, salted water; cover and cook.	15 min.
Greens (Mild Flavored) Chicory, Collards, Endive, Dandelion greens, Escarole, Lettuce, Romaine, Spinach, Watercress (Strong Flavored) Kale, Kohlrabi, Mustard greens, Swiss chard, Turnip Greens	Wash well in cold water. Save tender young leaves for salad. Remove imperfect leaves and root ends.	Cook mild flavored greens in just the water that clings to leaves. To preserve color, cook uncovered first 5 minutes. Cook strong flavored greens in water to cover. Leave cover off pot.	5 to 25 min.
Limas (Green)	Snap pods open; remove beans. Or cut thin strip from inner edge of pod with knife; push beans out.	In saucepan over medium heat, in 1 inch boiling salted water, heat beans to boiling, cover and cook until beans are tender.	20 to 30 min.
Mushrooms	Wipe of caps; cut off tips of stems. Leave whole or slice.	Add to melted butter in skillet; sprinkle with flour and mix. Cover and cook slowly, turning occasionally.	8 to 10 min.
Okra	Wash pods; cut off stems. Slice or leave whole	Cook covered in small amount of boiling salted water.	8 to 15 min.
Onions Small white, Yellow, Spanish, Bermuda,	Peel under running water (prevents tears); or chill onion. Leave whole, slice or quarter, depending on size.	Use as directed in recipes.	

Leeks	Cut off green tops with 2-inch white part.	Cook in 1 inch boiling salted water.	10 to 15 min.
Parsnips	Wash thoroughly; pare or scrape. Slice lengthwise or crosswise.	Cook covered in small amount of boiling salted water.	15 to 20 min.
Peas, Green	Shell and wash just before cooking	Cook covered in small amount of boiling salted water.	8 to 15 min.
Black eyed	Shell as green peas.	Cook covered in boiling water.	30 to 40 min.
Peppers, Bell	Rinse in cold water. Remove stem, seeds and membrane. Leave whole to stuff and bake.	Parboil, whole Bake at 350°F Saute (fry)	5 min. 25 to 30 min. 5 min.
Potatoes, White	Scrub with brush; remove eyes. Leave skins on whenever possible or pare thin. Leave whole or cut in large pieces or slices.	Boil whole Cut Bake	30 to 35 min. 20 to 25 min. 1 to 1½ hrs.
Pumpkin	Cut in half. Remove seeds and stringy fibers. Cut in smaller pieces; pare.	Boil in salted water, cover and cook. Bake (400°F)	25 to 30 min. 1 hr.
Squash (Summer) Straight Neck or, Crookneck, Chayote, Zucchini	(Soft Skin) Scrub gently with soft vegetable brush in cold water; do not pare. Remove stem and blossom ends. Remove large seeds (except in zucchini), coarse fiber, if any. Leave whole, slice or dice.	In saucepan over medium heat, in 1 inch boiling water, heat squash to boiling; cover and cooked halved squash. Bake whole (350°F)	10 to 15 min. 24 to 30 min.
(Winter) Banana, Butternut, Acorn, Table Queen	(Hard Skin) Rinse in cold water; cut into halves or quarters if desired, remove seeds and fibers, cut into serving pieces Acorn: do not pare, remove seeds.	For boiled squash, heat squash to boiling, cover and cook. Bake (375°F)	15 min. 45 to 90 min.
Spinach	Cut off roots and wash several times in lukewarm water; lifting out of water as you wash.	Cook covered in without adding water. Reduce heat when steam forms. Turn often while cooking.	3 to 5 min.
Sweet Potatoes	Scrub. When possible, don't peel before cooking, to save nutrients.	For boiled sweet potatoes, in saucepan in 1 inch boiling salted water, heat sweet potatoes to boiling, cover and cook until fork tender.	20 to 25 min.

		For baked sweet potatoes, preheat oven to 450°F and bake until fork tender.	45 min to 1 hr.
Tomatoes	Rinse in cold water. It is not necessary to peel tomatoes before using. If peeling is preferred, just dip tomatoes in boiling water for 1 minute, then cool in cold water; skin will peel off easily. Or with fork, hold tomato over direct flame, roasting constantly until skin pops; peel.	Cook slowly, covered without adding water.	10 to 15 min.
Turnips	Rinse in cold water. Peel thinly; leave whole or cut into slices or pieces.	In saucepan, in 1 inch boiling, salted water, heat turnips to boiling; cover and cook whole turnips; or sliced	20 to 30 min. 15 to 20 min.
Water Chestnuts	Rinse in cold water. Peel skin; use whole, sliced or cut into chunks.	Use in recipes as directed.	

HERBS and SPICES

Always try to use fresh herbs, but both frozen and dried ones can be substituted. Remember the dried herbs, generally have stronger taste (so use less dried than fresh). In the following table you will find a list of herbs and spices, with suggestions as to how you can make the most of them, and how you yourself can cultivate them. There's a certain knack to seasoning correctly – not too much, not too little – but it can be acquired by always tasting what you are cooking. The simple outline below is meant to be just that, specifying which herbs and spices go best with the food, but you can experiment. Just don't use them all at the same time!

Food	Herbs and Spices
Fish	Curry powder, turmeric, saffron, caraway seeds, coriander, mixed spice or spice herbs, dill, bay leaves, parsley, lemon balm chives, tarragon, chervil, fennel, marjoram
Pork	Curry powder, paprika, cayenne pepper, ginger, caraway seeds, bay leaves, parsley, rosemary, garlic basil, fennel, tarragon
Beef	Paprika, cayenne pepper, nutmeg, mixed spice or allspice beans, bay leaf, garlic, rosemary, thyme, sage, marjoram, watercress, horseradish
Veal	Curry powder, garlic, parsley, rosemary, dill, tarragon
Lamb	Curry powder, cayenne pepper, paprika, turmeric, dill, garlic, mint, marjoram, thyme, rosemary
Chopped meat and sausage dishes	Paprika, coriander, cayenne pepper, nutmeg, basil, marjoram, sage
Poultry	Paprika, curry powder, turmeric, cayenne pepper, tarragon, thyme, bay leaves, parsley, fennel, marjoram, sage, basil, lemon balm, garlic, horseradish
Game	Juniper berries, paprika, rosemary, thyme, bay leaves
Vegetables and salads	Nutmeg, paprika, curry powder, cayenne pepper, caraway seeds, parsley, chives, garlic, chervil, basil, marjoram. All herbs and spices are good in salads
Egg dishes	Curry powder, paprika, cayenne pepper, nutmeg, parsley, chervil, dill, tarragon, basil, marjoram, garlic
Rice dishes, pizza and pasta	Thyme, caraway seeds, rosemary, ginger, parsley, chives, oregano, basil
Desserts	Cinnamon, cardamom, vanilla, ginger
Breads and Cakes	Caraway seeds, mixed spice or allspice beans, cloves, cinnamon, cardamom, vanilla, saffron, fennel, sesame seed

COOKING SUBSTITUTIONS

Instead of	Use
Baking powder	¼ teaspoon baking soda plus ½ teaspoon cream of tartar
Bread crumbs, fine, dry ¼ cup	¾ cup soft bread crumbs, ¼ cup cracker crumbs **or** ¼ cup cornflake crumbs
Broth, beef or chicken (1 cup)	1 teaspoon **or** 1 cube instant beef broth **or** chicken bouillon plus 1 cup hot water
Cake flour, sifted (1 cup)	1 cup minus 2 tablespoons sifted all purpose flour
Chocolate, semisweet, 1 ounce square	1 tablespoon cocoa powder plus 2 tablespoons shortening plus 3½ teaspoons sugar
Chocolate, unsweetened, 1 ounce square	3 tablespoons cocoa powder plus 1 tablespoon shortening
Cornstarch, 1 tablespoon	2 tablespoons all purpose flour
Flour, sifted all purpose (1 cup)	1 cup plus 2 tablespoons sifted cake flour
Garlic, 1 clove	½ teaspoon bottled minced garlic **or** ⅛ teaspoon garlic powder
Herb, dried, 1 teaspoon	½ teaspoon ground herb
Herb, snipped fresh, 1 tablespoons	½ to 1 teaspoon dried herb, crushed
Half-and-half or light cream, 1 cup	1 tablespoon melted butter **or** margarine plus enough whole milk to make 1 cup
Honey, 1 cup	¾ cup sugar plus ¼ cup liquid
Margarine, 1 cup	1 cup butter, **or** 1 cup shortening plus ⅓ teaspoon salt, if desired
Milk, whole 1 cup	½ cup evaporated milk plus ½ cup water **or** 4 tablespoons nonfat dry milk plus 2 teaspoons shortening and 1 cup water
Molasses, 1 cup	1 cup honey
Mustard, dry, 1 teaspoon	1 tablespoon prepared mustard (in cooked mixtures)
Onion, chopped, 1 small (⅓ cup)	1 teaspoon onion powder, **or** 1 tablespoon dried minced

onion

Sugar, granulated, 1 cup   1⅓ cups brown sugar **or** 1½ cups confectioners' sugar

Tomato juice, 1 cup   ½ cup tomato sauce plus ½ cup water

Tomato sauce, 2 cups   ¾ cup tomato paste plus 1 cup water

Sour cream, dairy, 1 cup   1 cup plain yogurt **or** ⅓ cup butter and ⅔ cup milk

METRIC EQUIVALENTS

Ingredients: A standard cup measure of a dry or solid ingredient will vary in weight depending on the type of ingredient. A standard cup of liquid is the same volume for any type of liquid. Use the chart below when converting standard cup measures to grams (weight) or milliliters (volume).

Standard Cup	Fine Powder (Flour)	Grain (Rice)	Granular (Sugar)	Liquid Solids (Butter)	Liquid (Milk)
1	140g	150g	190g	200g	240ml
¾	105g	113g	143g	150g	180ml
⅔	93g	100g	125g	133g	160ml
½	70g	75g	95g	100g	120ml
⅓	47g	50g	63g	67g	80ml
¼	35g	38g	48g	50g	60ml
⅛	18g	19g	24g	25g	30ml

Temperatures & Liquid Measurements: Equivalents for cooking/oven temperatures are listed in the charts below.

EQUIVALENTS FOR LIQUID MEASUREMENTS BY VOLUME			
⅛ tsp.	= 0.5ml		
¼ tsp.	= 1ml		
½ tsp.	= 2ml		
1 tsp.	= 5ml		
3 tsp.	= 1 tbsp.	= ½ fl. oz.	= 15ml
2 tbsp.	= ⅛ cup	= 1 fl. oz.	= 30ml
4 tbsp.	= ¼ cup	= 2 fl. oz.	= 60ml
5⅓ tbsp.	= ⅓ cup	= 3 fl. oz.	= 80ml
8 tbsp.	= ½ cup	= 4 fl. oz.	= 120ml
10⅔ tbsp.	= ⅔ cup	= 5 fl. oz.	= 160ml
12 tbsp.	= ¾ cup	= 6 fl. oz.	= 180ml
16 tbsp.	= 1 cup	= 8 fl. oz.	= 240ml
1 pt.	= 2 cups	= 16 fl. oz.	= 480ml
1 qt.	= 4 cups	= 32 fl. oz.	= 960ml
		= 33 fl. oz.	= 1000ml

1 liter

DIMENSIONS
¹/₁₆ inch = 2 mm
⅛ inch = 3 mm
¼ inch = 6 mm
½ inch = 1.5 cm
¾ inch = 2 cm
1 inch = 2.5 cm

OVEN TEMPERATURES			
	Fahrenheit	Celsius	Gas Mark
Freeze Water	32°F	0°C	
Room Temperature	68°F	20°C	
Boil Water	212°F	100°C	
Bake	250°F	120°C	
	275°F	140°C	
	300°F	150°C	
	325°F	160°C	3
	350°F	180°C	4
	375°F	190°C	5
	400°F	200°C	6
	425°F	220°C	7
	450°F	230°C	8
	Broil		Grill

BAKING PAN SIZES			
Utility	Size in Inches/Quarts	Metric Volume	Size in Centimeters
Baking or Cake Pan (square or rectangular)	8 x 8 x 2	2 L	20 x 20 x 5
	9 x 9 x 2	2.5L	23 x 23 x 5
	12 x 8 x 2	3 L	30 x 20 x 5
	13 x 9 x 2	3.5 L	33 x 23 x 5
Loaf Pan	8 x 4 x 3	1.5 L	20 x 10 x 7
	9 x 5 x 3	2 L	23 x 13 x 7
Round Layer Cake Pan	8 x 1½	1.2 L	20 x 4
	9 x 1½	1.5 L	23 x 4
Pie Plate	8 x 1¼	750ml	20 x 3
	9 x 1¼	1 L	23 x 3
Baking Dish or Casserole	1 quart	1 L	
	1½ quart	1.5 L	
	2 quart	2 L	

ALTITUTDE COOKING

Approximate Boiling Temperature of Water at Various Altitudes

ALTITUDE	BOILING POINT OF WATER	
FEET	DEGREES (F°)	DEGREES (C°)
Sea level	212.0	100.0
2,000	208.4	98.4
5,000	203.0	95.0
7,500	198.4	92.4
10,000	194.0	90.0
15,000	185.0	85.0
30,000	158.0	70.0

Cake baking: Most cake recipes for sea level need no modification up to the altitude of 2,500 to 3,000 feet. Above that, it is often necessary to adjust recipes slightly in proportions of certain ingredients. Usually, a decrease in leavening or sugar (or both) and an increase in liquid are needed.

Each or all of these adjustments may be required to a greater or leasser degree, for every recipe is different in richness and in its balance of ingredients. Only repeated experiments with each recipe can give the most successful proportions to use.

In making very rich cakes at high altitudes, it is sometimes necessary to reduce shortening by 1 or 2 tablespoons. Recipes using baking soda may require a very slight reduction of this leavening agent. On the other hand, the amount of eggs may be increased at highest altitudes. This has possibilities in recipe adjustments for angel food and sponge cakes.

Cake Recipes Adjustment Guide for High Altitudes

ADJUSTMENT	3,000 Feet	5,000 Feet	7, 000 Feet
Reduce baking powder For each teaspoon, decrease...	⅛ teaspoon	⅛ to ¼ teaspoon	¼ to ½ teaspoon
Reduce sugar For each cup, decrease...	No change	Usually no change	1 to 2 tablespoons
Increase liquid For each cup, add...	1 to 2 tablespoon	2 to 3 tablespoons	3 to 4 tablespoons

NOTE: When two amounts are given, the smaller adjustment should be tried first; then if cake still needs improvement, the large adjustment can be used the next time.

A

Abalone: This red or pink mollusk or shellfish is found in the Pacific Ocean off the coast of California. The muscle of the shell is the edible part of the abalone and has a delicious clam-like flavor.

Absinthe: A famous (or infamous) liqueur. Absinthe takes its name from an aromatic plant (Artemisia) that contains an alkaloid used since ancient times as a tonic. Wormwood is the principal one of 14 herbs which are macerated in grape spirit, but hyssop and mint are also included. It is famous for its green color, and was called the <u>fée verte</u> (green fairy) in France (although the Swiss make a blue one). Because of the dangerous oils of wormwood, the sale of true absinthe is prohibited in most countries.

Accra: (akkra, akra) Originally a West African fritter, made throughout the islands. The traditional Jamaican akkra is a fritter made of ground black eyed peas or soybeans; the same thing is known as *cala* on the Dutch Islands. Accras are also made of a heavy batter into which a variety of ingredients are mixed, salt cod being the most popular. This combination is called ***stamp and go*** in Jamaica, ***acrat de morue*** in the French West Indies and ***bacalatias*** in Puerto Rico.

Achar: An Indian term for pickle. Relished throughout the Indian subcontinent, Indonesia and the West Indies and brought to Europe by the English in the 18th century, achar is made from a mixture of fruit and vegetables, which are chopped and steeped in a spicy sauce, often oil based and frequently flavored with saffron.

Acid: The term denotes a taste sensation as well as a chemical function. A weak acid, such as lemon juice, prevents artichoke hearts, avocadoes, sliced apples, and bananas from turning black through oxidation.

Acidulate: To turn a liquid or a dish slightly acid, tart or piquant by adding a little lemon juice, vinegar or the juice of unripe fruit. Acidulate also means to make sour cream by adding a few drops of lemon juice to fresh cream.

Acorn Squash: A fall and winter vegetable that belongs to the gourd family. It has a dark green rind, yellow-orange flesh, and many seeds. Its flavor is on the sweet side. Acorn squash is a Native American vegetable, and was unknown in Europe. In fact, the word squash comes from the Native American word **asquash**, which means, "eaten green."

Aerate: The process when dry ingredients pass through a sifter and air is circulated through, changing the composition of the material, (often referring to flour).

Agar-Agar: A viscous substance, also known as Japanese or Ceylon moss, agar-agar is an extract of seaweed from the Indian and Pacific Oceans. It is a vegetarian gelling agent and produces a firmer jelly, which does not melt as readily as gelatin.

Aillande: A feature of the cuisine of southern France, which varies according to the region where it is made. In Provence, it is either a vinaigrette sauce with garlic or a slice of bread rubbed with garlic, soaked in olive oil and grilled (broiled) (pain à l'aillande). In Languedoc, the aillande from the Toulouse region is a variation on aïoli mayonnaise made with blanched and ground walnuts, while in the region of Albi aillande is another name for aïoli.

Aïoli: Also known as ailloli. This French word comes from **ail**, meaning, "garlic". A Provençal emulsion sauce of garlic and oil; known in its mayonnaise form with egg yolks. It is served with cold poached fish, hard-boiled eggs, salad, snails, or cold meat.

Akee: Oblong egg shaped fruit of an evergreen tree widely cultivated in Jamaica. The scarlet pod enclosed cream colored flesh whose bland texture and taste is often compared to scrambled eggs. It is traditionally served in Jamaica with salt fish.

À la: This French terms means "in the manner of." It is usually followed by the name of the person who first created the dish, the name of the person for whom it was created, the name of the place where the dish originated, one of the main ingredients in the dish.

À la carte: This literal translation of this French term is "in the manner of the bill of fare." À la carte is used to describe a meal in which each dish is selected and paid for separately. The opposite term is **table d'hôte**, which means "the host's table." Here, one fixed price covers the cost of the whole meal.

À la king: A plain or rich white sauce that should contain any one or combination of these vegetables: sliced mushrooms, chopped green pepper, chopped or sliced pimientos. À la king sauce is most frequently used for cooked and diced chicken, but it is equally well suited for turkey, tuna, ham, hard boiled eggs, shrimp or lobster, and may be served on toast, in patty shells, on rice, noodles, or any food that needs a sauce or a dressing.

À la mode: In French, this means "in the fashion of." In cookery, a la mode has two completely different meanings. One is American, the other French. In American usage, a la mode describes cake, pie, pudding, or other desserts topped with a scoop of ice cream. In French cooking, a la mode describes a beef pot roast larded with fat, braised with vegetables, and simmered in a sauce, such as "boeuf a la mode."

Albacore: A fish in the tuna family. Albacore has the true white meat of all tuna and is used for the finest canned tuna and the most delicate dishes.

Alcohol: Only the alcohol used in beverages needs to concern us here. Alcohol in its pure form is a transparent, colorless strong liquid, volatile and very inflammable. It is distilled from a great variety of fruits and grains that contain either natural sugar or substances that can be transformed into sugar. The addition of natural or artificial yeast strains and mineral compounds change the sugar content by the process of fermentation into alcohol and other-by-products.

Al Dente: An Italian expression (meaning literally "to the tooth") indicating the correct degree of cooking pasta, which must be removed from the heat and drained while it is still firm enough to bite into.

Ale: Ale is a fermented malt beverage, beer is its brother. Ale, like beer, is brewed from malt, cereals, and hops, but the method of brewing ale is different from that of brewing beer. Ale is "top fermented", that is, during fermentation at a higher temperature its yeast rises to the top. The result is a brew with a more pronounced hop flavor than that found in beer. Porter and stout are two well-known varieties of ale, both sweeter and darker than the others. Porter has less hop flavor. Stout has a full hop flavor with a slightly burnt taste.

Allemande: This is a classic French sauce, golden yellow in color, creamy in consistency, with excellent flavor. It is used with boiled or poached fish, meats, or vegetables. The main ingredient is velouté sauce (a white sauce made with chicken, veal or fish stock instead of milk or cream), to which egg yolks, cream and lemon juice are added. In spite of its name, which means "German", it has nothing to do with Germany or German cuisine.

Allongé or **Américain:** a watered-down espresso. Also known as jus de chaussettes (literally "sock juice").

Allspice: Jamaican pepper is another name for the dried unripe fruit of the Pimenta dioica that is related to the myrtle family. The berries are picked green and dried in the sun. This wrinkles them, turns them a reddish brown, and intensifies their aroma. In spite of the name, allspice is not a combination of spices but one spice only; it is called so because its flavor resembles a combination of clove, cinnamon, and nutmeg, and is used with meats, egg dishes, soups, vegetables, fruits and desserts. Allspice Oil is oil extracted from the leaves of the allspice tree and used in making a Jamaican liqueur called *Pimento Dram.*

Almond: The word covers the tree and nut, the seed or kernel of *Prunus Amygdalus*, a subgenus that includes the peach tree. The almond closely resembles the peach in its blossom and young unripe fruit, although the almond tree grows larger. Basically, there are two types of almonds, sweet and bitter, although there are many varieties of these. Both are rich in sugar, albumen and oil. Bitter almonds are the source of almond flavoring, but are processed first since they contain prussic acid, a poison. However, used in tiny quantities in cooking, they are not dangerous. The Jordan almond is in fact from Spain, the name being a corruption of jardin (garden).

Almond Paste: A confectionery preparation consisting of ground sweet almonds mixed with their own weight of confectioners' sugar and a little glucose syrup. Adding the ground almonds to sugar syrup, then crushing the mixture is traditionally how almond paste is prepared.

Alsace: This easternmost province of France is famous for its food and wines. Its two gastronomic masterpieces are foie gras (goose liver, usually made into pâtés) with truffles, one of the world's most prized delicacies, and choucroute garnie, a robust dish of sauerkraut, pork products, and boiled potatoes cooked with white wine and juniper berries. The regions two best-known wines are the classic Riesling and the flowery Gewürztraminer; the best-known spirit is kirsch, a colorless brandy distilled from cherries.

Amandine: Made or garnished with almonds.

Anchovy: This small fish belongs to the herring family. The best anchovies are from the Mediterranean, and they have been used as appetizers or as ingredients to flavor foods from the days of the ancient Romans. Anchovies are used almost entirely in a preserved form, salted or pickled or packed in oil, and in fillets. Anchovy fillets come either flat or rolled around a caper. Anchovies are also made into a paste and into an extract.

Angel Food Cake: A high, delicate, fluffy white cake, which contains no fat and uses only the whites of eggs. Air, beaten into these, provides the leavening agent. Angel food cakes are usually baked in a tube pan. It can be decorated and frosted with fruits, icings, or whipped cream. It can be scooped out and filled with ice cream, custard, whipped cream, or fruit for a delicious dessert.

Angelica: The name of this aromatic herb means "heavenly" in Latin. Angelica was once considered a powerful protector against witches and fearsome creatures. In Elizabethan

England it was used as an antidote for the plague. All parts are aromatic. The dried roots and fruits flavor cakes, candies, beverages such as bitters, and liqueurs like Benedictine. The stems and leaf stalks are candied in sugar and used for decorating desserts because of their bright green color and pleasant flavor. The oil is used for flavorings, perfume and in medicine.

Anise or Sweet Anise: This culinary herb belongs to the parsley family. The plants and fruits have a distinctive licorice flavor. The dried fruits are called aniseed. Anise is one of the best-liked flavorings in European cuisine. In Italy it is used in liqueurs; Germans and Scandinavians flavor their breads with aniseed. It goes into stews and seafood cocktails, and it enhances carrot, cauliflower and beet dishes. To release the full flavor of the seeds in cooking, place them between two sheets of wax paper and crush them with a rolling pin, (meats, carrots, beets, green beans, mixed vegetable salads, breads, cakes, cookies, pastries)

Select green featherlike leaves and white bulbs. Season: October to March.

Refrigerate in crisper; use within 3 to 5 days

Annatto: (achiote) Rusty red dried seed of the Achiote tree (Bixa orellana), found in tropical regions from Mexico to Brazil. It is used primarily to color cooking oil or lard a bright orange- yellow, but also lends a delicate flavor.

Antipasto: An Italian term for cold hors d'oeuvres, the name derived from the Italian word pasto (meal) with the Latin prefix ante (before). An antipasto might consist of Parma ham with fresh figs, or a Piedmontese cheese fondue, raw vegetables accompanied by condiments and melted cheese sauce.

Aperitif: Certain plants have been known to have the property of restoring, or "opening" (from Latin aperire "to open") the appetite. The Romans had a liking for wine with honey; in the Middle Ages people believed in the benefits of wine mixed with herbs or spices.

Appareil: The French term for the mixture of different ingredients necessary to prepare a dish for cooking. The word *masse* is also used. Appareils are particularly common in cake and pastry making.

Appetite: Psychologists define under the term 'natural appetite' the tendencies, which instinctively cause us to satisfy the needs of the body. Hunger in reality is nothing more than the need to eat, whereas appetite is the lure of pleasure experienced while eating.

Apple: The fruit of any tree of the genus *Malus*. Apples come in many varieties. The ancient Romans know twenty-two of them. Who can describe an apple: In shape they can be found round like a McIntosh or egg-shaped like the Delicious. In size, it can vary from a two inch crabapple to a six inch Rome Beauty. The flesh can be white as a Cortland, yellow as in a Golden Delicious, crisp as a Northern Spy, mellow as a Baldwin, sweet as a Grimes Golden, or tart as a new Winesap. The skin is thin and glossy and ranges in color from bright or russet red to yellow to green. Apples fit into every course of every meal and are munched between meals too, they can be found in lunch boxes and fancy torts.

Select firm, crisp, well colored apples, the color depending upon the variety. Avoid brown spots, shriveled or soft fruit. Select apples according to their use: **eating**-Winesap, Red or Golden Delicious; **cooking**-Rhode Island Greening, York or Rome; **cooking and eating**-McIntosh, Jonathan, Yellow Newton, Stayman, Cortland or Northern Spy.

Refrigerate; use within 2 weeks. Season: all year; the best supplies are in October; the lowest from June to August.

Although available year round; the best supplies are in October; the lowest in June, July and August.

Apricot: Oval stoned fruit of a golden yellow color, which grows on a small tree belonging to the peach family. The name is derived from the Latin *praecoguus*, meaning, "Precious or early ripening." The ancient Greeks called the apricot the "golden egg of the sun". The tree is native to Asia, where it still grows wild. The first apricots in the United States were probably those the Spanish missionaries brought to California in the 1770's. Few fruits are more delectable or more beautiful.

Select plump, juicy looking orange-yellow fruit. Ripe apricots should yield to gentle pressure on the skin. Avoid dull looking, shriveled or soft fruit.

Refrigerate; use within 2 to 3 days. Season: June and July.

Aroma: The word means a distinctive, agreeable fragrance, which is more penetrating and persuasive than a smell, and has none of the negative meaning sometimes associated with the words smell and odor. The aroma of foods greatly affects our enjoyment of them since the connection between the senses of taste and smell is an extremely close one. Instinctively, one thinks that if the aroma of a food is pleasant, the taste will be too. This is true in most cases, but it can be otherwise.

Aromatics: Any fragrant plant that is used as a condiment or for flavoring. Various parts of the plant may be used: the leaves (basil, marjoram, mint, chervil and tarragon), the flower buds (caper and nasturtium), the seeds (dill, aniseed, caraway, coriander and mustard), the fruits (juniper and pimiento), the roots (horseradish), the stems (angelica, savory and wild thyme) or the bulbs (garlic and onion). Vegetables, such as carrots, celery, parsnips and leeks are also used in cooking as aromatics.

Arrowroot: The "starch" extracted from the rhizomes (underground stems) of several tropical plants. A fine white powder, it is useful in the kitchen as a last minute thickener of sauces and glazes. Arrowroot should be blended to a smooth thin paste with a little cold liquid before being added to a hot liquid. Unlike cornstarch, which gives a cloudy sauce, arrowroot clears when it boils.

Artichoke, French or Globe: Globe or common artichokes are the leafy buds from a plant resembling thistle. Artichokes, like other vegetables, may be eaten in many ways. One way is to eat them with the fingers; pull off the leaves one at a time and dip them in a sauce which may be hot melted butter and lemon juice, hollandaise or mayonnaise, sour cream, or a French dressing. Eventually a core of thin, light colored leaves is reached; this covers the choke and the heart. Eat the tender part of these leaves by drawing them between your teeth. Discard the remainder of the leaf. The fuzzy choke is scraped off with a knife or fork and discarded. The heart is also called the 'bottom' and is eaten with a fork. Very young artichokes are also eaten raw.

Select compact, plump artichokes, heave in relation to their size, with tightly closed, thick, green, and blemish free leaves. Size is not an indication of quality. Avoid over-mature artichokes with hard-tipped spreading leaves.

Refrigerate in plastic bag with a few drops of water, use within a few days. Season: all year; best supplies March to May.

Asiago: An Italian cheese made from unpasturized cow's milk. It has a supple but sliceable texture with numerous small holes. The flavor is slightly nutty, with lemon tones, which takes on a more tangy nature as the cheese matures.

Asparagus: This vegetable is a member of the lily-of-the-valley family. The name comes from a Greek word meaning "stalk" or "shoot". In Europe, asparagus is grown in a number of different varieties and ways. Especially prized is a variety of asparagus that yields very thick white fleshy stalks that are incredibly tender. Among the virtues of asparagus is that it not only tastes good with any kind of food, but it is equally good hot, lukewarm, or cold.

Look for straight stalks with closed, compact tips, good green color almost the entire length (the white area at the end is tough and should be discarded).

Refrigerate in crisper; use within 1 or 2 days. Season: March to July.

Aspic: A clear, savory, nonsweet jelly used to decorate or to mold entrées, salads, and canapés or meat, fish, poultry, eggs and the like. The origin of the word is French, meaning "lavender" and it may well be that the original aspic was a lavender-flavored jelly. In French culinary use, aspic refers not to the jelly, but to the whole decorated dish. The jelly itself is called "gelée."

Au beurre: With, or cooked in, butter.

Au gratin: With a browned covering of bread crumbs, often mixed with butter or cheese.

Au jus: Served with unthicken natural juices that develops during roasting.

Au lait: with milk.

Avocado: This fruit is native to Central or South America and references to it have been found in records kept by Spanish explorers as far back as 1519. The word is said to come from the Central American Indian word ahuacatl, which was modified by the Spanish explorers into aguacate. Avocados have a course shell like skin or a small thin skin, depending on the variety. They are yellowish-green with a fairly firm flesh and a single large seed, round or conical.

Select pear-shaped, round or egg-shaped green or purplish-black avocados, depending on variety. Firm avocados should ripen at room temperature in 3 to 5 days. They are ready to eat when they yield to gentle pressure on the skin. Avoid dark spots or broken surfaces. Light-brown irregular skin markings don't affect quality, however.

Refrigerate after ripening and use within 3 to 5 days. Season: Year round.

B

Baba: This French dessert cake is made with a yeast dough, which contains raisins. The finished cakes are steeped in rum and sugar syrup. Babas' come large or small and they are baked in tall, often fluted moulds.

Baba Ghannouj: A mezze or vegetable side dish eaten throughout the Middle East. The smoky flesh of grilled (broiled) aubergine (eggplant) is puréed with garlic, salt, lemon juice and good olive oil (sometimes tahini, a sesame paste) to make a paste known as "poor man's caviar".

Bacchus: His raised wine glass or basket of grapes may easily identify The Roman God of wine, portrayed in Greek and Roman paintings and sculpture. Called Dionysus by the Greeks in worship was banned by the Roman Senate in186 B.C.

Bacon: The cured and smoked fat and lean meat from the side of the pig, after the spareribs have been removed. Canadian bacon, which resembles ham rather than ordinary streaky bacon, is the eye muscle that runs along the pig's back. The word bacon, originally French, meant port and cured pork products.

Bagel: A bland doughnut shaped pastry made of non-sweet raised dough that is first simmered in water, then baked. This process gives the bagel a hard glazed crust and a chewy white interior.

Bagna Cauda: A hot dip (literally a "hot bath") the purée is made of olive oil with a little butter, pounded garlic and anchovy fillets, heated for some minutes, and then served over a small lamp, like fondue.

Bain Marie: A water bath for keeping cooked food or dishes, such as sauces and soups, warm without allowing them to continue cooking. It is also used for cooking delicate ingredients or mixtures, such as pâtes, custards or baked eggs, either on top of the stove or in the oven.

Bake: This basic cooking process is carried out with dry heat, at any kind of temperature, and usually in a confined space, such as an oven. However, foods have been baked over open fires, by hot coals and on hot rocks, under hot ashes, and even by the heat of the sun.

Baked Alaska: Cake, ice cream, and meringue are the ingredients of this spectacular dessert. The cake is topped with ice cream and covered on all sides with a meringue. Then the whole thing is browned in a hot oven and served immediately.

Baking Powder: This is a leavening agent used in batters and dough's to make them rise and become light and porous during baking. In mixtures it produces carbon dioxide, one of the three leavening agents (the other two are air and water vapor or steam).

Baking Soda: The chemical formula of this product is $NaHCO_3$. Its home use lies mostly in baking, to leaven cakes containing acid ingredients such as buttermilk, vinegar, molasses, and fruit juices. It is also used along with cream of tartar and baking powder where the amount of acid in the ingredients being combine varies a great deal, as it does when such things as chocolate, brown sugar, honey, sour cream, apples, etc. are used together. The acid in the ingredients combines with the baking soda to produce a gas when leaven the dough.

Baklava: A sweet pastry widely eaten in the Middle East consisting of sever very thin layers of phyllo pastry filled with chopped toasted almonds, pistachios and walnuts mixed with sugar and then cut into diamonds before baking. When they are taken out of the oven, a honey or sugar syrup flavored with rose water and lemon juice is poured over the baklavas.

Ballotine: A hot or cold dish based on meat, poultry, game birds or fish in aspic. The flesh is boned, stuffed, rolled and tied up with string, usually wrapped in muslin (cheesecloth) - sometimes in the skin -- then braised or poached.

Balm (Lemon Balm): A hardy perennial which has broad, dark green leaves, with a faint lemon flavor, and flowers growing in pale yellow clusters. Leaves and tender sprigs lend a subtle, charming flavor to lemonade, teas, meats, sauces, stuffing, soups, and salads even beer. Industrially, balm is used in making perfume and liqueurs, especially Benedictine and Chartreuse.

Bamboo Shoots: The inner white part of the young shoot of the bamboo, a tropical plant, prepared by stripping off the tight, tough, overlapping outer sheaths of the plant. Bamboo shoots are used mainly as fillers in Chinese cooking; their flavor is reminiscent of that of the artichoke. They can be deep fried, pickled, or put into soups, stews, and other dishes much in the way mushrooms are used.

Banana: Bananas are seedless fruit grown on a plant that resembles the palm, each plant bearing a single bunch of fruit. Bananas are harvested green, and their food value and flavor are the result of carefully controlled conditions and temperatures during ripening, when their starch is converted in sugar. There are some thirty species of bananas, which look and taste quite different from one another. There are red bananas, and greenish bananas, and bananas with a flavor reminiscent of apples and peaches, and some with a more delicate or a richer flavor. The **plantain** is the best known of these varieties, with a fruit that is larger, less sweet, and starchier than the usual banana.

Select solid yellow bananas with some browns flecks. Fruit with some green will ripen at home in a few days at room temperature. (Red bananas are a specialty in some areas.) Blackened skins usually indicate over ripened fruit.

Season: Available year round.

Banana Split: An ice cream dish created in the United States, the main ingredient of which is a banana split lengthwise. This is topped with three scoops of ice cream, of the same or different flavors, i.e., vanilla, chocolate and strawberry, coated with chocolate sauce and maraschino cherries.

Banbury Tart: It is a small pie or turnover filled with currants and raisins. It is also called a Banbury Cake. As with so many traditional pastries, the shape may very slightly, sometimes they are round, at other times oval, and again, they may be baked in a half moon (crescent) shape. Banbury tarts date back over 300 years; they brought fame and money to the small market town of Banbury in Oxfordshire.

Banquet: A banquet is a sumptuous, formal meal given for a large number of guests. The word comes from the French banc or bench, and may be interpreted to mean that people sat on benches while partaking of a common meal, rather than eating it haphazardly.

Barbecue: This familiar word has several related meanings. It covers food cooked over an open fire, over coals, in a pit, or on a spit in front of a fire. The food can be a whole animal, large or small, such as an ox or a pig, a bird, or a fish. It can also be cuts of any of these. A barbecue is an outdoor party, where these foods are prepared for a large group of people. The word also includes any equipment, simple or elaborate, used for the purpose, and finally sauces used for basting the foods that are being barbecued. The word barbecue comes from the Spanish word **barbacoa**, meaning a frame made of sticks, on which meat was set for roasting. This fame was set over a deep pit, which held the fire.

Bar-le-duc: A jam originally made in Bar-le-duc, France, from currants and honey. The seeds are laboriously bushed out with a needle. (Made in the U.S. with the seeds left in.)

Barley: This hard cereal grass is related to wheat, which it resembles. It comes in a number of varieties and seldom grows higher than three feet. Barley has an excellent, nutty flavor and is extremely satisfying as filler or as a side dish with meats, instead of potatoes. It is also an essential ingredient in brewing of beer and in the distillation of Scotch whisky. Barley water, a drink that is both refreshing and mild, was once a standard beverage in Victorian England.

Basil: There are five or six varieties of basil, which belongs to the mint family, all differing a height, color and taste. Each variety of this annual is very hardy and will grow in most climates. The basil most often used in this country is one of two varieties of sweet basil. Sweet basil is a delicious culinary seasoning. It is useful in almost any dish that can be herbed and is especially pleasing in seafood, salads, potatoes, vegetable soup, and dishes that contain tomatoes. Basil may be used fresh or dried. (meats, poultry, fish, stews, egg dishes, stuffing, vegetables, pasta, salads and dressing, breads, dips, sauces). Basil can be frozen, although it loses some of its flavor; and can dried, though not nearly so successfully.

Bass: The name cover more than a dozen North American food and game fish that belongs to at least halve a dozen different fish families. Some bass are fresh water fish, others, saltwater fish. The best-known saltwater basses are: common sea bass, from the Atlantic and the striped bass, originally native to the Atlantic, which is now also found in the Pacific. The flesh is delicately flavored, tender and juicy.

Baste, (to): The term for lightly moistening food cooking in the oven, on a rotisserie or under a grill (broiler) by spooning over melted fat or the cooking juices from the dish itself. A dish cooked au gratin may be basted with melted butter to facilitate browning.

Batter: A mixture of flour, liquid and other ingredients, to cook as is (as in pancakes or cakes), or to be used as an outer coating for foods that are to be fired. The consistency of the batter depends on its purpose. Batters containing beer are excellent for frying, since they are lighter, thanks to the fermentation of the beer. All alcohol vanished during the cooking. When coating foods with batter, it is essential that the foods are absolutely dry, or it won't adhere, and will come off in the frying. You should also remember not to over-beat the batter since this makes them tough. It is preferable to let a batter rest before using, if at all possible.

Bavarian Cream: A dessert made from an egg custard stiffened with gelatin and enriched with whipped cream. It is then molded and chilled, and served with or without a sauce. Bavarians were great favorites in the middle and latter part of the 19th century, which was the golden age of fancy puddings, with a special predilection for delicately quivering ones, such as Bavarians.

Bay Leaf or **Laurel Leaf**: The true bay or laurel leaf comes from the evergreen sweet bay or laurel shrub or small tree, native to the Middle East and the Mediterranean. Bay leaves are chiefly used dried and one leaf, crushed, can give a wonder flavor to a simple dish of potatoes, onions, and other vegetables and can add distinction to tomato flavored dishes. French cooking can't be imagined without a trace of Laurier, which is also one of the chief ingredients of the bouquet garni, a combination of herbs used for flavoring almost any French dish. (Corned beef, spaghetti sauce, fish, soups, stews, dried bean dishes, gravies, marinades)

Beans, Dry: Beans are the seed of many plants, both trailing vines and erect bushes, which are easily cultivated. They belong to the group of foods called legumes, which also include peas, lentils and peanuts. Next to cereals, it is the legume family, which contributes most substantially toward feeding the people of the world. Thanks to their high protein content. Dried bean varieties: black or turtle beans, blackeye and yelloweye beans (called peas in the South), chick peas (a.k.a. garbanzo beans), cranberry beans, Great Northern beans, Lima beans, marrow beans, navy beans, pinto and pink beans, red beans, red kidney beans, and soybeans.

Select packaged dry beans, peas and lentils free of stones and shriveled beans.

Béarnaise: A classic hot creamy French sauce made from egg yolks and reduced vinegar, whisked together over a low heat and mixed with butter. Though it takes its name from the Bearn, a French province in the Pyrenees, some authorities' say that the sauce did not originate in this region, where cooking with oil, nut butter is customary, but was created near Paris, in a restaurant called Pavilion Henri IV. Henri IV was the French king one called le grand Béarnaise. It is usually served with broiled meat or fish.

Beat, (to): To work a substance or mixture energetically, to modify its consistency, appearance or color. Beating not only mixes ingredients and makes them smooth but also, especially in the case of eggs, for example, makes them fluffy by incorporating air. In some baking, this air acts as a natural leavening agent.

Beaujolais: One of the best known red wines, made from the Gamay grape.

Béchamel: A white sauce made by combining hot flavored or seasoned milk with a roux. The classic recipe calls for milk flavored by heating it with a bay leaf, a slice of onion and a blade of mace or some nutmeg. Béchamel should always be made in a heavy-bottomed saucepan to prevent scorching and discoloring the roux.

Beef: Beef is the flesh of an adult animal of the *Bovidae* family of ruminants, which have been killed for food. Practically all the beef we eat comes from steers (males castrated when very young), heifers (females that have never borne a calf), and cows (mature animals that have borne at least one calf.) Some popular cuts: *Standing Rib Roast, Rib Steak, Delmonico Steak, Delmonico Roast, T-Bone Sirloin Steak, Wedge-bone Sirloin Steak, Flank Steak, Fillets, Short Ribs, Skirt Steak Fillets, Stew Beef, Round Eye Steak, Boneless Shoulder, Pot Roast or Steak, Brisket, Sirloin Tip, Boneless Sirloin, Top Round, Chuck,* to name a few.

Beer: A foamy, fermented beverage brewed from a malted cereal, with hops added. The introduction of hops came in the 15th century in England, whereas the brewing of beer goes back for thousands of years. Beer can be and has been brewed from a great variety of grains, such as wheat, millet, barley and rice. Beer is sometimes used in cooking, interchangeably with ale, especially in dishes with cheese and with certain seafood and meats. When cooked, the alcohol evaporates completely.

Beets: This vegetable is the enlarged red root of a plant, which is a member of the Beta genus and the first cousin to chard. Beet greens (the tops of the plants) are also edible, and some varieties are purposely grown for this purpose. Beets are also grown for sugar.

Select smooth, rich red beets of uniform size, with no ridges or blemishes. Soft spots are telltale signs of decay. Green tops should be fresh.

Remove tops; refrigerate tops and beets in crisper. Use beets within a week or so, preferably less. Use tops as soon as possible.

Beignet: This is the French word for fritter. Beignets may be of many different kinds. Some are bits of meat, poultry, fish, vegetables, fruits, rice, etc.; which are dipped into a batter and then fried in deep fat. Other beignets (sweet or not) are made from the same kind of batter of which éclairs are, with or without flavorings such as cheese, and then dropped by the spoonful into deep fat and fried.

Berry: The word describes not only the fruits that have berry as part of their names, but also cherries, tomatoes, and even rose hips, for the definition says that berries are any kind of small, pulpy fruit, no matter what its structure; Blackberries, Boysenberry, Dewberries, Loganberries, Raspberries, Blueberry, Cranberries and Strawberries.

Select plump, fresh-appearing, uniformity in color. Berries should be free of stems or leaves. Avoid fruit that is moldy or crushed, bruised or that has leaked moisture, staining the carton.

Refrigerate; use within 1 or 2 days. Season: Summer months, mostly June and July.

Beurre blanc: A classic French sauce made with reduced vinegar and shallots to which butter is added, called white butter sauce in English.

Beurre Manié: "Manipulated butter" is the literal translation of this French culinary term. Beurre manié is a thickening agent for sauces and it is composed of butter and flour kneaded or blended together into a paste. The thickening agent must be used at the end of the cooking process, and a sauce should not boil after it has been thickened with beurre manié.

Beuree Noir: Browned in butter sauce.

Beverage: The word comes from the Latin bibere, "to drink". It covers all liquids drunk by human beings, from water through milk to alcoholic drinks. By implication, beverages are manmade drinks, including coffee, tea, carbonated waters, fruit drinks, wine beer, spirits, alcoholic punches, etc.

Bind, (to): In culinary language this term means to hold separate solids or liquid together by adding an ingredient which serves as the cohesive agent, or by cooking. A bound dish is a thickened dish. Eggs are used to bind mayonnaise, stuffing, and custards. For croquettes, a cooked, thickened sauce holds the mixture together.

Birch Beer: The sap of the sweet birch, also called Black Birch or Cherry Birch, can be fermented into a mild or potent beer. Birches are tapped like the maples and their sap is delightful to drink, faintly sweet and tasting of wintergreen. Birch beer was one of the traditional beverages of the American frontier and the early settlers.

Biscuit: A term that includes a great many varieties of baked dough and batters. The word is French and means, "twice cooked", apply originally to thin, flatbreads used by travelers and soldiers. These breads had to be baked twice to expel as much moisture as possible to increase their shelf life. In America a biscuit is usually homemade quick breads made with baking powder or baking soda. In Great Britain and Europe, the word biscuit refers to every variety of cookie and cracker.

Bisque: 1. A seasoned shellfish purée flavored with white wine, cognac and double (heavy) cream, used as the bas of a soup. The flesh of the main ingredient (crayfish, lobster or crab) is diced and used as a garnish. 2. Or a frozen dessert, usually ice cream, with nuts in it.

Bittersweet chocolate: (a.k.a. as semi-sweet chocolate) contains at least 35 percent chocolate liqueur as well as cocoa butter and sugar. Semi-sweet, know to most Americans and Bittersweet, known to most Europeans vary only slightly in sweetness.

Black Bean: (frijoles negro, turtle bean) Small, flat charcoal-color bean no more than ½-inch long. It is a native of the Americas and related to the common navy and kidney bean.

Blanching: This term is used for several different operations; *par-broiling*: lightly cooking raw ingredients for varying amounts of time in boiling water with or without salt or vinegar. *Part-frying*: preliminary frying of certain potato preparations such as chips (French fries) so that they partially cook without changing color; soaking *briefly*: covering fruits, vegetables or nuts with boiling water for a few seconds to facilitate removal of skin.

Blancmange: In classic cuisine a much prized jellied almond cream, made with sweet almonds (and a few bitter almonds) which are then pounded pressed, sweetened and mixed with a flavoring and gelling agent.

Blanquette: A white, creamy stew of veal, chicken or lamb with small onions and mushrooms.

Blend, (to): To mix two or more ingredients so thoroughly that they cannot be separated. This can be done with an electric hand mixer or a blender. Blend is also a term used to describe mixtures of tea, coffee, cocoa, spices, etc.

Blini: This is the Russian and Polish version of pancakes. (In Polish the word is bliny.) They are usually small, made with buckwheat flour and raised with yeast. They are served as appetizers with various stuffing, such as salmon, cottage cheese, and best of all, caviar. When stuffed, they are called blinchiki.

Blintz: Blintzes are the Jewish version of pancakes, commonly attributed to Russian cookery where they are called blini or blinchiki. They are most popularly filled with cheese, but fruits, such as blueberries and cherries, can be used as fillings.

Blueberries: This is the edible berry of a plant of the same name. Blueberries belong to the Vaccinium genus, and there are many varieties of them, ranging in color from purplish-blue to the blue-black. They grow singly, or in clusters, on blushes and they need an acidic soil. Bilberries and whortleberries are blueberry varieties. You can find them canned (pie filling), fresh or frozen.

Select deep-colored berries of fairly uniform size. Silvery "bloom" on skin is natural protective waxy coating.

Refrigerate; use within 2 to 3 day, or may be frozen. Season: May to September.

Boil, (to): The word describes a movement of a liquid heated to reach the vaporizing stage, characterized by bubbles that break constantly on the surface. Water boils at a temperature of 212°F.at sea level, but the temperature decreases as altitude increases. When a liquid is boiling, the temperature remains constant.

Bologna: A mildly seasoned sausage made of finely ground beef, pork, or veal. The meat is packed into a casing and smoked. It originated in Bologna, Italy, during the Middle Ages. There are several varieties, ham bologna, all beef bologna (seasoned with garlic), and Lebanon bologna (all beef bologna which originated in Lebanon, Pennsylvania and requires long, slow cooking). In Italy the sausage is known as mortadella.

Bolognaise, a la: The French term for several dishes inspired by Italian cookery, especially that of Bologna, that are served with a thick sauce based on beef and vegetables, particularly tomato, popularly associated with pasta.

Bombe Glacée: The name of this elegant, molded frozen dessert is French and means "bomb". This goes back to the days when a bombe was molded in a round shape, the shape of the bomb at the time. Modern bombs are classically molded in tall, conical molds, or in melon-shaped molds. A bombe consists of an outer layer, usually of ice cream, sherbet, or whipped cream, and a softer filling, such as custard or a mousse. The dessert is then frozen in its mold. To loose from the mold, put a cloth rung out of hot water on the bottom of the mold and invert over a serving plate.

Bordeaux: The name covers a region and a city in southwestern France which are famous for their superlative cooking and wines. The city of Bordeaux, a beautiful one, is a gourmet's fondest dream come true, due to its combination of great wines and great hospitality. Bordeaux has produced incomparable wines ever since the Romans planted grapes there during the 3rd century. There are red, white and rosé Bordeaux wines. The red ones are dry and also known as 'clarets'. The white ones range from dry to very sweet. The most famous red Bordeaux wines are called Médoc, St. Émilion, and Pomerol, and the white ones, Graves and Sauternes.

Bordelaise: A classic French sauce which takes its name from the town of Bordeaux. It belongs to the family of brown sauces, is made with red wine and is rather highly seasoned. It is a sauce for meat, and usually served with steak.

Borsch: This is a dark-red Russian or Polish soup. The characteristic ingredient is beets. Borsch can contain other vegetables and also meat. It can be a thin soup or a substantial meal in itself. It can be served hot or cold, and usually with sour cream.

Bouillabaisse: A dish comprising fish boiled with herbs, which is traditionally associated with the Provençe region of France, especially Marseille, local people refer to it as a 'net full of fish'. It should contain at least eight different kinds of fish. Best choices for shellfish are lobsters and mussels. For heavy meated fish, try cod, haddock, and sea bass, for more delicate fish use sole, red snapper, flounder or sea perch.

Bouillon: The word is French and comes from bouillir, "to boil". A bouillon is a broth made by simmering meat, fish, or vegetables in water to extract their flavor. When clear broth is desire, the bouillon must be clarified, and a clarified bouillon is generally called "consommé". Today's canned bouillon and bouillon cubes are excellent.

Bouquet garni: An assortment of whole herbs and spices secured in a cheesecloth bag and used to flavor soups, stews and stocks. Typically, it includes fresh thyme, bay leaves and parsley stems, but it can also include other aromatics like celery and leeks. A bouquet garni should include at least one fresh herb. If a bouquet garni made from dried herbs is used, add a few sprigs of parsley to the bouquet

Braise, (to): A long, slow cooking method which utilizes moist heat in a tightly covered vessel at a temperature just below boiling. Braising is valuable for tenderizing tough meats and vegetables, since the long cooking breaks down their fibers. Braising should use a minimum amount of liquid, such as water, bouillon, or wine, which can be flavored in any preferred way to flavor the meat in its turn. Essentials for successful braising are a pot with a really tight lid to minimize evaporation, and heat so low that the liquid in which the food is cooked barely quivers. Braising can be done on top of the stove or in the oven.

Bran: The outer layers of food grains, obtained during flour making, are called by this name. Bran contains carbohydrates, vitamins, and minerals. It adds bulk to the diet and has a laxative effect.

Bratwurst: The word comes from the German and means "frying sausage" to distinguish it from ready-to-eat sausages. It is a fresh link sausage which is usually made from ground veal to which port or beef have been added. Bratwurst is mildly spiced with salt, pepper and/or coriander, ginger and mustard. Bratwurst is slowly fried in a pan until gently browned on all sides. It may also be browned first and then simmered in enough beer to cover. Or it may be grilled.

Brandy: This colorless spirituous liquid is obtained by the evaporation, by distillation, of most of the watery portion of wine. The alcohol content is usually fifty to sixty percent. Brandy is made from rather thin wines and it is matured in casks of many years where it becomes amber in color. Dark brand is artificially colored with a caramel solution. Good brandy is judges by is bouquet or aroma, and by its smoothness, as well as its taste, which differs with different brandies, making the choice a personal one, as with whiskies.

Brazil Nut: Botanically speaking Brazil nuts are not nuts at all, but the edible seeds of Bertholletia excelsa, the rough barked giant tree of the Amazon forest in South America. The fruit is globular; four to six inches in diameter, hard walled, and contains eight to twenty-four seeds, arranged like the sections of an orange. These seeds are what we know as Brazil nuts. The shell of the individual nut is triangular, dark brown, and very rough. The kernels are white with a rich flavor and quite oily.

Bread: Defined simply as a food made from flour or meal by moistening, kneading, and baking, bread, in its various forms, has been one of the most universal foods, indeed the staff of life, since prehistoric times. The bread of primitive man was unleavened and perhaps, as the story goes, the discovery of a leavening agent by a cook in ancient Egypt was pure chance. Egyptians literally earned their daily bread; workers were given bread at the end of the day as wages. It was the practical minded Romans who developed the circular millstone and enlarged the baking oven to mass production capacity. The commercial baker, in business by 168 B.C., carefully put his mark on each loaf. In the Middle Ages, as the cities and towns grew, trade guilds were established for bakers. Millers and bakers were not always high respected, for they were suspected, and in many cases rightly so of taking some of the grain or dough for themselves. During the Revolutionary War, bread was so important a part of our diet that the Continental Congress appointed a "Superintendent of Bakers and Director of Baking in the Grand Army of the United States". There are two basic kinds of bread, yeast breads, which are leavened by yeast and quick breads, which are leavened by baking soda or baking powder.

Bread, (to): To coat a food with bread or other crumbs, either directly or after dipping in first a beaten egg or milk. Breading is done prior to cooking the food; the cooking method is usually frying. Breading preserves the juices and provides a crust for texture. The crumbs used can be flavored with herbs, spices, cheese, etc. all ground fine. Some breading is done with fresh crumbs, depending on the taste and texture desired.

Breadfruit: Round or oblong fruit with a tough, yellowish-green and bumpy or prickly skin. It may measure up to 8 inches in diameter and weight as much as 10 pounds. The flesh is cream colored and has a flavor and texture that is often compared to grainy bread. It is eaten like a starchy vegetable, boiled, roasted or fried.

Breakfast: The first meal of the day is meant, as the word itself says "to break the fast". Life without doors has few pleasanter prospects than a neatly arranged and well-provisioned breakfast table", wrote Nathaniel Hawthorne. But breaking the fast is not the only function of breakfast. To be a good breakfast, the meal should be high in protein. The reason, protein is essential for building and maintaining healthy bodies and is best utilized when distributed evenly throughout the day. In addition to protein, a good breakfast should contain from one fourth to one third of all the other food values needed daily, carbohydrates, fats, vitamins and minerals.

Brie: This is one of the finest French cheeses, and one of the most famous. Brie is made from whole milk, and its shape is round and flat. The flavor varies from mild to pungent. The reddish crust is edible. Brie is fully ripened when the texture of the whole cheese is even; soft but not runny. Brie should be allowed to stand at room temperature before serving, to bring out the full flavor of the cheese.

Brine: A strong salt solution used in the preservation of fish, meats, vegetables, and in pickling. To keep foods in brine is one of the very oldest methods of preservation.

Brioche: Light, yet rich cake bread made with yeast dough, butter and eggs. The traditional shape of a brioche is round with a little hat, but here are also round, tall and slender and ring brioches.

Broccoli: This dark green vegetable is a member of the Brassica family and is closely related to cauliflower, less closely to cabbage and Brussels sprouts. Broccoli has tight small heads called curds (or florets), which sit like buds on a thick stem. Both heads and stems are edible.

Select tender, firm stalks and tightly closed, dark green flowerets.

Refrigerate in crisper; use within a week. Season: all year, lowest supplies are in July and August.

Brochette: This French word describes a small skewer on which meat, fish, or vegetables are cooked. The term en brochette means, meats cooked, and often served on a skewer. Like all skewered foods, en brochette foods can be grilled over an open file or under the broiler, or cooked in the oven.

Broil, (to): To cook directly under or above a source of radiant heat, which may be gas, electric, charcoal, or an open fire.

Broth: A thin liquid in which fish, meat, or vegetables have been cooked. Broth is often used interchangeably with bouillon, but is should not be confused with the word stock, which denotes richer extract.

Brown, (to): In cooking, to brown is to scorch the surfaces of a food, especially meat, in order to seal in juices within and to add flavor. Browning can be done either by exposing the food directly to the heat or by cooking it in a small amount of fat. For browned toppings, place foods under the broiler or in a hot oven.

Brownie: This rich, moist chocolate cookie has a universal appeal. Brownies are easy to make and they keep and ship well. Brownies fall into two main categories, the fudge type which is very chewy, and a true brownie, or cake type, with a lighter texture.

Brown Sauce: A dark basic sauce from which many other sauces are made. For this reason brown sauce, or Sauce Espagnole, as a similar sauce is called In France, is considered a "sauce mére", a mother sauce, in French cooking. Brown cause can be made in various ways, some elaborate, some simple, but it should always cook very slowly to become properly flavorful. Brown sauce freezes well.

Brûlé: The French term means "burnt"; Crème Brûlé, a dessert, in which the sugar topping is caramelized with a red hot iron, under the broiler or with a blow-torch.

Brunch: This meal is a combination of breakfast and lunch, and takes it name from the first two letters of breakfast and the last four of lunch. Brunches are a convenient form of entertaining, very popular on Sunday and holiday mornings, since they give hosts and guests a chance to sleep late.

Brussels sprouts: Brussels sprouts are a member of the cabbage family, and they look like miniature cabbages. The plant, instead of making one large cabbage heat, produces a number of rows of small heads where the leaves are attached. By pulling away the lower leaves the little heads are given room to develop, attached as they are to the long stalks of the plant. They should always be cooked in very little water. A dash of nutmeg is a good seasoning for a sauced or un-sauced dish of sprouts.

Look for firm, fresh, bright green (not yellow) sprouts with tight fitting outer leaves that are free from black spots. Puffy or soft sprouts are usually poor in quality.

Refrigerate in crisper; use within 3 to 4 days. Season: year round. Best supplies are from

September to February.

Buckwheat: The triangular seeds of this plant are used as a cereal although, botanically speaking, it is an herb of the genus Fagoypyrum. It is not a member of the family of cereal grasses to which wheat belongs. It is a staple grain of Russia and Poland, where cooked buckwheat is known as **kasha**.

Buffet: Literally translated, this French word means a "sideboard" or "cupboard". In French culinary language, a buffet indicates a good size tiered tabled on which various dishes have been arranged in a decorative manner and, by implication, a restaurant that has such an arrangement. In the United States, the word buffet is used as a term for a meal where the guests help themselves from a table on which the food, is placed in a decorative array.

Bulgur: Also known as boulghour, bulghur or burghul. It is made by cooking wheat, then drying and cracking it. It is then cooked in twice its volume of boiling water for about 10 minutes, or until the liquid is absorbed.

Bun: This is a small, sweetened or un-sweetened, round or oval cake or roll, and a very old form of baked food. Usually it is made with yeast. The best known buns are hot cross buns, marked with a sugar cross (originally baked for Good Friday, although now baked throughout Lent), and Swedish saffron buns, served on St. Lucia Day (December 13th). Young Swedish girls, dressed in white and wearing crowns with lighted candles, serve the saffron buns to their parents early in the morning. This custom inaugurates the Christmas season.

Burgundy: The name of a region of France which produces some of the greatest wines in the world. Outside of France, Burgundy is usually thought of as a red wine, but there are also superb dry white Burgundies, of which the best know is Chablis. Good Burgundy is a rich, mellow wine, rather on the hearty side. Burgundy as a region is also the home of some of the most glorious of all French cooking, famed throughout the world for the lusciousness of its food and the care taken in their preparation, and especially the king of all beef stews, bœuf bourguignon.

Butter: An edible animal fat, obtained from milk and cream which has been made solid by churning. Butter can be made from fresh or slightly acidic milk (this affects the taste and spreading consistency), it can be salted, unsalted or it can be sweet, this is, unsalted (Europeans prefer the later kind).

Butternut Squash: A winter squash, smooth and hard shelled, long and slender, with seeds contained in a small hallow in the base. The squash gets it name from the color, which for most of the year, is light brown or dark yellow. The flesh is almost orange. Its flavor is sweet, it mashes smoothly, and is comparatively quick cooking.

Butterscotch: This popular flavor is obtained by combining butter and sugar, usually brown sugar, and by cooking the two together in a number of different ways. Foods flavored with butterscotch, such as cakes, cookies, frosting, pudding, and sauces, take the name and become, butterscotch cake, butterscotch frosting, butterscotch pudding, etc. Butterscotch is also a hard candy.

C

Cabbage, Chinese: Napa, Bok Choy, Gai Choy (Chinese Mustard Greens), Gai Low (Chinese Broccoli)

Look for Crisp, fresh looking cabbage free from blemishes. For Napa, look for pale-green leaves on slender stalks. For Bok Choy, look for long, smooth, milk white stems with large, crinkly, dark green leaves. For Gai Choy, look for jade green cabbage with tightly packed, curled leaves. For Gai Low, look for broccoli-like cabbage with long, irregular stalks and many leaves with white or yellow flowers.

Refrigerate in crisper; use within a week. Season: all year.

Cabbage, Green and Red: Brassica is the Latin name of this leafy vegetable, which may be called man's best friend in the vegetable world. The word "cabbage" itself is an Anglicized version of the colloquial French word **caboche**, which mean "noggin'". Cabbage comes in many varieties, some with loose heads, some with firm ones, and others with flat, conical, or egg shape heads. Some cabbages are white, some green, some red, and some have plain leaves and some curly ones. Cabbage is eaten in one form or another in most countries of the world. It is a favorite food of the Slavic and the Germanic people, and an important part of their daily diet.

Select firm heads with fresh, crisp looking leaves. Green cabbage that has been held in storage is often trimmed of its outer leaves and lacks green color, but it is satisfactory if not wilted or discolored. Most popular green varieties include Danish, pointed and domestic. Savory type cabbage has finely crumpled green leaves, loosely formed heads; red varieties have distinctive reddish-purples color.

Refrigerate in crisper; use within 1 or 2 weeks. Season: Year round.

Café Arrosé: an espresso spiked with a shot of Calvados or eau-de-vie. Order it without the coffee - a calva or une eau-de-vie and you'll be taking part in an old French bar ritual known as tuer le ver ("killing the worm"), a folk remedy that is believed to kill intestinal worms.

Café Crème: an espresso with lots of warm, foamy milk. Ask for a grand crème if you want a large or a petit crème if you want a small.

Café noir or express: a small cup of strong black coffee; an espresso.

Caisses: Also known as caissettes. Cases used in cookery, pastry making in confectionery. Savory preparations en caisse (in cases) or en caissette (in small cases) are served as hot hors d'oeuvres or small entrées.

Cake: However inspired, no written definition of the word cake could approximate the glories of sweetened batter, baked, filled, frosted and made ravishing with edible decorations. The word "cake" comes to us from Middle English, and may have had earlier origins in Old Norse. From the earliest days of civilization, man has always considered cake, a food for the gods as well as himself. The Egyptians made cakes in animal, bird, and human forms for their various gods, Greeks offered honey cakes to their gods, and the north honey cakes were offered to Thor at the winter solstice to ensure a fruitful year to come. Few pleasures are greater than turning out a perfect cake. And perfect cakes can be achieved by any cook who is careful and who is willing to follow recipe directions. Cake making is an exact process, the ingredients and their relation to each other are balanced like a chemical formula, in fact, during the baking, a chemical process takes place, "transforming" the raw ingredients into a delicious new entity. There are two main classifications of cake in American fare, those made with fat and those made without.

Calabaza (West Indian pumpkin, green pumpkin) Pumpkins belong to the squash family, and in most parts of the Caribbean the term calabaza, or pumpkin, is used to mean squash. Sizes, shapes and skin coloring vary, but calabazas usually have firm yellow flesh and a delicate flavor somewhat like that of Hubbard or butternut squash.

Calorie: This word, which has caused grief to so many weight watchers, is used as a measuring unit for energy, just as ounces and pounds are used to measure weights, and pints and quarts to measure liquid. When the body takes on more calories than it needs to perform its daily routine, it store them away in the form of fat.

Callaloo: Caribbean wide soup made with callaloo greens and crab meat.

Callaloo Greens: The term is used both for the young leaves of the dasheen or taro plant and for the Asian potherbs known as Chinese spinach.

Canapés: A slice of bread cut into various shapes and garnished. Cold canapés are served at butts or lunches or with cocktails or apéritifs; hot canapés are served as hot hors d'oeuvre or small entrées.

Candied Fruit: To candy fruit is to preserve it in sugar (usually in sugar syrup) so that it keeps it original shape and color. Candied fruit is also called glacée fruit. The usual procedure in candying fruit is to boil it in a number of sugar syrups of varying degrees of thickness. The last boiling is in the glazing syrup, which gives the fruit its attractive, smooth, glossy appearance. Then the fruit is dried. Crystallized fruit,, a form of candied fruit, is prepared in the same manner, but without processing the fruit in the final glazing syrup. Thus the sugar crystallizes on exposure to air.

Candy: "Sweets to the sweet", said Hamlet, and who can resist? It is a rare person who is born without a sweet tooth. Egyptians used that age old sweetener, honey, to which they added figs, dates, nuts and spices. These early confections were made in various shapes and sometimes colored. It was the Arabs who made the biggest contribution to candy making in the early refining and processing of sugar. They spread the knowledge of sugar to the Mediterranean, although it was not until the crusades of the 14th century, that the acquaintance with sugar became widespread. Venice, that aristocratic lady of the Adriatic, carried on an extensive sea trade, and it was to this port that sugar was brought and made into tasty confections.

Canelling: The technique of making v-shaped grooves over the surface of a vegetable or a fruit for decoration, using a canelé knife. The fruit or vegetable is often sliced after the canelé grooves have been cut, to make decorative borders to the slices.

Cane Syrup, Pure: (ribbon cane syrup) Sweet dark brown sugar cane syrup, with a flavor somewhat like that of dark brown sugar. Available in 12, 24, 45 and 90 fluid ounce cans. As a substitute, combine two parts dark corn syrup with one part dark molasses.

Canning: Canning is a process of food preservation in which all organisms which might cause food spoilage are killed by heat. Canning can be done in a number of ways and the method selected must be suited to the kind of food to be canned. The food, once rendered completely sterile, is kept in sterilized hermetically sealed containers.

Cantaloupe: This is a variety of the muskmelon, with a sweet and fragrant taste. The cantaloupe was named for a castle in Italy. Like all melons, it originated in Asia, and was well known to the ancient Romans and other Mediterranean people.

Look for fully ripened fruit for best sweetness and flavor. Avoid bruised or cracked fruit. Scar at the stem end should be smooth and without any stem remaining; and rind around the blossom end should yield slightly with gentle thumb pressure; a pleasant melon odor should be perceptible; the coarse, corky netting or veining should stand out over the background rind; the cantaloupe rind should have no green color. Season: May to November.

Capers: They are the unopened flowers of the caper bush, a shrub native to the Mediterranean. During flowering season, the buds are picked before the petals can expand and preserved in vinegar and salt. Capers add liveliness to white and other sauces, to salads and creamed dishes, and, as condiments to appetizers, meats and seafood.

Capon: Capons are male chickens which have been castrated at six to eight weeks of age to produce birds with more tender flesh and a generous fat covering. Even though more expensive than roasting chicken, capons are a good buy for a large group of people. Capons can be roasted or braised. Roast capons for twenty-two to thirty minutes per pound.

Carafe: A glass or crystal vessel with a wide base and narrow neck, which can sometimes be sealed with a glass stopper. It is used to serve water or wine at the table.

Caramel, Caramelize: The word "caramel" has two meanings. It describes a candy with a chewy consistency and it is also a culinary term that refers to burnt sugar by itself or thinned with water. In the latter sense it is used by cooks to add color, flavor, and style to various foods, from stews and gravies to desserts. The more sugar is caramelized the less its sweetening power. To caramelize sugar, melt 1 cup granulated sugar in a heavy skillet and cook over medium heat to 338°F. Use a candy thermometer to check heat. Cook, stirring constantly, until sugar forms a golden brown syrup. Remove from heat immediately.

Caraway: This oval shape brown seed is named after the ancient district of Caria in Southeast Asia, demonstrating once more the antiquity of food seasonings. A most ancient herb, caraway was known to the Neolithic Swiss Lake Dwellers. Its medicinal properties were mentioned in the Medical Papyrus of These, dated from 1552 B.C. Greeks and Roman appreciated its culinary values as well. Caraway seeds are used to season soups, meats, and vegetables, breads such as rye, cakes, and pastries. Oil extracted from the seed provides the distinctive flavor of the liqueur kümmel. (meat loaves, pot roasts, stews, egg dishes, poultry stuffing, vegetables, salads, breads, dips, spreads)

Carbonated: This term is applied in beverages made sparkling, bubbling, or fizzing by charging them under pressure with a gas called carbon dioxide. Soda water is the best known as carbonated beverage. The term does not apply when the gas is produced within the beverage itself by the natural process of fermentation.

Cardamom: Cardamom seeds are brown, and they have an aromatic odor and a warm, spicy taste. They turn up in curries and in such meats as frankfurters and sausages, in pickling spice blends, and in baked foods. The spice is sold either whole in the form of bleached white pods; or ground. Whole cardamom pods must be crushed before using. They will disintegrate and disappear during the cooking. One word of caution; use cardamom with a light hand since a little goes a long way. Also, it should not be stored for too long since it rapidly loses its flavor.

Cardoon: (Cardoni) Also known as artichoke thistle in the sunflower family. A traditional Mediterranean vegetable considered to delicacy by many. Use a vegetable peeler to remove the tough outer strings of the ribs.

Look for stalks with small shanks and crisp looking leaves.

Refrigerate in crisper; use within 3 to 5 days. Season: fall and winter months.

Carob: The bean from the carob tree which is native to the Mediterranean region but cultivated in other warm climates.

Carpaccio: An Italian antipasto (appetizer) consisting of very thin slices of raw beef served cold with a creamy vinaigrette sauce made with olive oil.

Carrots: Carrots have been cultivated for over 2,000 years and have a long and honored history. The Greeks and Romans ate them in stews or as a vegetable. Elizabethan England adored them, and not only as a food, for when they were first introduced there, women adorned their hair with a wispy, fernlike leaves of the carrot. Carrots are not only a healthy fare, but also convenient vegetables since they store well and combine excellently with practically all slow cooking foods. They are at their best when young, slender and tender.

Select firm, well formed, bright colored carrots. Avoid flabby or shriveled carrots.

Refrigerate in crisper; if carrots have tops, remove tops and refrigerate. Use within 1 or 2 weeks. Season: all year.

Carve: In culinary terms the word is used to describe the process of cutting meat, game, and poultry to serve at the table.

Cashew: Evergreen tree and shrub native to the West Indies. It bears a tart, reddish, pear shaped cashew apple, from the bottom of which grows the kidney shaped nut, edible only when roasted.

Cassava: (manioc, yucca, mandioca) Long, irregularly shaped root at least 2 inches in diameter with a dark brown-rough bark-like skin and hard white starchy flesh. The bitter variety is poisonous until cooked. It is the base for tapioca and manioc meal.

Casserole: The word casserole has two meanings; 1) a deep cooking vessel of French origin, designed to retain heat and to be used for long slow cooking. A casserole container is usually round, with a tight fitting lid and with handles. 2) Casserole also means a cooked dish in which a number of raw and/or cooked ingredients are simmered together in the oven or on top of the stove.

Cassolette: A small container with lugs or a short handle made of heatproof porcelain, tempered glass or metal, which is used to prepare and serve hot entrées or certain hors d'oeuvres and cold puddings.

Cassoulet: This is a noble, garlicky bean stew with sausages and meats which comes to us from southwestern France. The name is from the cassole d'Issel, an earthenware utensil in which the cassoulet should be cooked. The ingredients must include a goodly amount of white beans, and they can include fresh pork, lamb, roast duck, various sausages, bacon, smoked ham, and confit d'oie, or preserved goose. A cassoulet must be cooked slowly, to blend the flavors.

Catfish: A fresh-water fish that derives its name from it *barbels*, or feelers, which resemble a cat's whiskers. The catfish lives in steams, primarily in the Mississippi valley. The most handsome member of the family and the best eating is the channel cat, which weighs from five to ten pounds. The smaller bullhead, up to a pound or so in weight is the most common. The channel cat is usually baked, the bullhead is fried.

Cauliflower: *Brassica oleracea* is the Latin name of this member of the cabbage family. The word is a combination of the Latin caulis, meaning "stalk", and floris, "flower". Cauliflower has been grown for centuries in the coastal regions of the Mediterranean. The oldest records date to the 6th century, B.C. and the Romans naturalist Pliny wrote about the vegetable in the 2nd century A.D. The entire white edible portion is called the "curd".

Spotted or bruised curd should be avoided unless it can be trimmed without causing waste. Size of the head does not affect quality.

Look for creamy white, compact, tightly packed flowerets with a granular appearance. Leaves around base should be fresh and green.

Refrigerate in crisper; use as soon as possible, within 3 to 5 days. Season: all year, best supplies are from September to November.

Caviar: Caviar is fish roe which has been sieved, lightly pressed, and treated with salt. It may come from any of the following fish among others; beluga (which of course is a member of the sturgeon family), sterlet, sturgeon, salmon, carp, herring, whitefish, or cod.

Cayenne: The hot, pungent red pepper known as cayenne is prepared by grinding the dried rip fruit of several species of the Capsicum plant. Cayenne is an ingredient of sausage seasonings and curry powders. When used with a light hand, it gives a zestful flavor to meat, fish, poultry, cheese, and egg dishes, and to sauces. (Mexican dishes, cream soups, dips, spreads, sauces, French dressing)

Celeriac: This dark, turnip rooted European variety of celery also goby the name of celery root or celery knob. Celeriac is seldom eaten raw. It is excellent creamed, au gratin, or chilled and served as a salad or hors d'oeuvre with a French or mayonnaise dressing.

Select firm small celeriac without sprouts on top of the root. Bulb roots should be clean and tops fresh looking.

Refrigerate, use within a week.

Celery: A popular stalk vegetable which is cultivated version of a white flowered herb that few wild in both Europe and Asia. The leaves, stalk, and root of cultivated celery are all edible. Splendid as a fresh, crunchy raw stalk, celery is also a delicious cooked vegetable. Fried, braised, or with a sauce, it makes an excellent accompaniment to roast meats and poultry (roasts, stews, egg dishes, stuffing, salads, breads, sauces, relishes, spreads).

Select fresh, crisp, clean celery of medium length and size, pale green in color. Thin, dark green stalks may be stringy.

Refrigerate in crisper; use within a week. Season: all year.

Celery Salt: The product of a combination of ground celery seed and fine salt. Use as a seasoning in vegetable and clam juices, soups, salad dressings, croquettes, eggs, and with fish and potato dishes.

Celery Seeds: Celery seed is a tiny olive-grown seed obtained from the celery plant in its wild form. The flavor of celery seed is almost identical with that of the vegetable celery. This seasoning is excellent in pickling, salad dressings, and in fish and vegetable dishes.

Cereal: An edible seed, also called grain, of the grass family. The most common cereal grasses are barley, corn, oats, rice, rye, and wheat. (Buckwheat, millet, and sorghum are not true cereals in the botanical sense, though they are used as cereals.) Cereal grains are used in the making of bread, flour, pastas, and breakfast foods, which are also called cereals. The word cereal goes back to Ceres the Roman goddess of grain. Spring festivals beseeching her for fruitful harvests were called Cerealia.

Cervelat: A smoked sausage made of finely ground beef chuck and pork, seasoned with salt, sugar, and red and black pepper.

Chafing Dish: This handsome cooking utensil is used to cook at the table, and has its own source of heat, such as an alcohol lamp, candle, solid fuel burner, or an electric unit. The word developed from the Latin *calefacere*, "to make warm", through the Middle English *chaufen* which mean the same thing.

Champignon: Champignon is the French word for mushroom. It comes from **champ**, French for "field", implying that mushrooms grow in fields.

Chantilly: This French word describes whipped cream that has been sweetened and flavored; it is also used for any dish, such as potatoes or sauce, to which whipped cream, sweet or unsweetened, has been added. Name derived from that of a castle north of Paris.

Chard or **Swiss Chard**: This vegetable is a variety of beet, of which the leaves and stalk, not the root, are eaten. Chard is a wholesome vegetable, with all the attributes of green leafy vegetables. It is an excellent source of Vitamin A., a very good source of iron, and a good source of vitamin C. Look for tender, fresh green leaves and crisp stalks of white or reddish hue.

Charlotte Russe: This elegant lady of the dessert family consists of a molded shell of ladyfingers filled with a sumptuous Bavarian cream. Sisters of this dessert are the ***Charlottes des Fruits,*** and in particular the ***Charlotte des Pommes***, or apple charlotte. This kind of charlotte is always served hot, and consists of a shell of crisp bread filled with cooked fruit.

Cerviche: Also known as cebiche. A dish characteristic of Peruvian cookery, that is based on raw fish marinated in lemon juice and is served with sweet limes, raw onion rings, tomato and boiled sweet corn.

Châtelaine, À la: A method of garnishing simple dishes. For egg dishes, the châtelaine garnish includes chestnuts, for meat, artichoke hearts.

Chaud-Froid: A dish that is prepared as a hot dish, but served cold. Chaud-froid's are pieces of meat, poultry, fish or game, coated with brown or white sauce, then glazed with aspic. It should contain some stock made from the food it is to coat, such as chicken stock for a chicken chaud-froid.

Chayote: (christophene, choco) This gourd-like fruit of a trailing vine, which is eaten as a vegetable, chayote has a deeply ribbed, greenish white rind and one soft seed. Chayote is more delicate in flavor then summer squash, and its main virtues are that it is low in starch and that it keeps its shape even when overcooked. Louisianans call it Mirliton or vegetable pear.

Cheese: A natural miracle and a universal food, cheese is made from milk which has been thickened and separated into two substances; a liquid called "whey" and a soft semisolid called "curd". Generally it is the curd which is pressed, treated and ripened into a great variety of cheese.

Cheesecake: The earliest published recipe appears in a famous 18ᵗʰ century cookbook, *The Art of Cookery Made Plain and Easy, by Mrs. Glasse.* This recipe begins; **"Take a pint of cream, warm it, and put to it five quarts of milk warm from the cow, then put rennet to it and just give it a stir; and when it is come, put the curd in a linen bag, let it drain well away from the whey bud do not squeeze it much. Then put it to your mortar and pound as fine as butter."** Today we only need to go to the nearest grocery store, and buy cream cheese, ricotta cheese, or cottage cheese to make a cheesecake.

Chef: In French, the word means "chief", but in both French and English it as become a culinary term for a superior male cook, head of his/her kitchen. To be a chef means that a man or woman has embraced a definite profession, studying, serving an apprenticeship, and working his/her way through specialized cooking positions until he/she become the head cook.

Cherries: The small, smooth, long stemmed, round stoned fruit of a tree that has a birch like bark and charming pink or white flowers. Cherries are divided into two groups; sweet and sour. Sweet cherries are the larger of the two, heat shaped, and firm yet tender. Sour cherries are a rounder, softer textured fruit.

Select, bright cherries with color ranging from light to bright red to purplish-black, depending upon variety. Tart or sour cherries are best for cooking. Sweet cherries can be eaten fresh or used in cooking. Avoid too soft or shriveled fruit.

Refrigerate; use in 2 or 3 days. Season: May to August

Cherry Liqueur: A member of well known European liqueurs and brandies are made from special strains of cherries cultivated for the purpose. The best known ones are Kirsch, a strong, colorless spirit made in France, Switzerland, and Germany.

Chervil: This delicate herb, used to flavor soups, salads, and stews, is a favorite in American herb gardens. Chervil is an annual, in appearance, it resembles a delicate parsley with lacy leaves. Chervil may be used fresh or dried. It is more flavorful when fresh.

Chestnut: The edible nut of a tree of the same name. Chestnuts are peeled (both the hard brown outer shell and the thin bitter brown inner peel), and are eaten in a variety of ways. They may be boiled or roasted, and served with a glass of wine. With turkey, goose, wild duck, or pheasant, they serve as a glorious stuffing, with all of these meats, as well as with pork and sausages, they go well as a vegetable mashed or whole brained form. Braised chestnuts also combine deliciously with red cabbage, Brussels sprouts, mushrooms, onions and carrots.

Chicken: This domesticated bird, whose meat and eggs are such an important and popular source of food, originated in the jungles of southeast Asia. The market types of ready to cook chicken are: *Broiler* or *Fryer*, *Capon*, *Roaster*, *Cornish Game Hen*, and *Stewing* chicken. Fully cooked young chicken sometimes appears underdone due to the red color around the bone. This is caused by internal pigment moving from the inside to the outside of the bone and does not affect eating quality.

Chicken, with its fine-textured, mildly flavored, lean and easily digested meat is popular with both adults and children. It is available year round, and is ideal for a huge variety of dishes.

Chickens are given different names according to their size, the quality of their meat and the way they are raised. The smallest, most tender chickens are described as squab and weighs 1 to 2 lbs. A spring chicken weighs around 2½ lbs. Ordinary fresh or frozen chickens, usually labeled as roasting or oven-ready come in the middle range of weights, and are fed to provide the maximum amount of meat for your money. They weigh up to 4½ lbs. sometimes a little more. The largest chickens on the marked are plum capons, which are castrated male birds specially raised for the table. They weigh up to 11 lbs.

Cutting a raw chicken: *1. a chicken can be cut into10 parts; 2. Place chicken breast side up. Grip the drumstick firmly and cut through the skin, close to the body. Pull thigh away from body and cut through the joint at the top of the thigh; 3. Place skin side down, and then cut through the joint between drumstick and thigh. (If chicken is small leave as one piece.) 4. Press wing against the body. The shoulder joint will now be visible under the skin. Make an incision between the ball and socket parts of the joint; 5. Place the knife inside the cavity of the chicken and pierce one side between the shoulder joint and the rib cage. Cut through the ribs parallel to the backbone. Repeat on the other side; 6. Pull the breast away from the backbone. Cut between these bones to detach breast section. Cut the back in half at the point where the ribcage ends; 7. Place* *the breast skin side up and cut down through the breastbone and meat on one or the other side of the keel.*

Stuffing and battering breast fillets: *1. Halve the breast. Remove any ligaments fat, etc; 2. Cut a pocket into the thickest side of the breast making sure not to cut through to the other side; 3. Fill the pocket; squeeze the edges together and close with small skewers; 4. Coat the stuffed breast first in seasoned flour, then with beaten egg, and finally breadcrumbs.*

Chick Pea: The chick pea, also known as garbanzo bean, Spanish bean, or ceci pea, is native to and extensively grown in southern Europe. Chick peas have a nutty flavor, which lends itself to cooking in many ways, and are one of the most nutritious of the legumes. They can be served as a vegetable, added to soups and stews, used in sauces, and salads, or marinated and served as an appetizer.

Chicory: The salad green is a member of the endive family, with finely cut, feathery leaves that have dark green edges and almost white centers. Its slightly bitter is a welcome addition to salads.

Chiffon: The word is used to describe both a cake and a pie, each of which, not surprisingly, is light textured and fluffy. A professional baker invented chiffon pie in the early 1920's. It was so fluffy with beaten egg whites that his mother side it reminded her of a pile of chiffon. This pie is always served chilled. The cake was invented by another professional baker in the 1940's, and the novelty of it was that it used a liquid shortening, cooking oil, instead of the usual solid shortenings.

Chiffonade: Literally translated this French term means "made of rags". In French culinary usage, it stands for a preparation of sorrel, chicory (endive), lettuce or other leaves, cut into even shreds or strips. Cutting en chiffonade is the term for shredding green leaves. Chiffonade is also a salad dressing in which shredded vegetables and hard boiled eggs are added to a standard French dressing.

Chili: A tropical plant from whose small elongated pods, or peppers, we get cayenne (red) pepper and hot pepper sauce. Chili powder is a blend of dried ground chili pepper pods, which may or may not contain other powdered herbs and spices. Most blend contain some ground cumin and oregano. In addition garlic, cloves or allspice may be used. (meats, poultry, fish, stews, egg dishes, vegetables, French dressing, croutons, spreads, dips)

Chili Sauce: This is a thick tomato sauce similar to ketchup, but spicier; it has bits of whole tomato, onion and other seasonings added. It is used like ketchup when a more distinct flavor is desired.

Chill, (to): To remove the heat from food or beverages by placing in a cold, but not freezing temperature, in the refrigerator, on ice, or as in the case of wine, in an ice and water pack. Chilling does not mean icing or freezing. Over chilling deprives most foods of flavor, especially seafood, salads, and fruits.

Chinquapin: A tree and its edible fruit which, like chestnuts, belongs to the genus *Castanea*. Although not of the same quality as chestnuts, chinquapins are eaten in the same way.

Chitterlings: The intestines of young pigs that have been emptied, turned inside out, and scraped clean while still warm. They are then soaked for twenty-four hours in cold salted water to cover, and washed at least six times before being cut up into two-inch lengths. Chitterlings are very popular in the South, and are a surprisingly tasty dish, eaten either boiled or deep fried.

Chives: A member of the onion family, it grows in clumps of slender, green, tubular leaves. Chives may be used to flavor any food in which a mild onion flavor is desired. Fresh chopped leaves are excellent in soups, casseroles, eggs, vegetables, appetizers, cheeses, cream and other sauces, and in salad dressings. They should be cut and added to foods just before serving. Chives can be frozen but are best fresh.

Chocolate: The result of roasting fermented cocoa beans and removing the shells, leaving the meat, or nibs. The word comes from the Mexican Indian choco, "foam", and alt, "water". It is said that Columbus brought some home to Spain with him, but the first Europeans to see it used were the Spaniards who invaded Mexico under Cortez in 1519. There they found chocolate in common use, flavored with spices, but unsweetened. It was the royal drink of the Aztecs, the Emperor Montezuma drank his chocolate from gold ceremonial goblets. Cocoa beans were also used a money. Chocolate, apart from its palatability, has a considerable stimulating effect on the heart and the general musculature of the body. It is more than a delicacy; it is good solid food and nourishment and considered as such my many countries. Chocolate should be stored in a cool, dry place at a temperature of about 60°F. If chocolate becomes warm, the fat in it rises to the surface, forming a grayish film. This is not harmful, and the chocolate is perfectly usable. But if the wrapper gets oily, the chocolate has deteriorated. When confronted with a choice of desserts, just remember "when in doubt, make it chocolate".

Chokecherry: This small, wild cherry grows on a large shrub, and is a native of North America. Chokecherries have a "puckery" taste, and though they can be eaten raw, they are best used for jams and jellies. Chokecherries are not be confused with chokeberries, which belong to a different species, and are the inedible fruits of a purely ornamental shrub.

Chop, (to): This can be either a noun or a verb. As a noun, a chop is a small tender cut of lamb, pork, or veal with a part of the rib or bone attached. The verb "to chop" means to cut into small pieces, smaller than cubes or dices but larger than minces. For efficient chopping you need sharp knives, hold the knife by both ends and chop up and down rapidly, using the tip of the blade as a pivot. Keep pushing chopped food together under the knife.

Chorizo: A Spanish or Mexican sausage made from coarsely cut meat, usually pork. It is seasoned with garlic, sweet red pepper and hot paprika, which gives it a piquant flavor and colorful appearance. Chorizo can be purchased either fresh, or dried and uncooked.

Chowder: This is a thick hearty soup that probably originated in New England, but takes it name from a large French kettle, the *chaudière*. It usually contains fish or seafood, salt pork, vegetables, and milk. There are also all vegetable chowders.

Choux Paste: Although it is often referred to as choux pastry. Choux is completely different from other types of pastry, such as short crusts, flaky, puff, and phyllo and so on. The mixture is based on a paste of flour and water, enriched with butter, and then lightened with and by beating thoroughly. When cooked the paste rises to form a crisp shell with a tin moist lining of cooked paste and a hollow center.

Chutney: This word of Hindustani origin, describes a well-seasoned relish that originated in India. It is made from a mixture of chopped fruits (mangos are one of the characteristic ingredients) and spices. Chutney can be served with other dishes as well as curries; stews poultry, meat, and vegetables.

Cider: Cider is the juice of apples that have been ground to a pulp and pressed to extract their juices. Cider may be "sweet" or "hard", that is, non-fermented or fermented. Hard or fermented cider is the drink Europeans who are great cider drinkers, usually refer to when they speak of cider. Its alcoholic content varies. Another form is Applejack, a potent spirit distilled from hard cider.

Cider vinegar: A mild, yellow brown vinegar, made from hard cider.

Cinnamon: This reddish brown spice comes from the dried bark of the shrub like evergreen trees of the *Cinnamonomum* family, which belongs to the laurel group. The kinds of cinnamon most commonly used are cassia and Ceylon cinnamon. Perhaps the sweet smell of cinnamon is the embodiment of the scent of all spices. When we read Milton's **Paradise Lost**, *"Off at Sea North-East winds blow Sabean Odours from the spicie-shoare of Arabie the blest"*, we cannot help but think of cinnamon. Ground cinnamon is widely used in baking and in flavoring fruits and desserts. Whole cinnamon comes in sticks in order to minimize breakage. A one inch piece of stick cinnamon will work wonders for the stock from corned beef or smoked pork shoulder; (pork chops, beef, stewed chicken, vegetables, fruits, salad dressings, breads, French toast, cookies, pastries, desserts, beverages)

Cioppino: This delectable fish stew is one of California's great contributions to gastronomy. Cioppino is a complicated stew and the versions are many. Traditional seasonings vary from area to area and the fish used vary with the day's catch. In addition, individual cooks often change the ingredients to suit their own tastes. Some prefer white wine to red, others use sherry. Many like to make it with the addition of exotic tidbits such a octopus, squid, or eel.

Citron: A citrus fruit originally from China and similar to the lemon, but larger and slightly pear-shaped, with a thick glassy skin. It is rarely eaten raw and gives little juice, which can be used like lemon juice. It's used mainly for its peel which is candied and used in baking.

Citron presse: freshly squeezed lemon juice with sugar and water on the side.

Citrus: A family of fruit trees, native to tropical Asia where they have been grown for thousands of years, but now grow in all parts of the world where the comate is favorable. The best known species are oranges, grapefruit, tangerines, lemons and limes, which are eaten for pleasure and health since they are outstanding sources of vitamins.

Clabber: This is milk which has soured naturally and thickened. It contains definite cuds, but they have not yet separated from the whey. Chilled clabbered milk is a pleasant, refreshing, wholesome dish that can be flavored in any desired way or eaten with fruit.

Clam: The name is used to describe many bivalved mollusk found in various parts of the world. There are the round, hard shelled clam, and the long, soft shelled clam. Soft shell clams are generally steamed or used in chowders. Hard shell clams are fished by raking, or dredged, like oysters, New Englanders often call them by their Native American name, "quahog". As early as 1616 Captain John Smith was so thrilled by his adventures as an amateur clam digger that he wrote this account to his fellow Englishmen *"you shall scarce find any bay or cove of sand where you may not take any clams, or lobsters or both at your pleasure."* Unfortunately ruthless harvesting has diminished the supply.

Claret: Properly speaking, this is a red wine from the Bordeaux region in southwestern France. Claret is famous for its jewel like color and its delicate flavor and bouquet. The principal grape variety used in red Bordeaux wines is Cabernet Savignon.

Clarify: In cooking, as in general usage, this word means to make pure and clear. It is generally applied to liquids and fats and it involves separating the solid parts from the liquid parts. The most commonly clarified foods are consommé and butter. Liquids are clarified by filter; fats are clarified by slow heating; fruit juices and wines can be clarified by slight fermentation or by the addition of other substances, such as isinglass, a very pure animal gelatin.

Cloves: Cloves are sold whole or ground, and are one of the most useful spices. They are used in gingerbreads, spice cakes, and fruitcakes; chili sauce and pickles. A clove studded ham looks and tastes much better than a plain one. Cloves studding a whole onion give zest to creamed dishes and sauces, an apple studded with cloves should be added to mulled wine and cider (pork, lamb, vegetables, fruit salads and dressings, cakes, cookies, pastries, marinades).

Coat: To coat food is to cover it with a thin layer of flour, fine crumbs, sugar, nuts, or frosting. Food is coated to preserve the inner moisture and to add flavor and texture contrasts between food and coating. When coating, make sure dry coating materials are very finely crumbled. When coating with crumbs, it is necessary to dip the food first into a liquid, such as milk, cream, or beaten eggs, to make crumbs adhere to it. Once coated, chill the food before frying, in this way a crisper, firmer coating is formed.

Cobbler: There are cobbles to eat and cobblers to drink. The first are desserts resembling a deep dish fruit pie, where sugared fruit is covered with a single biscuit or pastry crust and baked. Cobblers to drink consist of refreshing cold summer dinks spiked with wines or liquors, and garnished with fruits, such as oranges, lemons and/or berries, and with mint.

Cocktail: The word is used to describe drinks, both alcoholic and non-alcoholic, and also a certain type of appetizer. The alcoholic beverage is a short, iced, and rather potent drink, made with liquors and flavoring ingredients. The non alcoholic cocktail may be a chilled vegetable, fruit, or clam juice. The appetizer called a "cocktail" is chilled cut up fruit or vegetables, or chilled seafood, served with a highly seasoned sauce.

Cocoa: The word comes from the Mexican Indian *cacahuatl* and describes a beverage and dessert flavoring made from the beans of the cacao tree which flourishes only in tropical climates. Regular cocoa contains from 10 to 22 percent cocoa butter. Dutch process cocoa has been treated with alkali to give darker color and a slightly different flavor.

Instant cocoa is a mixture of cocoa, sugar, milk solids, flavor and an emulsifier which enables it to dissolve more readily, it can e prepared hot or cold with water or milk.

Cocoa Butter: This is the fat removed from cacao beans during the conversion into chocolate and cocoa. It is used primarily in making candy and pharmaceutical products.

Cocoa Powder: powdered chocolate liqueur.

Coconut: The fruit of a palm, native to Malaya, which has been transplanted to all parts of the tropical and subtropical world. It takes about a year to mature. The outer covering is smooth, the husk fibrous, and a woody brown shell encases a layer of firm white meat with a milky fluid at its center. The coconut itself produces a white meat which can be grated or shredded and eaten as is or used for cooking, fresh or preserved.

Select coconuts heavy for their size and with juice that sloshes around inside when coconut is shaken. Avoid fruit with moldy or wet "eyes".

Refrigerate and use within a week. (Fresh shredded coconut will keep in refrigerator 1 or 2 days.) Season: all year with best supplies from October to November.

Cod: This soft finned salt water fish. Cod is eaten fresh or salted. There are a number of varieties, such as Greenland and Pacific cod, which are found in the Alaskan waters and the Bering Sea and off the cost of Japan, but most code comes from the North Atlantic and the Baltic. **Scrod** is a young cod weighing one and a half to two and half pounds. The flesh is firm, white and delicious. Its vitamin rich liver gave strength to the Norwegian people long before it was made into cod liver oil; to this day the livers are boiled and then sometimes sautéed.

Coddle: To coddle is to cook gently by letting the food stand in water that has been brought to the boiling point and then removed from the heat. The pan should be tightly covered. What happens in coddling is that the food cooks gently in the cooling water and thus acquires a delicate, yet firm texture. Eggs are the most commonly coddled food.

Coffee: This is a beverage brewed from roasted and ground coffee beans. Coffee may be sold roasted whole, roasted ground, or as instant. Around 1720 it was brought to the French West Indies, then on to Brazil, which is now the largest coffee producer. However Colombia, Guatemala, San Salvador, Costa Rica, Java and Malaya also depend on coffee for much of their economy. In colonial America coffeehouses were common. Here coffee consumption was given additional impetus by the imposition of taxes on tea. Coffee in the early coffeehouses was served in shallow bowls and the habitué called for a "dish of coffee". Handles on the cups in which coffee was served were introduced in the middle of the 18th century. Made dozens of ways, drunk thick or thin, dark or light, strong or weak, pure or diluted with other substances such as chicory, coffee stands as a symbol of hospitality throughout the world.

Coffeecake: Coffeecakes are actually breads, usually with a sweetened filling or topping, which are served with coffee and especially with breakfast coffee. They are made with or without yeast, in both large and individual sizes. Toppings and fillings include sugared crumbs, confectioners' sugar, frostings, fruit juice glazes, fruits, nuts and cheese.

Cola: The word covers a tree, a nut; as well as complex syrup used for making America's favorite carbonated beverage. Native to tropical Africa, the cola tree produces fruit containing numerous seeds. These brownish bitter seeds are the cola nut from which the cola extract is obtained. Containing a small amount of caffeine, the cola nut is a mild stimulant

Cold Cuts: Assorted meats and poultry known as cold cuts and served cold, in slices. The meats may be roasted or boiled; fresh cured, smoked, or corned; they may be canned, they may be jellied; they may be sausages which require no cooking; bologna, salami, liverwurst.

Coleslaw: The Dutch words *kool* and *salade*, meaning "cabbage" and "salad", provide the most direct definition of coleslaw. Uncooked green or red cabbage is shredded and served with dressing. Other ingredients, such as chopped onion or celery, may be added. There are as many version s of coleslaw as there are cooks. To prepared cabbage properly, cut cabbage into halves; remove leaves and trim rough ribs. Roll up leaves and shred very fine with a sharp knife or use a food processor, dry well. Place in refrigerator until ready to mix if crisp coleslaw is required.

Collards: Collards are a member of the cabbage family and most closely related to kale. Their leaves are smooth, tall, and broad, but they do not form a head as cabbage does. The usual method of cooking them is to boil them with a piece of bacon or salt pork. Collards can also be cooked like spinach, chard, cabbage, or kale.

Coloring: In cookery, artificial tints, usually in the form of vegetable extracts are added to foods to strengthen the natural color or, as in candies, to create a purely decorative effect. When using food colorings, it must be remembered that they are extremely concentrated, and that even two or three drops may be more than enough. Start with a drop at a time, and blend thoroughly into food before adding the next drop.

Combine, (to): In cooking terms, the word means to put a number of different ingredients together in a bowl or sauce pan. This is done prior to incorporating the ingredients by mixing, blending, stirring, etc.

Compote: This is a dessert of fresh, canned, or dried fruits, cooked gently to preserve their shape, served in their own juices hot or cold. Compotes may be flavored with spices, wines, liqueurs and/or fruit juices. They may consist of single fruits or a combination of fruits. The word compote comes from Old French **composte** and conveys the thought of something that has been composed or put together. Compote is also the name given to the stemmed bowl from which the fruit is served.

Conch: (lambi) Pronounced "conk", this large shellfish, encased in a handsome spiral shell, inhabits southern waters. The muscle is edible, but is usually tough and must be tenderized. The most effective methods are: pounding with the edge of a heavy plate, parbroiling, or marinating.

Condiment: This word is applied to a seasoning an acid, salty, spicy addition to food to enhance flavor. Condiments have come to mean prepared sauces or accompaniments, such as ketchup, mustards, pickles, or chutney, and steak sauce or other sauces.

Confection: The word comes from the Latin word *confectus*, "prepared". Strictly speaking it can mean any prepared dish, but it especially applies to a sweet dish. Candies are often referred to as confections, and confectioners' shops are places where candy is sold.

Conserve: A sweetmeat or preserve made of a mixture of fruits, generally with nuts added. Conserves are soft and spread easily.

Consommé: This is a clear soup made from the broth of slowly simmered meat or poultry which has been clarified to become sparkling clear. The word comes from the French **consommer** which means "to accomplish", or "to boil down". Consommé is an essential in French cooking and eating. Good, strong consommé is used as a curtain raiser to any meal. Served in cups with a salty cracker, consommé makes an excellent first course in any cuisine.

Cookies: At one time, what we now call a cookie was referred to as a small cake or sweet biscuit. We must thank the Dutch for providing us with a special name for it. It is derived from *Koekje* or *Koekie*, meaning "small cake". Cookies are usually classified according to the way in which the dough is shaped. The six classifications are: 1) bars and squares, 2) drop cookies, 3) rolled cookies, 4) pressed cookies, 5) molded or shaped cookies, and 6) refrigerator cookies.

Coquille: In French, a coquille is a shell. In culinary language, it is a little dish in the shape of a shell, made from fireproof china, glass, or metal or an actual shell, preferably the shell of a scallop. A coquille is also food placed into this kind of dish with or without a sauce, but covered with breadcrumbs and/or grated cheese and browned in the oven or under the broiler.

Cordial: A beverage, often sweet, which is generally alcoholic and aromatic. It is supposed to have a tonic effect, as the etymology of cordial suggests, from the Latin "cor", which means heart.

Cordon Bleu: This was originally a wide blue ribbon worn by members of the highest order of knighthood, L 'Ordre des Chevaliers du Saint-Esprit, instituted by Henri III of France in 1578. By extension, the term has since been applied to food prepared to a very high standard and to outstanding cooks.

Coriander: (cilantro, Chinese parsley) This spice seed is the dried fruit of a herb which belongs to the parsley family. Coriander has a pleasant flavor, not unlike that of a combination of aniseed, cumin, and orange. It has the delightful quality of becoming more fragrant the longer it is kept. Like so many spices, it can be used in a great variety of foods, depending on personal taste. Ground, it flavors cookies, candies, soups, Danish pastries, and gingerbreads. Cheeses, meats and even salads benefit by the addition of this fragrant seed.

Corn: To botanists, corn is very specifically the tall grass Zea mays, which is also known as maize. It seems to have originated in Mexico the word "maize" comes from the Native American word mahiz - and is America's great contribution to the cereal group. Its edible grain is cultivated for human food and for livestock feed, the entire plant is used for forage. Its usefulness was not limited to food from the grain, for the Peruvians obtained sugar from its stalks, the Mexicans a honey-like substance, and a kind of beer or wine was made from it by all natives of the tropics. When selecting fresh corn, look for bright green, snug husks with dark brown silk at the husk end (a sign of well filled kernels). Buy for quick use. Texture, flavor, and half of the sugar content is lost in the first 24 hours after picking in summer temperature.

Look for medium size ears with right, plump, milky kernels that are just firm enough to offer slight resistance to pressure. Tiny kernels indicate immaturity; corn with very large, deep yellow kernels may be over mature and tough.

Refrigerate in crisper; use as soon as possible. Season: all year, best supplies are from May to September.

Corn Flour: Yellow or white corn, milled to the texture of wheat flour. It tastes like cornmeal.

Cornish Pasties: A pastry turnover traditionally made with short pastry but often made using puff pastry. It is filled with a mixture of diced beef, onions, potatoes and other root vegetables. Originally from the country of Cornwall in England, they were lunchtime snacks for miners.

Cornmeal: This is corn, coarsely ground after the hull and germ of the kernel are removed. Italy's famous *polenta* and Rumania's *mamaliga* are cornmeal cooked into a thick mush, served by itself, or with a sauce, milk, meat, or vegetables, or fried.

Corn Oil: Non hydrogenated oil obtained from the kernel of corn. After refining it has no taste or order. It is used extensively for salad dressings, for frying, and as a shortening in baking.

Cornstarch: This is a starch obtained from the endosperm portion of the kernel. It is used as a thickener in sauces, gravies, and puddings.

Corn Syrup: This syrup obtained from cornstarch and is made in two kinds: light and dark. Light corn syrup has been clarified and decolorized. Dark syrup has a stronger flavor.

Coulis: A thick sauce made with fruit or vegetable puree, used as a base or garnish.

Coup de rouge: a glass of red wine.

Course: A course is a part of a meal consisting of one dish or of one dish plus the accompaniments served with it. There was a time when formal dinner demanded no fewer than eight and often ten or twelve course. The eight course dinner was served in the following order; **hors d'oeuvre** (small cold appetizers), **soup** (preferably clear), **fish** (often more than one kind), **entree** (a variety of light dishes such as rissoles and croquettes plus fillets and cutlets) **remove** (the main course and usually a joint of meat served with vegetables although poultry could be served instead or as an addition), **roast** (poultry or game), **entremets** (three minor courses comprising dressed vegetables, hot or cold sweets such as jellies and puddings, and savories such as cheese and sardines), **dessert** (fruit, ices, petit fours) and coffee.

Court Bouillon: "Short broth" is the literal translation of this French term, which stands for a liquid in which fish or seafood is poached. A court bouillon can be as simple as salted water or it can be a broth made with wine and seasonings. A salt water bouillon is used for sea bass, red snapper, striped bass, and for fish that have a distinctive flavor in themselves so that they do not need artificial seasonings. The proportions used are one and a half teaspoons salt to one quart of water. Salmon, halibut, cod and seafood profit from a court bouillon pleasantly flavored with wine or lemon or vinegar, herbs, and spices, to which the bones and heads of fish may or may not be added for additional flavor. A flavored court bouillon may also be cooked down and used as an ingredient for fish sauces or as the base for aspics and glazes.

Couscous: A traditional North African ingredient made with hard wheat semolina and sometimes with barley, or, in Tunisia, with green wheat.

Crab: One of a large group of crustaceans characterized by a wide flat body protected by a hard shell (carapace). Crabs are decapods having five pairs of legs; these vary in size according to species, but the first pair (pinchers), are generally much larger and equipped with strong claws.

Cranberries: The red berry of any of several related shrubs of the genus Vaccinium. In both the northern part of North America and in northern Europe different varieties of cranberries grow on low trailing woody plants in bogs and places with wet acid soil. Wild cranberries were cooked with honey or maple syrup by the Indians and also dried for winter use long before the first settlers arrived on these shores. The mountain cranberry is found in heath and woodland in cold mountainous regions. Also known as loganberry and cowberry, it is eaten mainly in the United States, Scandinavia and Germany.

Select plump, firm berries with high luster. Some varieties are rather large, right red and quite tart; others are smaller darker and sweeter. Avoid shriveled, discolored or moist cranberries. Refrigerate; use in 1 to 2 week; may be frozen. Season: September to January.

Crawfish, **Crayfish:** The crawfish is a salt water crayfish. Crayfish, a fresh water crustacean resembling a small lobster; the species found in Europe grow 6 to 8 inches long. Crayfish are among the most exquisite of shellfish and greatly prized by connoisseurs of fine food in France, Germany and especially Scandinavia. In Sweden in particular, Midsummer Day (June 24) is the time for a national crayfish festival, where these delicious crustaceans are consumed by the ton and washed down with aquavit and beer.

Cream: A dairy product consisting of the part of milk, rich in fat, which has separated by skimming. Often an increase in the thickness of cream denotes an increase in fat content, but this is not always true as the viscosity of cream can be controlled by manufacturing processes, giving a variation in the thickness of creams the same fat content. Half-and-half is a mixture of milk and cream containing 10 to 12 percent milk fat; Sour cream usually has about 18 percent

Cream, (to): A cooking term meaning to make foods soft and creamy by mashing or beating them with a spoon, or any other tool. The word is frequently applied to fats such as butter which must be creamed before flavorings or sugars are added, or the fat won't be receptive to them. "To cream" is also used instead of "to blend", although the two processes are not quite identical. Creaming butter and sugar means that minute particles of each are thoroughly amalgamated, so that they don't show up separately. To blend the two means almost the same thing, but indicates that their combining is done to a somewhat lesser extent.

Creamed: This is said of a food cooked or served in a creamed or creamy sauce, creamed chicken, or creamed carrots, for example. Creaming a dish is a good way of stretching it.

Cream of Tartar: A natural fruit acid in the form of fine white powder made from pressed grapes. It is an ingredient in commercial baking powders.

Cream Puff: This is any airy little cream filled cake, brother to an éclair. Cream puffs are round éclairs are oblong. They are of French origin and made by an entirely different method from other pastries. Cream puff pastry is also called choux pastry. Perfect puffs should be firm, tender, and dry.

Cream Sauce: A classic cream sauce or Béchamel sauce which contains milk. It may also be made with cream rather than milk.

Crème: A sweet liqueur with a syrupy consistency. Crèmes are obtained by soaking various substances in brandy or a spirit containing sugar syrup: fruits (pineapple, banana, black currants, strawberries, tangerines, and raspberries), various plant parts (vanilla, mint, cocoa, tea, coffee) or flowers (violet; rose).

Crème Fraîche: Cream to which a lactic bacteria culture has been added, which thickens the cream and gives it a slightly sharp but not sour flavor.

Crenshaw: This is a melon with a cream and green colored rind which is smooth, with no netting and very little ribbing. As the melon ripens the rind takes on a yellower cast. The flesh is salmon-colored, thick, juicy and full of flavor. Crenshaw melons are at their best in the last summer and early fall.

Look for a deep golden yellow, sometimes with small areas of lighter yellow; the rind especially around the blossom end should yield slightly to gentle thumb pressure; it should have a pleasant aroma.

Let ripen at room temperature; refrigerate and use within 3 to 4 days. Keep melons with area well-wrapped; after cutting melons, cover cut surface with plastic wrap.

Creole: There are those who say that Creole cooking is America's most original contribution to good food, and that it ranks with Europe's finest cuisines. Be that as it may, there is no doubt that Creole cooking has made its hometown, New Orleans, a mecca to which gourmets from every part of the world come joyfully. Creole cooking is a combination of classic French, Spanish and Anglo Saxon cuisine, prepared with skill, by cooks, and spiced and seasoned with ingredients used by the local Choctaw Indians. It is a product of abundant native foods such as game, salt water and fresh water fish, oysters, crayfish and shrimps and of history and geographic circumstances. It is the seasoning - leaning heavily on pepper, onions, garlic, green peppers, and spices - that makes many Creole dishes so individual.

Creole Mustard: Pungent prepared mustard made from brown mustard seeds. As a substitute, use any strong flavored prepared brown mustard.

Crêpe: The French word for a type of pancake. It is a very thin, delicate pancake made of flour and eggs, without or without flavoring, sweetened or unsweetened. Sweetened crêpes are served for dessert with fruit or a sauce or just with sugar. The most famous member of the dessert crêpe family is Crêpe Suzettes, which are folded into quarters and served with a flaming liqueur sauce. Unsweetened crêpes are stuffed with meat, vegetables, fish, or cheese, rolled or folded, and sauced to be served as a main dish. The word comes from the Latin *crispus*, meaning curly or wavy.

Crimp, (to): This culinary term refers to two widely different methods of food preparation. In pastry making, crimping means pressing down a fork or similar tool on the outer edges of uncooked pastry. This is an easy way to achieve a decorative pattern and, in the case of two crust pies, it seals the supper and lower crusts together so that the filling won't escape. When crimping a pie, moisten the edges of the pastry with cold water first, thus holding them together. In preparing fresh fish, crimping means gashing a freshly caught fish on both sides of the body at 1 or 2 inch intervals; the fish is then plunged into icy water for between 30 minutes to 1 hour, depending on the size. This firms the flesh of the fish.

Crisp: When used as a verb, "to crisp" means to revive freshness by placing in chilled liquid or moist air, as celery is crisped, or by placing in a warm oven, as crackers are crisped. "To crisp" also means to make firm by frying as fritters. As an adjective crisp implies that the texture of a food is brittle and crackly, a crisp crust of bread, a crisp dry cereal, or crisp bacon.

Croaker: The name is given to a number of different fish that make croaking or grunting noises. They include the Atlantic croaker, the fresh water drum, and the queen fish. The noise is produced by the air bladder. Croakers are usually small fish, and are eaten either fried or broiled.

Croissant: This French word means "crescent" and it describes a buttery, flaky roll baked in the shape of a crescent. The French, Swiss, Austrians and other central Europeans eat freshly baked croissant for breakfast, a habit enthusiastically embraced by foreigners visiting these countries. This delicious pastry originated in Budapest in 1686, and was used to commemorate the withdrawal of invading Turks. Bakers working at night heard the Turks tunneling into the city and spread the alarm, which lead to the defeat of the Turkish troops. As a reward for their vigilance, the bakers were commissioned to produce a commemorative pastry, shaped like a crescent, the emblem of Turkey.

Croquette: The word is a derivative of the French word **croquer** which means "to crunch" or "to crackle under the teeth". The culinary term covers a little savory morsel, which should be crisp on the outside and creamy on the inside. Croquettes are made in the shape of a cone or a sausage, and consist of such cooked foods as minced fish, eggs, meats, vegetables, and fruits, held together by a thick sauce and deep fried.

Croustade: A term used in French cooking for a browned case or shell made of bread, rice, potato, hominy or pastry and used to hold a creamed meat, seafood, vegetable or hors d'oeuvre mixture.

Crouton: A small piece of bread which is toasted, lightly browned in butter, fried in oil or simply dried in the oven. The word "crouton" is derived from the French word for the crusty end of a long loaf of bread. Croutons are served principally as a garnish for soup or scrambled eggs, in salads, stuffing, or bread puddings, or as a casserole topping. The name crouton is also given to small decorative aspic shapes used to garnish cold dishes.

Crudités: Raw vegetables or fruits served as an hors d' oeuvre, generally thinly sliced, grated or cut into little sticks and accompanied by cold sauces. A plate of crudités may also include a hard-boiled egg in mayonnaise.

Cruller: A fried cake, sister to the doughnut, which takes its name from the Dutch word **krulle**, meaning "twisted cake". Crullers are made by rolling out dough, cutting it into strips, doubling the strips, twisting them, and pinching the ends together. They are then fried in deep fat and brushed with sugar. French crullers are made in a round shape with a cream puff batter, and fried in deep fat. They have a thin icing.

Crumb, (to): This phrase has two related meanings in culinary practice. "To crumb" can mean to coast food with bread, cereal, or cracker crumbs, then food may simply be topped with plain, buttered, or sweet crumbs, or it may be dipped into a liquid such as milk or beaten eggs first, and then coated with crumbs. "To crumb" is also used to describe breaking, crushing, rolling, or grinding food into small pieces. Bread is torn into crumbs either by hand or in a food processor, cookies and crackers are crushed by placing them into a plastic bag and rolled with a rolling pin or other heavy object.

Crumpet: A small, patty-cake-shape, unsweetened, leavened brad made of flour, milk, butter, salt, yeast and egg. The word comes from the Middle English word for "wafer". Although they are similar to their English muffin cousins, crumpets are softer in texture with surface holds appearing during the pan cooking, these holes enable them to absorb great quantities of butter.

Crust: The word has several meanings in cookery. It is used to describe a firm, hardened covering formed as a result of cooking, in meats, poultry, or breads for example. It also describes a thin layer of pastry, as used in pies, or to top a casserole, or to encase a pâté, a ham or other meat in order to seal in the juices. Crusts are made from flour liquid, and shortening. They can be savory or sweet and they may be flavored with herbs, spices, cheese, citrus rind, or nuts. Sometimes the word crust is used to describe a hard, dried outer coating which forms on a food. With foods such as custards and puddings, a crust is not desirable. To prevent one from forming on top of a pudding or thick custard, either sprinkle with sugar, place wax paper directly on pudding, or cover tightly with a lid or plastic wrap while still warm.

Cube, (to): When used as a culinary term, "to cube" means to cut food into small, uniform, and sometimes decorative chunks, cheese, bread, potatoes, or carrots, for example. When the size of a cube is important (½-inch or 1-inch cubes), it will generally be specified in a recipe. "To dice" is the term used for cutting foods into cubes less than ½-inch in size.

Cucumber: The succulent fruit of an annual climbing plant of the gourd family, which is generally eaten raw but is also good, cooked. The word comes from the fruits Latin name, *cucumis*. A native of southern Asia, the cucumber has been cultivated since early historic times. Cucumbers have always been a staple vegetable, both fresh and pickled. Indians, Hebrews, Greek and Romans referred to them as long as 4,000 years ago. Cucumbers are available year round. Look for cucumbers that are well shaped, crisp, firm, fresh and bright green in color with a whitish tip. Over mature cucumbers are dull in color, yellowish, or puffy.

Look for firm, well shaped cucumbers with good green color. Over mature cucumbers, generally seedy, are dull or yellow and have overgrown, puffy look. Smaller varieties are preferred for pickling.

Refrigerate; use within 3 to 5 days. Season: all year, best supplies are from May to August.

Cuisine: This French word means two things, first, a kitchen and second, the style of cooking of a restaurant, or a nation.

Culinary: This adjective means "of, or pertaining to, the kitchen or cooking". It comes straight from the Latin word of the same meaning, *culinarius*, which was itself formed from culina, "kitchen". Culinary is used in such expression as "culinary arts" or "culinary standards".

Cumin: The cumin plant, source of the aromatic cumin seed, is a delicate member of the parsley family. The seed is tiny and oval, with a strong, warm, and slightly bitter taste. Cumin is one of the herb seeds used b the ancient Persians, Greeks and Romans. In the Middle Ages it was believed that cumin had the power to bind a person to a place or another person. For this reason in Germany the bride and groom carried cumin seeds in their pockets during the marriage ceremony. Since cumin resembles caraway seed in flavor as well as looks, its uses are much the same. Cumin is stronger, however, and should be used sparingly at first. Cumin is available whole and ground.

Cupcake: This small cake is baked in the shape of a cup, from a special kind of cake batter. The cup may be a muffin pan, a custard cup, a small cup mold. If muffin tins are used, they must be greased and floured for easy removal.

Curaçao: Liqueur produced in the Caribbean from the peel of bitter oranges.

Cure: The word, when used as a verb relating to food, refers to an age old method of preserving meat, poultry, and vegetables using salt as a preservative. Sugar is sometimes added for flavor and counteracts the tendency the saltpeter has to harden the meat. Pork is the most frequently cured meat.

Curd: Milk coagulated either by the action of rennet or by natural fermentation. Curdling is the first stage in the manufacturing of cheese.

Currant: This name is applied to two totally different fruits. One, a fresh currant, is a berry of the genus Ribes, a member of the gooseberry family, the other, a dry currant, is a dried grape of the genus Vitis. Since the fresh currant is first mentioned as a garden plant in the 15th century, it probably took its name from the dry currant, which had been cultivated for centuries before that time and which it resembles.

Curry: The idea of curry as a dish flavored with curry powder was a British invention, or more appropriately, a misrepresentation of spiced Indian dishes. Curries are native to India, where they are mentioned as early as 477 A.D. The word from the Tamil **kari**, is recorded in the English language in the 16th century and from then on, throughout the world. In India the spices in kari vary according to the individual cook, the region, caste and customs, as well, of course, as the main ingredient or dish which it is intended the compliment. In general, southern Indian curries are more pungent, northern Indian ones milder. (beef, pork, poultry, lamb, fish, egg dishes, seafood salads, vegetables, rice, fruit compotes, sauces, salad dressings, dips, cheese spreads)

Custard: A hot or cold mixture set or thickened with eggs or egg yolks. The term primarily refers to sweet mixtures of milk or cream with eggs. There are several basic types of sweet custard and numerous variations on them; they also form the base for a wide variety of desserts.

Cut, (to): As a noun used in connection with food, the word refers to a natural or customary segment of meat. Porterhouse steak and brisket are cuts of meat, for example. As a verb, "to cut" means anything done with a knife or other sharp instrument. Cutting includes, chopping, slicing, dicing, mincing and slashing.

Cut In: In culinary terms, this phrase means to break fat into small particles and combine them with dry ingredients. Cutting in is done with two knives or a pastry cutter.

Cutlet: A small piece of meat, cut from leg or ribs, for broiling or frying. A shaped cutlet (côtelette composée) consisted of boned minced ground meat, poultry or fish that is bound with a sauce and shaped into a cutlet.

D

Dab: (limande) Any of several related flat fish found in the North Sea, the English Channel and the Atlantic, north of the Bay of Biscay. The true (or European) dab is lozenge-shaped; its upper surface brownish with orange-yellow spots. They are sold either whole or filleted, and are usually grilled or baked.

Dacquoise: A traditional gâteau of southwestern France, also Palois (the dacquoise are inhabitants of Dax, the palois those of Pau). It consists of two or three layers of meringue mixed with almonds (or almonds and hazelnuts). The layers are sandwiched together with whipped cream or French butter cream, using a variety of flavors.

Daikon: Also known as dai-co, mooli, Japanese radish, or satsuma radish. A type of white-skinned radish, widely cultivated as a vegetable in the Far East, for use raw, in cooked dishes or as a garnish.

Daiquiri: Rum cocktail named after a small village on the Cuban coast near Santiago, where, in the 19th century, the Americans supposedly landed after defeating, the Spanish.

Dandelion: A perennial flowering plant that grows wild in Europe. Pissenlit in French, the English name is derived from the alternative French name den-delion (literally "lions tooth"; referring to its serrated leaves); pissenlit is a reference to its supposed diuretic properties. Wild or cultivated, dandelion leaves are eaten as a vegetable, raw or cooked. They have a somewhat bitter flavor. They should be harvested in the spring, before the plant flowers, when the leaves are still young, tender and delicate. The roots can be roasted and ground and made into a root coffee. To make dandelion root coffee, roast the roost in a slow oven for 4 hours. They should snap easily and show a very dark brown interior; grind and use as you do coffee.

Dash: A small quantity or portion added to or put on a food with a quick stroke of the hand, i.e. a dash of salt or pepper.

Dashi: The Japanese name for stock. Stocks used in Japanese cookery are very light, made by soaking dried **konbu** seaweed and/or other ingredients in water. Dried cured bonito flakes (katsuobushi) may be used with the konbu. **Niboshi**, small dried fish, may be used instead of bonito flakes, depending on the type of dashi required.

Dates: The fruit of the date palm, Phoenix dactyifera. Dates are one of the oldest and most valuable food plants, with a history of more than 5,000 years. Brown and fleshy, about 1½-inches long, growing in clusters, the date is rich in sugar. Cleopatra of Egypt ate dates and drank wine made from them, and so did the Greeks, who called it **dakulos** (finger) because of its shape, used it in sauces for fish or meat and included it in various cakes and pastries. The Greeks thought of the date as a symbol of light, fertility, and riches, and dedicated it to Apollo, the god of music and poetry. There is a charming Jewish legend that the female palm tree wept for her lover until a branch of the male tree was brought to her.

Look for lustrous golden brown fruit.

Keep tightly wrapped, when refrigerated, will keep for several weeks. Season: Year round, with best supplies in November.

Daube: A method of braising meat (beef, mutton, turkey, goose, pheasant, rabbit, pork, chicken), certain vegetables (boletus mushrooms, palm hearts), and some fish (tuna). Meat cooked en daube is braised in red wine stock well seasoned with herbs; the name is thought to come from the Spanish **dobar** (to braise).

Dauphine: A soft cow's milk cheese from Hainaut in France, with a brown rind and containing at least 50% fat.

Déca: decaf.

Decant: To transfer a liquid from one vessel to another after allowing suspended impurities to settle.

Deer: The meat is called venison and its quality varies according to the type of deer, its age, sex and habitat. Deer have been valued for their meat since prehistoric times and there is evidence of attempts to capture them in ancient Egypt. In the Middle Ages, deer were the most highly prized game animals, reserved exclusively for nobility.

Deep Fry(ing): The term means to cook food in enough fat to cover the food completely. When food is properly deep fried; a thin coating forms on its outer surface, keeping its juices inside and preventing the fat from penetrating the food. Success in deep fried foods depends largely on the heat of the fat. It must be hot enough to cause rapid browning of the food's surfaces but the fat should not be so hot that it smokes. The right temperature for most foods is 375°F., although some foods require a higher temperature. Recipes will generally specify the correct temperature when this is so.

Deglaze: To add a small amount of liquid (usually water or wine) to a pan after sautéing food and stirring to loosen the browned bits. This mixture is then used to make a sauce or reduced and served with the food.

Dehydrate: The word means "to take away water" and refers to the process of drying foods in machines which use controlled heat. The nutritive value of the food is not impaired in the process.

Delicatessen: A shop, or department in a store or supermarket, selling high quality, luxury food and/or special products. The word, meaning delicacies originated in Germany, in the 18th century.

Demi-Glace: A rich brown sauce made by boiling and skimming espagnole sauce and adding white stock or estouffade. It usually has the addition of Maderia, sherry or a similar wine.

Demitasse: A French word which means "half a cup". It applies to a small cup for, or of, black coffee.

Dessert: Dessert is the final course of a meal. The word comes from the French verb **desservir**, which means "to clear or take away", and in French gastronomy it includes the service of cheese, entremets (or sweets) and fruit.

Devilled: In French, á la diable; the name given to dishes with a piquant or hot marinade, spice mixture or sauce, usually based on mustard. Worcestershire sauce, cayenne pepper and paprika are other typical seasonings.

Devil's Food Cake: One of America's most popular chocolate cakes, with a true chocolate flavor, a deep rich color, and a light fluffy texture. Devil's food is probably so called to contrast it with the snowy white Angel Food Cake.

Devonshire Cream: This English country delicacy, from the county of Devonshire, is a thick, clotted cream made from non-homogenized fresh farm milk. It is eaten with scones or toast, accompanied by jam, with fruit pies, or with fruit.

Dice, (to): As a culinary term, it means to cut into cubes with a sharp knife. First the food is cut into slices, then slices are cut into strips, and the strips are bundled and cut crosswise into cubes. Ordinarily size is assumed to be small, less than ½-inch. If size is important, it is generally indicated in a recipe by such expression as "finely diced".

Diet: The word is derived from the Greek *diata*, meaning "manner of living", and when used about food, refers in general to the food and drink regularly provided and eaten. It also means, more specifically, "to eat and drink sparingly or by prescribed rules". Although we think of dieting in the second sense of the word as a comparatively modern development, this is by no means true. Demosthenes, in the 3rd century B.C., wrote, "Like the diet prescribed by doctors, which neither restores the strength of the patient nor allows him to succumb..." The Roman poet Horace, in the 1st century B.C. was saying more positively, "Now learn what and how great benefits a temperate diet will bring along with it. In the first place you will enjoy good health."

Dijon mustard: Prepared mustard (originally made in Dijon, France); which may be either mild or highly seasoned. When a recipe calls for Dijon mustard it is generally calling for the highly seasoned version.

Dijonnaise, a la: The description a la Dijonnaise is given to various dishes prepared with a specialty of Dijon, particularly mustard (for savory dishes) or black currants (for sweet dishes). Dijonnaise sauce is a mustard flavored mayonnaise-type sauce served with cold meats.

Dill: An aromatic umbelliferous plant originating in the East and introduced into Europe in ancient times. It is commonly called false anise or bastard fennel but in fact it has an excellent and distinct, yet delicate flavor of its own. It is used in preparing and serving soups, cheese, fish, meats, poultry, vegetables, potatoes, breads and apple pie. Dill is available as fresh leaves, dill weed, and as whole or ground dill seed (beef, lamb, poultry, fish, seafood, egg dishes, vegetables, salads and dressings, breads, sauces). The stems and seeds are used in flavor pickling vinegar. Dill is very popular in Scandinavian cooking, traditionally used with raw, smoked and pickled salmon.

Dim Sum: A Cantonese specialty, consisting of a collection of steamed and deep fried snacks; usually served mid-morning, right through the afternoon. Traditionally served in teahouses, dim sum is now offered in many restaurants during the day.

Dinner: The main meal of the day eaten from noon onward. The Norwegians eat dinner between four and five in the afternoon, the French between seven and eight, and the

Spaniards after nine at night, while American eat between six and seven.. There is no hard and fast rule for dinnertime.

Dissolve, (to): In cookery, to dissolve means to add a solid to a liquid, hot or cold, and cause the solid to become one with the liquid. This is done, for example, when sugar is dissolved in hot coffee, gelatin in water, a bouillon cube in hot water, salt in a sauce, and yeast in water.

Divinity: A creamy candy produced by cooking sugar, water, and corn syrup to the firm ball stage (248°F. on a candy thermometer) and then slowly beating this hot syrup into stiffly beaten egg whites. The mixture is dropped by the spoonful onto wax paper and allowed to harden and cooked, or it is turned into a butter pan, allowed to harden, and cut into squares. Melted chocolate, nuts, coconut or candied fruits may be added for variety. Divinity is usually made with white sugar but occasionally brown sugar is used. When Divinity is made with brown sugar, it is called "Seafoam".

Djon Djon: Tiny Haitian mushrooms with caps considerably smaller than a dime. When cooked, they give off a dark brownish-black liquid and color.

Dot, (to): "To dot" means to place a small amount of an ingredient over the top surface of food. It usually appears in recipes in such phrases as "dot with butter", "dot with melted chocolate", etc. The appearance and flavor of the foods are improved by this procedure.

Dough: Wheat flour and water and basic dough ingredients, but other cereals and liquids may be used. Salt is often added for flavor and sugar for sweetening. Fat (lard, butter, shortening or oil) and eggs enrich dough. Milk or other liquids may be used instead of water to bind the ingredients. Raising agents, such as yeast or baking powder, may be used to make the dough rise during baking.

Doughnut: A doughnut is a small cake, deep fried or baked and leavened with yeast or baking powder. Doughnuts are ring shape with a hole in the center. Crullers and dried cakes are closely related to them. Both are made of the same kind of dough and deep fried, but technically crullers are shaped in a twist, and fried cakes are made round or square, without a hole. The origin of the doughnut, or more particularly the doughnut hole, has caused considerable speculation. The most popular story regarding the whole in a doughnut, centers around a New England sea captain named Hanson Gregory. In 1847, when Captain Gregory was a boy in Camden, Maine, he complained to his mother that dried cakes were never completely cooked in the center. To alleviate the problem of a doughy center she poked holes in them before they were cooked. Americans have enjoyed doughnuts with holes ever since.

Drain, (to): To pour a liquid off a solid with the primary intention of saving the solid.

Dredge: To sprinkle a food with a dry substance, such as flour, cornmeal, or sugar. The purpose of dredging is to add flavor, facilitate browning, or improve appearance. Veal cutlets are dredged in flour, and doughnuts and cookies with granulated or confectioners' sugar.

Dressing: In culinary language, the word has three meanings; 1) A sauce, usually cold, added to fish, meats, fruits and most commonly, salads; 2) A solid, well seasoned mixture used to stuff fish, poultry, or meats, or to be baked by itself, this type of dressing is often called a "stuffing"; 3) A method of preparing food for cooking. Fowl is dressed by plucking, drawing, singeing, trimming and trussing, fish is dressed by scaling, gutting, and trimming.

Dried Fruit: Fruits, which the solids have been greatly concentrated by evaporating a large portion of the original water content, are called dried fruits. The purpose of drying is preservation, but the resulting decrease in bulk affords great savings in transportation and storage costs. Dried fruits have a great variety of uses. They may be eaten as is, cooked and used as a sauce, used in pies, cakes, cookies, quick breads, puddings, and in stuffing, or served as meat accompaniments.

Drink: The simplest and most natural drink, and the only one essential for survival of all living organisms, is water. The average consumption of liquid in a temperate climate is 1 liter (1¾ pints or 4⅓ cups) per day, but needs vary according to the climate and the diet.

Drip: This refers to a steady flow of liquid, drop by drop. The word is most often used in reference to making jelly; fruit juice is allowed to drip through several layers of cheesecloth. It is also used when making mayonnaise or hollandaise, oil or butter is dropped into other ingredients to prevent curdling, or in cheese making, when whey drips out of the curd.

Drippings: The term applies to any fat or juices that is drawn from food during cooking, i.e., bacon drippings, roast beef drippings, roast chicken drippings, etc. Fat from drippings can be used as shortening in making gravies, sauces, pie crust, cookies, biscuits, breads, etc.

Drop: In reference to food and food preparation, the word has two meanings. In its first sense it is a unit of measure for a minute amount of liquid which is usually measured out with an eye dropper or glass tube with a rubber squeeze top. It is used for measuring flavoring extracts and food colorings as well as to indicate the rate or flow as in "add oil drop by drop". In its second sense, the word 'drop' describes a batter or dough of a certain consistency, which needs a spoon for shaping, such as drop cookies, drop biscuits, drop dumplings, etc.

Drumstick: The lower leg of a fowl or game bird, consisting of the bone, meat and a thin layer of fat, giving it the shape of a pestle (hence the France name pilon, which means pestle). It is fleshier and juicier than white meat, but inferior to the thigh.

Dry: To dry food is to remove the moisture in it naturally by exposing the food to the sun or air. The reason for drying foods, a practice as old as history, is to preserve them by reducing water spoilage, such as molding, fermentation, or rotting. Dry can also mean to remove moisture from the surface of a food by wiping it with a dry cloth, such as "wash chicken and pat dry". In still another meaning, dry is used to describe wines lacking sweetness.

Duck: The duck is a dark fleshed, web footed water fowl closely related to swans and geese. Ducks have been hunted since the beginning of recorded time. Egyptians depicted them in their hieroglyphics, and were in the habit of drying and salting them in order to have a constant supply on hand. The Chinese were the first people known to have bred ducks for food, and by the 1st century of the Christian era ducks have been domesticated in Europe. The Romans fattened their ducks on figs and dates and served them sprinkled with wine and perfumed with truffles. Apicius, the Roman gourmet, gives us a number of sauces suitable for crane or duck. All domestic ducks are derived from either the mallard; Anas platyrhynchos, or the Muscovy duck Cairina moschata. In France, the most common breeds are Nantes duck and the Barbary duck. The mallard duck, produced by crossing these two breeds, is reared mainly in southwestern France for the production of foie gras since the 1970's and is highly esteemed by gourmets. Whatever breed, duck should be consumed within three days of killing.

Ducks are mostly available frozen; and the average duck weighs 2¾ to 5½ lbs. and serves and serves 3 to 6 people.

Dumplings: A ball of dough, originally savory and served as an accompaniment to meat or as a dessert. Although dumplings are part of standard English and Scandinavian cooking, there is a "dumpling belt" in Central Europe, stretching from Alace to Poland, and taking in southern Germany, and northern Switzerland, and the whole of Austria. Here the dumpling reigns supreme. Dumplings are closely related to pasta. Italian gnocchi are good examples of small dumplings. A simple satisfying good, dumplings were boiled and served to extend small amounts of meat.

Durum Wheat: A type of hard wheat with a high gluten content, valued particularly for making semolina and pasta. Pasta products made from it do not disintegrate in cooking, but become tender while remaining firm.

Dutch Chocolate: Dutch-processed cocoa which is treated with a mild alkali, mellowing the flavor and making it easier to dissolve.

Dutch Oven: A large, heavy cooking pot with a close fitting lid, authentically made of cast iron and hung over an open fire. Thought to be of 16th century Pennsylvania Dutch origin, the pot was used for stewing and braising; however, other types of dishes, such as breads, were also cooked in it.

Duxelles: A basic preparation of chopped mushrooms, onions and shallots sautéed in butter. Duxelles are used as a stuffing or garnish, as a complimentary ingredient of a sauce, and in the preparation of various dishes called á la duxelles.

E

Ear: A piece of offal, usually from pigs of calves, used in cooking or in the preparation of brown (head cheese) and various other forms of charcuterie.

Eau-de-Vie: A French term meaning "water of life"; from the Latin *aqua vitae*. It is also generally applied to brandy (not necessarily cognac or Armagnac) and also to the alcohols blanc (white alcohols) -- spirits distilled from fruits or herbs and kept in glass (not wood) without any sweetening.

Éclair: A small, log-shaped bun of choux pastry filled with cream and coated with chocolate fondant icing (frosting). The paste is piped onto a baking sheet until crisp and hollow.

Écot: A French term meaning each diners' share in a meal paid communally. The word, which comes from the Old French skot (contribution), is hardly used at all now, except in the expression "payer son écot" (to pay one's share).

Eel: A snake-like fish with a smooth slippery skin. Eels were popular with the Romans and widely eaten during the Middle Ages. Jellied eels are famous in Britain, served cold in the jellied stock in which they were cooked. Smoked eel is a popular dish in Scandinavia and northern Germany. Eels are particularly popular in Japan, especially opened and skewered, then grilled as **kabayaki**. It is also served on rice or cooked **nabemono** style as part as a one-pot meal prepared at the table.

Egg: The round or oval reproductive body laid by the female of many animals, containing the developing embryo and its food reserves and protected by a shell or skin. The word "egg" comes from the Middle English **egge**. The Latin word for egg is *ovum*. Although the eggs of many birds, fish and even reptiles can be used as food, the word "egg" unqualified applies exclusively to hen's eggs. Eggs are a basic food. Their taste, their nutritive values, and their availability are matched only by their versatility. In addition to their use as a food in their own right, eggs are used in cooking to thicken, as in custard, and puddings, to leaven, as in soufflés, angel food and sponge cake, and puffy omelets; to coat for proper adherence to breading, to bind, as in meatloaves and casseroles, to emulsify, as in mayonnaise and salad dressings, to clarify, as in consommé and boiled coffee, to add color, as in sauces and cakes, to hinder crystallization, in candy making, and to garnish as in canapés, salads, and soups.

Egg Custard: The name often given to baked sweet custard, a dessert made by pouring sweetened hot milk on to beaten eggs lightly sweetened with superfine (caster) sugar. The milk is usually flavored with vanilla.

Eggnog: A nourishing drink served either hot or cold. To make it, beat an egg yolk with a tablespoon of sugar. Add a glass of hot milk and lace with rum or brandy.

Eggplant: The eggplant is an erect branching plant, Solanum melongena, closely related to the potato. The fruit, which in reality is a berry, varies in length from two to twelve inches. Its shiny surface may be dark purple, white, red, yellowish, or even striped, depending on the variety. Eggplant is grown in different sizes and shapes, round, oblong, and pear shaped. Possibly the first variety known to Europeans was that resembling a hen's egg, hence the name eggplant. The original home of the eggplant is believed to have been the East Indies although it is first mentioned as being used as a vegetable in India. Look for eggplants that are heavy firm, smooth, and of a uniform dark glossy color. Large rough spongy places indicate poor quality.

Select firm and heavy eggplant that has a uniformly dark, rich purple color and a bright green cap, and is free from scars or cuts. Wrinkled or flabby eggplant will usually be bitter tasting.

Refrigerate; use within 1 or 2 days. Season: Year round.

Egg Sauce: A hot English sauce made of diced hard-boiled eggs and butter, most often served with poached fish.

Elixir: A solution of aromatic substances in alcohol. In the Middle Ages elixirs were used as potions to which magical properties were sometimes attributed. The word comes from the Arabic al-iksür (essence), from the Greek ksêron (dry medicine).

Empanada: A pie or pastry filled with meat or fish popular all over Spain and in parts of South America. The classic empanada comes from Galicia and is made with chicken, onions and peppers.

Emperor Fish: Fish of the Beryciform family, which lives at great depths of the eastern Atlantic from Ireland to Spain, and in the Pacific around New Zealand. Sold as fillets, its excellent flesh is similar to monkfish, and it is cooked in the same way.

Emulsifier: A food additive used to preserve the texture of emulsions. Among natural emulsifiers are lecithin's, extracted from almonds or other seeds (especially soybeans in making chocolate) or from egg yolks.

Emulsion: A preparation obtained by dispersing one kind of liquid (in the form of tiny droplets) in another liquid, with which it does not mix. An emulsion consisting of a fatty substance, such as oil or butter, dispersed in vinegar, water or lemon juice will only remain smooth and stable if it is bound with an emulsifier, usually egg yolk.

En brochette: French term for cooked on a skewer.

En-cas: The French term for a light meal, usually cold, eaten between main meals (the word literally means "in case"; of hunger in this context). In the old châteaux, an en-cas nuit, consisting of cheese, fruit and cold meals, was arranged on a pedestal table for the refreshment of travelers returning home late at night.

Enchilada: A tortilla, stuffed, rolled and served with a highly seasoned sauce.

Endive, French or Belgian (Witloof): This salad green is a member of the family of plants called Cichorium, to which chicory also belongs. The endive is a plant with narrow, finely divided curly leaves and is often called "curly endive". Two other salad greens closely related to endive are escarole, which has broad waved leaves and a blanched heart, and witloof, or Belgian endive, which is four to six inches in length and one to two inches thick. The leaves of Belgian endive are white with light green tips pressed close together to form a cylinder which tapers off to a point. Most varieties have bitter leaves. The variety commonly used is the curly endive. The hearts, known as gourilos, may also be eaten. Look for crisp, fresh, tender plants. Avoid tough, dark green outer leaves; look for a tightly packed head. Browning of the outer leaves indicates bruises.

Select small compact stalks with white leaves with pale green edges. Avoid wilted outer leaves.

Refrigerate in crisper; use within 1 or 2 days. Season: September to June.

English Muffin: This English tea bread is a yeast raised, unsweetened bread about three and one half inches in diameter and about one inch thick. Usually English muffins are cut and allowed to rise on a surface dusted with cornmeal, and then baked on a griddle. The baked muffins are then split and toasted and spread with butter or jam.

Enriched: Resupplied with vitamins and minerals lost or diminished during processing of food.

Entre côte (Rib Steak): A piece of prime quality beef, which should be cut from "between two ribs (côtes) hence the name. However, it is usually cut from the boned set of ribs.

Marbled and tender entre côte steak should be grilled or fried. Steak cut from the lower ribs are prepared the same way but tend to be firmer.

Entre-deux-mers: An AOC white wine from the Bordeaux region. Some red wine is also produced from Merlot and Cabernet Sauvignon grapes and is sold as Bordeaux AOC. They provide a good accompaniment to most fish and shellfish dishes, including oysters.

Entrée: The word comes directly from the French word meaning "entrance". In culinary terms it is used to describe one of the dishes of a meal, or the course during which the dish is served. Today, the entrée is usually the main course of the meal, but in a full French menu it is the third course, following the hors d' oeuvres (or soup) and the fish course and preceding the roast.

Entremets: The sweet course, which in France is always served after the cheese (the word is used to mean a specific dessert). In restaurants, the word still embraces the vegetable dishes.

Epergne: A centerpiece composed of a ornamental stem with branches holding three, four, six, and even eight dishes or receptacles. Epergnes are used to hold hors d'oeuvres, or fruits and little cakes.

Esau: The name of this biblical character, who sold his birthright to his brother Jacob for a mess of pottage, is given to a thickened soup made from lentil purée and white stock or consommé.

Escabéche: A spicy cold marinade intended for preserving cooked foods and originating in Spain. It is used chiefly for small cooked fish (sardines, mackerel, smelt, whiting, red mullet). The fish are headed (hence the name, from cabeza "head"), then fried or lightly browned; they are then marinated for 24 hours in a cooked and spiced marinade. The fish then keeps for up to a week in the refrigerator.

Escalope: (Escallop): A thin slice of white meat. The word comes from the Old French **eschalope** (nutshell), probably because the slice tends to curl up during cooking (it is sometimes snipped on one end to prevent the flesh from shrinking). In English the word is spelled escallop, in Italian, **scaloppine**.

 Escargot: An edible snail.

Escarole: A vegetable, also called batavia, similar to curly endive (chicory), but with broader leaves. Escarole is generally eaten raw, in a green salad (often with seasoning flavored with mustard or shallots), possibly with tomatoes or scaled French green beans, or in a winter salad with nuts and raisins. It can also be cooked like spinach. Look for crisp, tender, fresh plants with no brown edges or wilted leaves. Leaves should be easily snapped, and a yellow green color.

Espagnole Sauce: A brown sauce, which is used as a basis for a large number of derivative brown sauces, such as Robert, genevoise, bordelaise, Bery, Madeira and Perigueux. It is made with a brown stock, to which a brown roux and a mirepoix are added, followed by a tomato purée. Espagnole freezes well. It will keep for four to six weeks.

Espresso: A strong coffee, brewed by a distinctive method, which comes to us from Italy. An espresso coffeemaker is needed to brew the specially roasted, strong, dark, coffee blend which is used.

Essence: In culinary usage, an essence is a concentrated substance possessing the predominant qualities of a food, its coloring, flavor, or nutritive value. Often it is an alcoholic solution of an essential oil obtained by distillation, infusion, etc., and essence of peppermint, or essence of oranges.

Evaporate: To evaporate means to expel moisture from a liquid or solid, thus concentrating the solid portions. Evaporation is usually accomplished by heat, and any boiling process used in cooking involves evaporation to some extent. In canned evaporated milk, half the water has been removed, thus concentrating the milk solids.

Extract: A concentrated aromatic liquid used either to enhance the flavor of certain culinary preparations or to flavor certain foods that have little or no flavor of their own.

F

Farce, **Farci**: Farce is a French word meaning "forcemeat" or "stuff". Farci means "stuffed".

Farina: This is a cereal, made from hard (but not durum) wheat, from which the bran and most of the germ have been removed. It is creamy colored, rich in protein, and very easy to digest. Farina is used as a breakfast cereal, cooked in either water or milk. It is also made into sweet puddings. Since it is very bland, farina combines well with other foods.

Fat: In cooking, this is an edible oily or greasy substance occurring in animal cells, in milk, in olives, and in the seeds of certain plants. The most commonly used fat of animal derivation are butter, lard, bacon fat, suet, and poultry fat. Vegetable fats include the various oils such as olive, corn, safflower, cottonseed, soy, peanut and sesame.

Fennel: This is an aromatic plant belonging to the carrot family. There are three different types of fennel, all of which have a feathery foliage of bright green. Common fennel, Foeniculum vulgare, is a tall perennial with finely divided feather leaves and yellow flowers. It has a flavor reminiscent of anise. All parts of the plant can be utilized. The shoots are eaten raw or cooked, the leaves are used for salads and seasoning, and the seeds, which are oval, greenish or yellowish-brown are used as a culinary spice for cooking, candy, and liqueurs. Fennel oil is used in medicine, perfume and soaps. Sweet fennel, Foeniculum vulgare dulce, is a dwarf variety, also call **finocchio** or Florence fennel. The third type is Foeniculum vulgare piperitum, known as Italian or Sicilian fennel or **carosella**. Its tender young stalks are eaten raw.

Fermentation: A chemical change in food or other organic compounds caused by the action of enzymes produced by yeasts, bacteria, or microorganism. The kinds most useful in foods and cooking are those which produce a gas or gasses, most frequently carbon dioxide, within the food to give effervescence or leavening. Foods and beverages in which fermentation is most often usefully employed are breads, wines, spirits, and beers, cheese, buttermilk, cultured milks and yogurt, cider and vinegars.

Fiasco: An Italian wine bottle with a wide, round base and a thin neck. The neck can be long or short. The bottle is wrapped in straw, and has a straw base so that it can stand. The French word for his kind of bottle is **flasque**, the source of our word "flask". The Italian plural for fiasco is fiaschi. Fiaschi are the traditional old fashioned Italian wine or olive oil bottles. They are especially characteristic of the red "Chianti" wines.

Figs: Figs are the fruit of the tree Ficus carica; originally native to Asia, Africa and Southern Europe. The fruit consists of a soft pulp covered by a thin skin. There are between 600 and 800 varieties of figs, varying shape from round to oblong and in color from almost white to purple black. Apart from its value as a food tree, it was regarded as sacred by many people. The Jews looked upon the fig tree as a symbol of peace and plenty. Mohammed's followers called it the "Tree of Heaven". The Romans sacrificed the milky sap of the wild fig tree to Juno; and some central African tribes built huts for the spirits of their ancestors in the shade of the sacred fig trees. Varieties of figs include: Adriatic, Calimyrna, Celeste, Kadota, Magnolia or Brunswick, and Mission.

Select slightly firm fruit which yields slightly to gentle pressure on the skin. Varieties range in color from greenish-yellow to purple to black. Avoid too-soft fruit or fruit with sour odor.

Refrigerate; use within 1 or 2 days. Season: May to September.

Filbert: This nut is the fruit of shrubs or small trees of the family Corylus. It is also known as a hazelnut or cobnut. Generally speaking the name "filbert" is applied to the oblong nuts of two varieties of hazel native to Europe. Corylus avellana pontica and c.maxima, "cobnut" to another native European variety, c. avellana grandis which produces a large round nut, and "hazelnut" to the American varieties c. americana and c. cornuta, which bear small round nuts. Filberts are drier than almonds or walnuts. When chopped or ground into fine meal, they are used in baking, particularly in Central Europe.

Filé: This is a seasoning and thickening agent made from the dried and powdered young leaves of the sassafras tree. It is an essential element in Creole cooking, and one of the basic ingredients in gumbo. Filé came to us through the Choctaw Indians who once lived in the New Orleans area, and who used filé constantly in their cooking. Filé - the word may be derived from the French word filé meaning "made into threads" - was a useful thickening agent in an age that knew no gelatin, cornstarch, or other modern thickening agents. As the name suggests filé can go stringy in a dish. It must be added to a boiling liquid gradually, stirring constantly, after the dish has been removed from the heat. _Under **no** circumstances must the dish be boiled again after the filé has been added._

Filet or Fillet: A fillet, the French word for the same thing as filet, is usually a flat slice, strip or piece of lean boneless meat or fish. When talking of beef or pork, a filet is also a specific cut.

Filling: A sweet or non-sweet mixture; used in pastry shells; or between layers of such foods, as cake or bread to add content flavor or color. Sweet fillings are most generally found in pies, tarts, cream puffs, éclairs, cakes and cookies, non-sweet fillings in sandwiches and non-sweet pastry shells. Omelets can have either type of filling.

Fines herbes: A French term meaning "fine herbs". In culinary language its precise meaning is a combination of two or more finely chopped fresh herbs, such as parsley, tarragon, chervil, basil, thyme, and chives. It is also used to describe chopped parsley, as in an Omelette aux fines Herbes. A properly composed combination of fines herbs adds great distinction to fish, chicken, meat, eggs and salads. **For Beef or other red meats**: thyme, chervil, and basil, or chives, basil and parsley. **For Chicken, Meat, Eggs or Salads:** chervil, parsley, and chives. **For Fish, Chicken or Veal:** parsley, rosemary and tarragon.

Finnan Haddie: This is smoked haddock and was named for the village of Findon near Aberdeen in Scotland, which was famous for the curing of the fish. The fish is lightly salted and smoked. Originally, the smoking was done over peat fires which gave the fish a wonderful flavor.

Fish: Fish are cold-blooded aquatic animals and, broadly speaking, include shellfish as well as the tapered, scaly animal with backbone, gills, and fins. Here, we are concerned only with edible types of fish, which are usually divided into three groups, **salt water fish**, such as sea bass, pompano, cod, haddock, halibut, herring, mackerel, salmon, shad, sole, sturgeon, swordfish, and tuna, **fresh water fish** such as bass, catfish, trout, perch, and **shellfish**, such as abalone, clams, crabs, crayfish, lobsters, mussels, oysters, scallops and shrimps. Fish lends itself to a wide range of preparations. It can be sautéed, broiled, baked, braised, fried, poached or steamed.

Flageolet: A small green haricot bean which looks like a baby Lima bean and is used either fresh or dried. Flageolets are delicious whole or puréed, and are used as a garnish for meat dishes, especially lamb or mutton.

Flake: A flake is a small, flat, thin, loose piece of food which looks like a scale rather than a crumb. To flake is a term used in fish cookery. When fish flakes easily at the touch of a toothpick or fork, it is cooked.

Flambé: The French word describes foods which are served flaming. This can be done by pouring a warmed spirit, such as brandy, over the food and setting it alight. This most frequently used spirits for flambé are brandy, rum, and kirsch.

Flan: A flan can be either of two things: One, a straight sided, open faced tart that stands alone in its own pastry shell with any savory or sweet filling. The second culinary meaning of the word flan is a custard or caramel cream thickened with eggs or with other thickening agents such as Irish moss or gum arabics. This kind of flan is a standard dessert in Spanish speaking countries.

Flank: A cut of beef taken from the side of the animal between ribs and hip. It is available as flank steak and as flank steak fillets and is most often braised or broiled.

Flannel Cake: A griddle cake. This name, used most frequently in New England, implies a thick pancake made in plate size.

Flapjack: Call them flapjacks, hotcakes, wheat cakes, flannel cakes, or pancakes; they are all griddle cakes and their batters resemble each other closely.

Flatfish: Any of a very large group of fish found in seas throughout the world. The best known food fish in the group are flounder, halibut, turbot, and sole.

How to skin Flatfish: *1. using a very sharp knife; make an incision across the tail on the dark skin side of the fish. The white skin on the other side is usually left on; 2. Slip your thumb into the slit and gently loosen the skin. Work your way down the side by the fins until it is free all around; 3. Hold the tail firmly, and pull the skin quickly towards the head. You may need the sharp knife to help you.*

Flavor: The qualities of a substance affecting the senses of smell and taste are called "flavor". When applied to food, flavor is more specifically the blend of taste, odor, and feeling sensations obtained from a substance in the mouth. The subject of flavor is a complicated once since flavor itself has an elusive and highly individual nature. Ordinarily, we think of flavor as "taste" and it may come as a surprise that not only the sense of taste, but also the senses of smell and feeling are involved in determining a flavor. Taste is affected by temperature, by texture and by a person's sensitivity to its various components. For instance, when ice cream is melted at room temperature, it tastes much sweeter than when cold and it is much more flavorful when eaten slowly in small spoonfuls, rather than quickly. To taste a food reliably for seasoning, it should be neither very hot nor very cold.

Flavoring: A substance added to flood to give it a particular flavor. Spices, condiments, grated fruit rinds, and liqueurs are considered flavorings, but more specifically, the word is used in reference to essences or extracts of spices, nuts, herbs, fruits, and some flowers in alcoholic solutions.

Flitch: This is an English term for a whole side of salt pork or more specifically, a side of bacon.

Floating Island: This poetically named dessert consists of a soft custard topped with puffs of meringue baked in the oven until slightly brown; or a soft custard topped with puffs of meringue which have been cooked until firm in scalding milk.

Florentine: This is a cooking method which uses spinach as its base. Eggs, fish or chicken are most often cooked a la Florentine.

Flounder: The name is used for a large family of salt water flatfish. The flounder family also includes gray sole, summer flounder (also called fluke), winter flounder, lemon sole, and dabs.

Flour: Flour is finely ground meal made from grain. It is usually bolted (sifted) to obtain the very finest particles. When the term flour is used without any further description, it refers to white wheat flour. However, flours made from different grains are available. These include flours made from barley, buckwheat, corn, cottonseed, Lima beans, peanuts, potatoes, rye, rice and soybeans. Flour, when it is first milled, has a slightly yellow color. In addition, freshly milled wheat flour does not bake as good a loaf of bread as matured flour. Natural aging will bleach and mature the flour without the use of chemicals, but this requires several weeks for most flours. Chemicals are often used to bring about these changes quickly. An oxidizing agent - chlorine dioxide is a typical one - is used to increase the whiteness of flour as well as to mature it. **Cake Flour**: Is specially milled from selected "soft" winter wheat's to make exceptionally delicate, fine textured cakes. It has a texture softer than most all-purpose flour. **Rye Flour**: Flour made from rye. Wheat flour is usually used with it to make bread light. **Self-Rising Flour**: an all-purpose flour to which leavening agents and salt have been added in proportions suitable for much reads, popovers and egg-leavened cakes such as angel food and sponge cake. **Whole Wheat or Graham**: The fine or coarsely ground whole kernels of wheat including bran and germ.

Flour, (To): "To flour" means to coat or dust something lightly with flour. Foods are coated with flour before being sautéed or fried so that they will brown and be crisp outside and juicy inside. Pans are dusted with flour for the easy removal of a cake, cupcakes, or breads. Pastry boards, rolling pins, and hands are dusted with flour to keep the dough from sticking. Dough is dusted with flour to prevent it from sticking when it is shaped.

Flummery: An old New England dessert prepared by simmering berries in water and thickening with cornstarch. The dessert is sweetened and served cold with cream.

Flute: To make decorative indentations.

Foie Gras: Literally translated, these two French words mean "fat liver". In culinary language, they are applied to the lives of geese which are bred to be used for foie gras, and are a specialty of Alsace and southwest France. There are a great many uses for foie gras. It can be eaten as an appetizer spread, or as a main dish with a green salad.

Fold, (To): In culinary language the phase "to fold" has several meanings. It can mean "to enclose", as when the dough is folded over the filling or over butter in puff pastry; "to mix", as when mushrooms are folded into a sauce; and most often "to incorporate", as when egg whites are folded into a soufflé or cake batter.

Fondant: A crystalline, soft, white candy made by cooking sugar, water, light corn syrup or cream of tartar to the "soft ball" stage. The mixture is then cooled and beaten and kneaded until it is perfectly white. It is used as a base for such candies as bonbons and chocolate creams.

Fondue: The origin of this French word is *fondre* that is "to melt". In culinary language, it often means a hot dish made from melted cheese, and wine or brandy into which pieces of bread are dipped. Dessert fondue may be made of chocolate or other sauces. The term also denotes a soufflé-like dish made with bread, and a dish in which cubes of beef are cooked at the table in hot fat and eaten with a variety of sauces. Fondue is the national dish of Switzerland.

Fool: This surprising word describes a very old but still popular English fruit dessert. It is based on a fruit purée (any soft fruit, especially berries, will do). The fruit is cooked with very little water, sweetened to taste, strained, and chilled. Just before serving, chilled whipped cream is added to the fruit purée, in the proportion of two parts whipped cream to one part fruit. The fool is served in sherbet glasses.

Forcemeat: Forcemeat, the French word **farce** is synonymous, are mixtures of finely chopped raw or cooked meats, raw or cooked poultry or game, fresh or canned fish, variety meats and game, all blended with herbs and spices into a thick smooth paste. Forcemeats can also be made of potatoes, cornmeal, chestnuts, or even fruit. Fruit forcemeats are excellent for stuffing duck or other poultry. The main ingredient in forcemeat must be ground several times to achieve as smooth a texture as possible. The remaining ingredients are then beat in carefully to incorporate air and give the mixture lightness.

Fork: The fork is a table utensil consisting of a handle and two or more prongs, used for serving and eating food. Though ancient in origin, it did not make its appearance in the kitchen or on the dinner table for many centuries after its discovery. The first two-pronged forks were used to hold sacrificial meat. Sophisticated Venetians became acquainted with the art of the fork from a Byzantine princess in the 11th century. Members of the aristocracy used the fork more as a lark than as a method of serious eating. Not until the 17th century did eating with forks catch on as the fashionable thing to do. Then people carried their precious forks in special cases with them when invited to dinner. The fork in many instances was as elaborate as a piece of jewelry.

Fortified: Supplied with more vitamins and minerals than were present in the natural state.

Fowl: The term covers any large edible wild or domestic bird. Specifically, it is used to describe a mature female chicken, also called a hen or stewing chicken, more than ten months old and weighing three to six pounds. This bird is best cooked by moist heat.

Frangipane: This is a name given to a mixture made with flour, egg yolks, butter, and milk. It is cooked like a cream puff pastry and used for poultry and fish forcemeats. Frangipane cream is a thick, custard filling, made with crushed macaroons or ground almonds and used for cakes, tarts, crêpes, and other desserts.

Frankfurter: Frankfurters (or wieners or hot dogs) are a type of sausage, made from beef, pork and sometimes veal or combinations of these meats. The meats are combined with seasonings and curing nitrates and in some cases, fillers, then stuffed into casings, smoked, cooked in steam, and quickly chilled. Although recipes vary, in general those labeled "all meat" are a combination of beef and pork, but without fillers. Those labeled "all beef" contain only beef, are sometimes kosher and frequently heavily seasoned with garlic. Frankfurters are extremely versatile and easy to prepare. They may be barbecued, boiled, braised, broiled, fried, roasted or steamed, used along with other foods, whole, sliced or in chunks.

Frappé: Literally translated, this French word means "beaten". In culinary language, it refers to a drink or a dessert, partially frozen and stirred. Frappés are served in glasses and are very pleasant hot weather fare. At the end of a meal, a frappé can double as a drink and a dessert. Liqueurs, poured over a glass of shaved or cracked ice, are also called *frappé*.

Freeze, (to): The freezing of food is the process of chilling a liquid, or a solid which contains varying amounts of liquid, until it is hardened.

Fricassée: This is the French word for hash. In culinary language, a fricassee, though not a hash in the American sense, is an extremely thrifty food dish of fowl, veal, and other meats, which generally utilizes less-tender cuts. These are first cooked in fat until a pale gold, then a liquid, such as bouillon, water, milk, or wine, is added to the dish, along with vegetables and seasonings.

Fritter: This is a small amount of batter which may be mixed with chopped fish, meat, vegetables, or fruits are used to coat these foods. The trick to making successful fritters lies in having the food dry and, it is to be coated with the batter; make sure that it is completely coated so that the food can't ooze out during frying.

Frog's Legs: The hind legs of the frog are eaten as a delicacy. Their taste resembles chicken in texture and flavor but is more delicate. Frog's legs can be broiled, sautéed, cooked with a sauce, or deep fried, since they are small, they take only a short time to cook.

Fromage: French word for cheese.

Frost, (To) and **Frosting:** In culinary language to "to frost" means to coat a cake, cookie or pastry with a frosting. Frostings are made of sugar combined with water, milk, or egg whites, flavorings, and often coloring. They can be cooked or uncooked and should be soft enough to spread easily but firm enough to keep from running off. Frostings should be applied while the cake is fresh. In order to keep crumbs from mixing with the frosting, the cake should be crumbed or be spread over with a thin layer of frosting which is allowed to dry before the remainder is put on.

Fruit: This is the reproductive body of a seed plant. Although, strictly speaking, acorns, beans, peas, chestnuts, and tomatoes are all fruits, when we think and speak colloquially of fruits, we mean the more or less sweet pulped products of vines, shrubs, or trees, ranging from apples to tangerines. Fruit has always sustained a delighted mankind, whether he found it wild, or grew it scientifically. Aside from its health giving properties and its culinary versatility, it is the most ravishing of the products of nature, appealing to the eye as much as to the senses of smell and taste.

Fruitcake: The term is applied to a cake which is composed mainly of fruits and nuts, held together with a rich batter. In some cakes there is just enough batter to hold the fruit and nuts together, in others, considerably more. Fruitcakes rage from the very dark ones containing molasses or brown sugar and a large varied amount of spices to those called golden or light, in which lighter colored batter, generally made with granulated sugar, light colored fruits, and no spices are used.

Fry: As a verb "to fry" means to cook food in pieces or serving size units, in fat or oil. When only a small amount of fat is used, the process is called "pan frying" or "sautéing". Sometimes the fat is supplied by the food itself, as in the case with bacon. When larger amounts of fat are used, enough to cover the food, the process is called "deep frying".

Fudge: This creamy smooth confection is one of the basic candies; it is also one of the best loved ones, and one that is frequently made at home, to the joy of all concerned.

G

Galantine: A galantine is a French dish made from boned poultry, meat, or fish which has been stuffed, pressed into a symmetrical form, cooked in a broth, and covered with aspic.

Game: Game literally means any wild bird or quadruped judged to be suitable for table use. It should also encompass many of the game birds which have been domesticated for the market. Such birds include quail, pheasant, turkey, partridge, and pigeons, to name only a few.

Garlic: The garlic, a hardy bulbous plant, is a member of the lily family, which also includes leeks, chives, onions, and shallots. Like the onion, the edible bulb of the plant grows beneath the ground. The compound bulb is made up of small sections or bulbets called "cloves" which are encased in thin papery envelops. Garlic can be grown from the cloves of the bulb. It does best in full sun. The green stems from a clove of garlic can be chopped and added to salads or sprinkled over boiled potatoes, etc., to give a mild garlic flavor. Crush garlic for casseroles, etc, and if you want only a subtle taste of garlic, rub the inside of the casserole or bowl with a split clove. The juice of garlic is a very strong antiseptic and was used by the French during World War I. Garlic is also available in dried powdered form, as well as minced and sliced.

Look for firm, dry bulb.

Refrigerate or keep at cool room temperature in container that allows good circulation of air. Keep dry. Will keep for several months. Season: all year.

Garnish: The word is used to describe an ornament, which should be edible, added to a finished dish for the purpose of enhancing its appearance and appeal.

Gastronome, **Gastronomy**: These culinary terms drive from the Greek words *gaster* and *nomos*, "belly" and "law". Gastronomy means the art of good food and a gastronome is a person who recognizes good food and takes great pleasure in it.

Gâteau: The literal translation of this French word is "Cake", and the French use it as casually as we use the word cake, there being *grand gâteaux* and *petits gâteaux*, that is, big and little cakes, which can be as plain or as fancy as desired.

Gazpacho: A Spanish dish of cold, uncooked soup, which typically contains, tomatoes, cucumbers, onions, garlic, oil and vinegar.

Gelatin: A protein substance which swells on contact with a liquid, dissolves in hot water, and forms jelly when it cools. The word gelatin and jelly both come from the Latin *gelatus*, meaning "frozen". In cooking gelatin is used as a thickening agent.

Génoise: A sponge cake made with melted butter. It is a very fine-textured cake used as the basis for many elegant creations, such as gâteaux.

Geranium or **Pelargonium**: There are more than 250 varieties of this popular perennial. The leaves make an attractive and unusual garnish. A few leaves placed in the bottom of a pan of baked apples, custards, puddings, or ice cream is a good idea.

German Chocolate: (a.k.a. sweet cooking chocolate) has a higher sugar content then bittersweet and contains at least 15% chocolate liqueur.

Ghee: This is the anglicized version of the Hindustani word *ghi*, which means "clarified butter" and is a basic ingredient in the cooking in India. Indian butter is made from buffalo's or cow's milk. The reason for clarifying butter in a hot climate is that it will keep without refrigeration for quite a long time, depending on the temperature.

Gherkin: These very small cucumbers grow to a length of about one to three inches. They are used to make either sweet or sour pickles. Gherkins are good condiments; they can be chopped into salads, sauces, stuffing, and fish dishes.

Giblets: The gizzard, liver, and heart of any kind of poultry are called giblets. They are an inexpensive, good quality source of protein and minerals. Poultry livers cook quickly, but the remaining giblets must be simmered in water to cover, with seasonings added, for about 1 hour, or until they are tender. Giblets are rich in vitamins and minerals. Finely chopped they can be added to stuffing's, sauces, or used on their own for pâtés, and soups.

Ginger Root: Ginger is a spice obtained from the root of *Zingiber officinale*, an erect perennial plant, has large brilliant yellowish flowers with purple lips, which are borne in a spike. Ginger is used crystallized, preserved, or dried; whole, cracked or ground to a powder. Wrapped in plastic bag and refrigerated, the fresh root will keep for two weeks. (Oriental dishes, meats, poultry, vegetables, salad dressings, marinades, fruit, breads, desserts, cookies pastries)

Select firm, irregular, knobby roots without any soft spots.

Refrigerate; and use within 1 or 2 weeks. Season: all year.

Gingerbread: A flat, square, spicy bread-cake made with brown sugar or honey and molasses (or just molasses), leavened with baking powder and baking soda (or just baking soda), and heavily spiced with ground ginger and other spices.

Glacé: In American culinary language this French word refers to a coating of sugar or sugar syrup used on fruits, cakes, and breads. In French culinary language, glace (or glacee) either frozen or glazed. In the latter case, the glazing need not necessarily be sweet, but may be done with butter, sauce, or gelatin or, of course, with sugar.

Glaze: A glaze is a smooth glossy surface. In cooking, "to glaze" means to cover food with a mixture, often liquid, which hardens, becomes glossy, and gives an attractive finish to either hot or cold dishes.

Gnocchi: Gnocco, the plural is gnocchi, is the Italian word for dumpling. Italian gnocchi are small and delicate. They are made from potatoes, farina, or flour, and sometimes with eggs; they are cooked in fast boiling, salted water and served with a sauce or with butter and grated Parmesan cheese.

Goose: The goose is a waterfowl, first cousin to the duck and the swan. Geese are traditional Christmas birds of many European countries, especially Austria, Germany, Hungary, England, and the Scandinavian countries. Since geese are fat, it is essential to cook out as much fat as possible. The fat should be poured from the pan as it accumulates during roasting. Apples, prunes and oranges go well with this bird because they take the edge off the richness of the meat.

As well as traditional roasting, geese may be smoked, fried, salted and boiled with excellent results. The meat is good cold.

Gooseberry: This round juicy berry, a first cousin of the fresh currant. There are a number of varieties; red, green, white, or yellow, and smooth or hairy. Gooseberries require cool weather to flourish.

Goulash: This is the national meat dish of Hungary and a popular one all over the world. It is a thick stew that always contains meat, onions, and sweet or hot paprika. The meat is usually beef or veal, but there are other goulash dishes which incorporate three kinds of meat.

Gourmand, Gourmet: These are two words taken directly from the French which characterize a person by his eating habits. A gourmand is a hearty sometimes, greedy, eater who delights in luxurious food. A gourmet is a connoisseur who knows and appreciates fine food and wine.

Granité: This is an ice made from fruit syrup and frozen without stirring. It is slightly granular in consistency, accounting for its name, which means "granulated" in French. *Granités* are served in sherbet glasses.

Grapefruit: This important member of the citrus family, also called "pomelo" is large and round with a rind colored from pale yellow to bronze, a juicy pulp which may be yellowish-white or pink, and a slightly bitter flavor.

Look for well-shaped, firm but springy to touch, fruit that is heavy for its size. Russet or brownish discolorations on skin usually don't affect eating quality. Varieties include seedless, with seeds, pink or white-fleshed. Avoid fruit that is soft or discolored at stem end.

Refrigerate; use in 1 to 2 weeks. Season: all year with best supplies in October to April.

Grapes: Botanically speaking, the grape is the berry of any vine of the Vitaceae family. Grapes grow wild in many temperate zones of Europe, Africa, Asia and America, there are thousands of varieties. The cultivated species include varieties grown for wine making, for sweet juices, for the production of raisins for the table. One of the best known native American grape is the northern fox grape, from which come hybrids such as the Concord grape and the muscadine, which grows in the Atlantic and Gulf states. Other varieties of grape are: Almeria, Cardinal, Emperor, Olivette Blanche, Red Malaga, Ribier, Thompson Seedless, Tokay or Flame Tokay, White Malaga, Catawba, Delaware and Niagara.

Look for plump, grapes with individual berries firmly attached to stems. A color for variety usually means good flavor. Avoid dry, brittle stems or shriveled grapes or ones leaking moisture.

Refrigerate; use in 1 to 2 weeks. Season: all year with best supplies from July to November.

Grate, (to): In cooking term means to reduce a hard food into smaller pieces by rubbing against a rough or indented surface. The resulting pieces may be very fine and dust like or coarse. It depends on the size of the grater used.

Gratin (or **Gratian**): Gratin is the French word for a dish which has been gratinated; this is, it has acquired a crisp golden-brown crust after having been exposed to high heat; gratin is also the word used to describe the crust itself. Generally, a covering of buttered crumbs or grated cheese is used to gratinate a dish.

Gravy: Gravy is a sauce that utilizes the fat, meat drippings, and juices of the meat or poultry with which it is to be served. It also contains a thickening agent, such as flour, cornstarch, potato starch, or gingersnaps, in a liquid, such as water, broth, bouillon, milk, or sweet or sour cream.

Grease: The word covers any animal fat, usually pork, beef, or lamb that is rendered. It also refers to spreading a pan thinly with fat (greasing the pan) to keep foods from sticking during cooking or baking.

Greens: Beet or Turnip Tops, Swiss Chard, Endive, Collards, Escarole, Kale, Mustard Greens, Rappini, Sorrel, Spinach.

Gremolata: A classic Italian seasoning mixture of flat-leaf parsley, grated lemon rind, and garlic. Used primarily for flavoring soups and stews.

Grenadine: Syrup flavored with pomegranate, used as flavoring and in sauces.

Grenouilles: French for frogs' legs.

Grill: "To grill" means to cook by direct heat by (1) broiling in an oven; (2) cooking over a gas flame, briquettes, charcoal, or heated stones, either indoors or out; (3) cooking on a griddle or grill, either electric or non-electric. As a noun the word grill refers to the utensil or piece of equipment on which food is grilled, rotisserie, brazier, camp stove, or stationary barbecue pits.

Grind: To grind is to crush food into small pieces by passing it through a grinder. A grinder may be mechanical or electrical and can grind foods into particles from coarse all the way to fine, depending on the blade used.

Grits, Groats: Both words refer to hulled and coarsely ground cereal grains and both have the meaning of "fragment" or "part". Grits are smaller than groats; and more finely ground, usually from corn, but also from buckwheat, rye, oats, or rice. Grits ground from corn are known as hominy grits. Groats are most often ground from buckwheat, oats, barley, and wheat, as well as corn.

Grouper: Groupers are salt water fish which live in warm waters, at the bottom of the sea, and in rocky nooks and crevices. They resemble sea bass. Groupers can be cooked like sea bass or red snapper. The fillets are excellent when broiled or stuffed and baked.

Grouse: There are many varieties of this plump game bird. Grouse are related to the pheasant. The meat is dark and rich and is best broiled or roasted.

Gruel: An old fashioned dish made from a cereal boiled with water to the consistency of a thin porridge. It can be flavored with sugar, honey, wine, butter, salt, or lemon peel, and eaten plain or with milk.

Grunion: A small, salt water fish, somewhat similar to smelt. The grunion is found in the water off the California coast. Grunions are cooked like any other small fish; boiled, sautéed, or deep fried.

Guava: There are many varieties of guavas, usually oval in shape, with fruits from the size of a walnut to that of an apple. Guavas are usually from 2 to 5 inches in diameter, the guava has a thin skin and its flesh can be yellow or red; it is very aromatic, sweet, and juicy and has high vitamin content. They are also made into jams, jellies and guava paste, a rich preserve. When buying fresh guava, choose firm fruit on the verge of softening, but not spotting.

Select red or yellow fruit, depending on variety. Ripe guavas should yield to gentle pressure on the skin. Avoid cracked skins.

Refrigerate after ripening and use within 2 to 3 days. Season: September to December.

Guinea Fowl: This small fowl, originally wild, has been domesticated and is now raised chiefly for food. The taste of guinea fowl is slightly and pleasantly gamy. It can be prepared in any way chicken or other small birds are cooked, but the meat is drier and must be treated accordingly.

Gumbo: A gumbo is a well seasoned Creole dish which takes its name from a corruption of the African Bantu word for okra. It maybe thickened with okras or with filé powder. The consistency of a gumbo is between that of soup and stew. It is usually served over cooked rice. Gumbos can be made with seafood, poultry, meat, especially salt pork or ham, and with vegetables.

Gumdrop: This is a colorful, soft candy made of sugar and water with flavoring and coloring added. Gum arabic gives it a chewy gelatinous texture. Gumdrops can be used to decorate cakes and puddings.

H

Haddock: This salt water fish is one of the most important food fish of the North Atlantic, from Nova Scotia to Cape Hatteras. The flesh is firm and white, with a pleasant flavor which is on the bland side. Haddock can be successfully cooked in any desired way.

Half and Half: A dairy product consisting of a mixture of milk and cream. The mixture is usually homogenized, and used for coffee or table cream.

Halibut: A cold water fish which lives in all the seas of the world. The flesh is white and excellent in flavor and texture.

Ham: The rear leg of a hog, from the aitchbone (hipbone) through the meaty part of the shank bone, is called a ham. The differences in the taste of ham lie in the breed of the hog and the food it is fed. In the case of cured hams, taste is also affected by the flavors of the brines used in curing, and the fuel, such as hickory logs, over which the meat is smoked.

American Country-Style Hams (Georgia, Kentucky, Smithfield, Tennessee and Virginia) are heavily cured and smoked, but uncooked. Italian **prosciutto,** Spanish **jamón** and German westphalian hams are cured, pressed, smoked, aged in spices and ready to eat. They are usually sold sliced paper-thin.

Hamburger: This term stands for ground beef prepared form the less tender cuts. After steak, hamburger is America's favorite meat, it is good, it is fast, it is inexpensive, it is easy to serve either in patties, or in meatloaves and countless other ways.

Hard Sauce: This sauce is made by creaming butter with sugar, and flavoring it with brandy, rum, whisky, wine, or with extracts or spices. The sugar can be granulated, confectioners' sugar, or brown sugar. It takes time to make a good hard sauce. This sugar must be creamed into the softened, but not melted, butter slowly, and in small amounts.

Haricot: A French word meaning "bean". Haricots blancs are "white beans", haricots verts are "green beans. In French culinary language, a haricot can also be a mutton or lamb stew made with potatoes and onions. A "haricot" does not contain beans; the name is a corruption of the French hacher, meaning "chopped very fine".

Hash: A mixture of food chopped into small pieces and mixed. The word is most commonly applied to a mixture of meat or poultry, potatoes, and seasonings.

Haute cuisine: A style of cooking that emphasizes elaborate meals with many courses.

Hazelnut: This grape size, smooth shelled nuts grows on shrubs and tress. The nuts grow in clusters and each is wrapped in a fuzzy outer husk that opens as the nut ripens. The nuts are often toasted for a browner color and a better flavor; they are never blanched.

Head Cheese: Head cheese is a well seasoned cold cut made of the edible parts of a calf's or pig's head such as the cheeks, snouts, and underlips, to which sometimes brains, hearts, tongues, and feet are added.

Heart: The hearts of beef, veal, lamb, and pork are used in cooking, especially in Scandinavia and in central Europe. Poultry hearts are usually used as giblets. Hearts are tasty meat when properly cooked. Since they are the least tender cuts, they must be cooked slowly in moist heat, by braising and stewing. Hearts can be used in any recipe calling for sliced, diced or ground meat.

Herbs: An aromatic plant used to add flavor to food. Strictly speaking only seed plants which do not develop a woody persistent tissue can be considered herbs. When cooking with herbs, here is a word of caution; be selective about the kinds of herbs used and conservative about the amounts. Use ⅓ to ½ teaspoon dried herbs for every tablespoon fresh herbs. Crumble dried herbs before using to release flavor.

There's a certain knack to seasoning correctly – not too much, not too little – but it can be acquired by always *tasting* what you are cooking. A simple outline below is meant to be just that, specifying which herbs and spices go best with the main ingredient, but you can experiment. **Just don't use them all at the same time, though!**

Herbsaint: Greenish-amber anise flavored liqueur.

Herbes de Provence: An assortment of dried herbs that usually includes thyme, bay leaves, rosemary, basil and savory.

Hermit: A dark, spicy cookie filled with fruits and nuts. The dark color comes from molasses or brown sugar and ground spices. Hermits may be served plain or with a glaze.

Herring: These small, salt water fish belong to the family *Clupeidae*, the shad, and sardine are related to them. Kippers and bloaters are two herring specialties of England. The fish are cured by salting and smoking. They are baked or broiled just long enough to heat them through.

Hibachi: Small, portable charcoal grill.

Hoecake: This is the cornmeal cake of the early settlers, which often served as bread. The inventive settlers baked a cornmeal and water mixture on the blades of their hoes on hot coals in front of a wood fire and called them hoecakes.

Hoisin Sauce: A thick sauce made of soy beans and seasonings used in Chinese cooking.

Hollandaise: Hollandaise sauce is not only a classic accompaniment for asparagus, broccoli, and other vegetables, it is the base of other famous sauces, Béarnaise, Mousseline, Maltaise, and Choron, and a necessary ingredient for many dishes including eggs Benedict.

Hominy: Kernels of hulled dried corn from which the germ has been removed. Ground hominy is called grits. Hominy is cooked in water or milk, and may then be fried, baked or served with a sauce.

Homogenize: This is a word of Greek origin, composed of homos, meaning "the same", and "genous", kin or kind. In culinary language, "to homogenize", is to reduce an emulsion to particles of the same size and to distribute them evenly.

Honey: A sweet sticky liquid made by honeybees from the nectar of plants. When honey is substituted for sugar it is necessary to adjust the amount of liquid in the recipe. To substitute honey for sugar; 1 cup honey contains about ¼ cup water, therefore deduct ¼ cup liquid from the amount in the recipe for each cup of honey used.

Honeydew Melon: These melons belong to the muskmelon family, whose varieties include cantaloupes, honeydews, casaba, and Persian melons. Honeydews have a smooth yellowish-white rind, and their flesh is sweet and green.

Select yellowish to creamy-white; should have a soft, velvety feel; the rind should be slightly soft around the blossom end and have a faint, pleasant aroma. (Ripeness is difficult to judge.)

Hors d'oeuvre: The literal translation of these French words is "outside of the main work". Hors d'oeuvres are small appetizers that are not part of the menu, but serve as an introduction to a meal. Many hors d'oeuvres can be prepared beforehand, frozen, and reheated at serving time.

Horseradish Root: Peeled and grated, served as is or in vinegar, it is used as a condiment for fish, seafood, meats, game, and in sauces. It has been used since antiquity, long before Christian times. It is one of the five bitter herbs of the Jewish Passover, when it is served symbolically during the Seder services. Fresh horseradish should be grated as soon as possible after purchase. Dried horseradish root is also available. The flavor of dried horseradish is not as strong as that of fresh grated horseradish.

Look for firm roots with no decay or soft spots; avoid shriveled roots.

Refrigerate; and use as needed. Keeps for several months.

Hot Cake: This is another term for a griddlecake, pancake, flannel cake, or flapjack.

Hydrogenate: Hydrogenation is a process which converts liquid oils into semisolid, malleable fats. Further processing incorporates air or an inert gas resulting in a solid bland fat which is soft and creamy in consistency and creamy white in color.

I

Ice: When water solidifies, it is called ice. Water, like all liquids, when sufficiently cooled becomes solid. The freezing point of water is 32°F, or 0°C. Ice is transparent in color and lighter than water, which accounts for the familiar sight of ice floating on water.

Ice(2): This word ice is used to describe a frozen mixture of a fruit juice or purée, a sweetener, and water. Occasionally ices are made with coffee or wine instead of fruit juice. Such mixtures are often called "water ices" to distinguish them from the sherbets, ice creams, and other frozen desserts to which eggs, milk, cream, etc. are added.

Ice cream: America's favorite dessert is a frozen food made from milk products, sweetener, flavoring, and other ingredients, depending on whether it is homemade or made commercially. Ice cream may contain cream, fresh or evaporated milk, a sweetener such as sugar or honey or an artificial sweetener. Fruits, nuts, and flavorings are added to suit the fancy. The choice of flavoring is varied; from vanilla to liqueurs.

Infuse/Infusion: To infuse something in cooking usually involves a solid, aromatic ingredient, and a liquid such as water, milk, or even oil.

Irish Moss or **Carrageen**: A species of small edible seaweed, varying in color from greenish yellow to purplish brown, named after Carrageen, Waterford county, Ireland. The plants are washed in salt water and spread out to dry and bleach. Used for clarifying malt beverages, it is also sold through druggists and health food stores.

J

Jack Fruit: (jaquier, jaca) Oblong fruit with green, lumpy skin, closely related to the breadfruit but enormous – it sometimes weighs as much as 70 or cooked; it is especially popular in curries.

Jam: A preserve of fruit which is usually crushed, or may even be ground, cooked with sugar until thick, and store in sterilized jars.

Jambalaya: A Creole dish, made with combinations of ham, sausage, fowl, shrimp, oysters, tomatoes, onions, garlic, and other seasonings. The Spanish *paella*, a mixture of rice, meat, and seafood, is a close relative.

Jardinière: Garnished with vegetables.

Jaune: A pastis, a popular anise-flavored apéritifs.

Jellied: This adjective describes; (1) A semitransparent, semisolid, and somewhat elastic consistency of foods, due to the presence of such substances as agar, gelatin, Irish moss, isinglass, or pectin; (2) A complete dish containing, or covered with, gelatin such as jellied eggs, jellied salads, jellied meats, etc.

Jelly: A mixture of fruit juice, sugar, acid, and pectin, either natural or added, cooked to a stage at which gelatin occurs. Unlike jams, which require only one cooking, jellies require two; one cooking prepares the fruit for juice extraction; the second cooking the juices mixed with sugar and cooked to the gelatin stage.

Jerusalem artichoke: Edible tuber of a variety of sunflower native to the United States. The tubers look like small rough-skinned sweet potatoes, but their flesh is white.

Julep: An alcoholic drink made with spirits, most often bourbon, but sometimes rum or brandy; and sugar, crushed ice, and mint.

Julienne: The term, of French origin, refers first to food cut into thin match like strips. Vegetables, meats, poultry, and cheese can be cut in this manner.

Juniper Berry: The fruit of the evergreen *Juniperus communis*, a small tree or shrub. They should be crushed before using, since this releases the flavor. The flavor of freshly dried juniper berries is intense but is dissipates fairly quickly so that dried juniper berries should not be kept too long.

K

Kabob: The word means a small piece of roasted meat. The addition of the word shish, or "skewer", means that the meat was threaded on a skewer and then roasted.

Kachouri: Deep fried fritter of Indian origin made with chick pea meal and chopped scallions.

Kale: This member of the cabbage family, is also called "borecole", "cole", or "colewort". It is high in vitamin content. Kale can be cooked in any of the ways spinach is cooked, but the leaves should be chopped.

Ketchup: This highly seasoned thick condiment sauce is also called "catsup". Ketchup is a smoothly textured and brightly colored sauce, usually made with red tomato pulp, mildly seasoned popular as a topping for meats and fish and an ingredient of many foods such as barbecue sauce, meat loaf, salad dressing. It can also be made from green tomatoes, fruits, berries, and vegetables.

Kid: This is the meat of a young goat slaughtered before being weaned. Kid is a surprisingly bland and delicate meant, which is prized in the cooking of Latin countries in Europe and South America.

Kidney: Known as a variety meat, this is one of the glandular organs of animals. The kidneys of beef, lamb, veal, and less frequently, pork are used in cookery. Kidneys may be served alone or combined with other meats or in omelets.

Kielbasa: A highly seasoned sausage of Polish origin, made of coarsely ground lean pork and beef, flavored with garlic and other spices. It comes fresh or smoked, uncooked or cooked.

Kipper: As a verb the word means to cure fish by cleaning, salting, spicing, and then drying or smoking. The best known kippered fish is herring, and when the word kipper is used alone, it refers to kippered herring.

Kiss: A small chewy mound shape confection prepared with egg white and sugar. To these basic ingredients coconut, chopped nuts, chopped dates and chocolate or chopped candy are added. Since the name is derived from the shape, other small mound shape confections may be referred to as kisses.

Kiwi: It grows on trees and is the same shape and size as a lime. The berry has a thin brown skin covered with coarse fuzz. It can be peeled or spooned out of the skin. The flesh is soft, brilliant green in color, and is filled with tiny edible black seeds. It has a refreshing tart-sweet subtle taste.

Look for slightly firm fruit with fairly fuzzy skin. When fully ripened, kiwis should yield to gentle pressure on the skin. Season: June to December

Knackwurst: A smoked and cooked sausage also called knockwurst, or knoblauch, made from a formula similar to that used for the frankfurter. The chief difference between a frankfurter and knackwurst are in the size and the seasoning: knackwurst is larger around and shorter, and it contains more garlic.

Knead: A method of mixing with the palms and heels of the hands to make dough or fudge smooth and elastic. In culinary language, the word is most often applied to the working of a yeast dough with the hands in order to develop the gluten of the flour and give better grain and texture to the final product.

Kohlrabi: This member of the cabbage family is a native to northern Europe. The name comes from the German and means "cabbage turnip". Kohlrabi has an unusual appearance which distinguishes it from other members of the cabbage family. Instead of a head of closely packed leaves, there is a globular swelling of the stem, about three to four inches in diameter, just above the ground, and the leaves sprout from this. The leaves are similar to turnip leaves. Kohlrabi is a popular vegetable in Europe. It makes an excellent accompaniment to roast or broiled meats when cut into julienne strips or thin slices and steamed and buttered.

Select small or medium-size kohlrabi with fresh top, tender rind.

Remove tops and discard; refrigerate; use within 2 or 3 days. Season: May to November, best supplies are in June and July.

Kosher: From the Hebrew word **kasher** meaning "fitting", "lawful", or "pure". The word is applied most often to food and utensils which have undergone the operations and rituals laid down for orthodox Jews in conformity with the law of the Talmud. The regulations as to the types of food which may or may not be eaten and those foods which may or may not be eaten together derive from the interpretations of Biblical injunctions.

Kumquat: The smallest of the citrus fruits, the kumquat grows on small evergreen shrubs which have aromatic white flowers. The kumquat themselves are oblong and the size of a small plum. They have a thick golden-orange spice rind, acid, rather dry flesh, and small seeds. Generally speaking kumquats are better eaten cooked than raw. If used raw, they should be very ripe or else they will be unpalatable. They can be cut up or sliced and used for salads or fruit cups.

Look for firm, bright orange kumquats. Avoid blemished or shriveled fruit.

Keep a few days at room temperature or refrigerate and use within a week. Season: November to February

L

Lamb: A lamb is a young sheep of either sex that has not reached maturity. Some popular cuts: *Loin Chops, Sirloin steak, Blade steak, Round steak, Rib Roast, Rolled Rump Roast, Shank.*

Langosta: (langouste) Spiny lobster, native to Caribbean waters, high prized for the mean of its tail. It lacks the large claws of the northern lobster.

Lard: Fat separated from the fatty tissue of pork. It has a characteristic nutty-flavor and is usually white in color. It is often used in piecrusts, biscuits and other baked foods, and for deep-fat and pan frying.

Lasagna: A broad noodle, about two inches wide, with a ruffled or a plain edge. Lasagna is also used to denote a dish of cooked and drained lasagna noodles baked with several kinds of cheese and in a tomato sauce. The dish may contain meat.

Layer Cake: A cake baked in layers, held together by filling, and covered with thick luscious frosting is typically American and a favorite dessert.

L'eau Ordinaire: Tap water.

Leaven: These are various substances which lighten dough or batter while it is baking and make it more palatable. The word comes from the Latin *levare* which means "to raise".

Lebkuchen: A spice cake of German origin and one of the oldest of cakes. Originally it was always made with honey.

Leeks: Once known as the poor man's asparagus, the flavor is soft and sweet. This first cousin of the onion and garlic family has a cylindrical stalk with a small simple bulb, and flat, juicy, compactly rolled up leaves which are dark green at the top and white towards the bulb. They're excellent sautéed and in soups, and leeks are the key ingredients in classic vichyssoise. Raw, they can be used as a garnish. Clean thoroughly as they tend to trap dirt and sand.

Look for white bulb base with fresh green tops, usually trimmed. (Leeks are larger, milder than green onions, and give different flavor in recipes.)

Refrigerate; wrapped; use within 3 to 5 days.

Legume: Food plants which have pods that open along two seams when the seeds are ripe are called legumes. The seeds are usually the edible part of the legume. Peas, chick peas, beans, Lima beans, soybeans, peanuts, and lentils are the best known food legumes. Next to cereals, legumes are the most important food plant for humans. They contain proteins, carbohydrates, fats, minerals and some vitamin B.

Lemon: The lemon tree, a member of the citrus family. The light yellow fruit is small, oval, and ends in a blunt point. The pulp of the fruit is juicy and acid, containing half of one percent sugar and five percent citric acid. There are many varieties of lemons. Some have thin skins and other very thick ones. The first are used for their juice, the second for making candied lemon peel which is used in baking and for desserts.

Look for bright, firm lemons, heavy for their size. Pale or greenish-yellow color usually means fruit of higher acidity. Avoid soft, shriveled or hard-skinned lemons.

Keep a few days at room temperature; refrigerate and use within 2 weeks. Season: all year.

Lemonade: Lemon juice, sugar, and water are the ingredients of one of the most popular and refreshing beverages invented by man. Lemonade is usually served icy cold and often garnished with fruit or mint.

Lentil: This legume is one of the first plants whose seed were used for food. The lentil seed is small and lens shape. It is never used green, but is dried when it is fully ripe. The lentil is extremely nutritious and is one of the staple foods of the Middle East.

Lettuce: This is a vegetable whose nutrients are found in the part of the plant that grows above the ground. Varieties include: Bib, Boston, Romaine, and Iceberg.

Look for clean, crisp, tender leaves, free from decay. For Iceberg lettuce, look for solid head, heavy for its size; for Bibb and Boston look for soft textured leaves with lighter color inside leaves; for Romaine look for crisp, coarse leaves.

Refrigerate in crisper use within a week. Season: all year.

Licorice: A perennial herb of the pea family. It grows wild in southern Europe and in western and central Asia. Its dried root, or an extract made from it, is used to flavor medicines, tobacco, cigars, cigarettes, soft and alcoholic drinks, candy and chewing gum.

Lima Bean: This round, full, slightly curved bean is truly an American native, for although a number of beans were known and used in Europe before the voyage of Columbus, Lima beans as well as green beans, kidney beans, peas, pinto beans and other were unheard of before the New World was discovered.

Limes: Resembles the lemon in shape. The rind of the lime is green and thin. The flesh is light green, with a very acid and juicy pulp which yields a pungent juice.

Look for firm glossy-skinned limes, heavy for their size. Irregular purplish-brown marks on skin don't affect flesh quality. Avoid hard, dry or soft limes.

Keep at room temperature a few days or refrigerate and use within 2 weeks. Season: all year.

Liqueur: Liqueurs are spirits that have been sweetened, flavored, and **sometimes colored according to** formulas which usually remain well kept secrets. Unlike spirits or wines which are made by straightforward processes of distillation or fermentation, the alchemy of a liqueur lies in the choice of blending of the flavoring ingredients (caraway and orris, aniseed and peppermint, cocoa and coffee beans, to name a few) that give the sweetened spirit a distinctive taste.

Liver: Liver has outstanding nutritional properties and, when properly prepared, it is delicious. Beef, calf's, lamb, pork and poultry livers are used in the cookery of many nations. Goose liver is used in France and Hungary to make the famous pâtés de foie gras.

Liverwurst: A ready-to-eat sausage made of finely ground lean pork and pork liver mixed with spices and seasonings. Liverwurst is usually boiled or smoked.

Lobster: A member of the family of crustaceans, to which shrimp and crabs also belong. They lack spinal columns and have "crusty" outer skeletons or shells with jointed bodies and limbs.

Loganberry: This berry resembles a blackberry in shape but its color is red and, when fully ripe, it takes on a purple tinge. In flavor it resembles the raspberry, but is more acidic.

Loquat: A tropical evergreen tree its fruit that is also known as a "Japanese medlar". The fruit is small, round, downy, and yellow-orange in color, with large black seeds. The flesh is pale yellow to orange, very juicy, with a delicious, slightly acidic flavor, not as rich and sweet as most tropical fruit. The loquat fruit is best eaten fresh.

Select deep colored, orange-yellow fruit that yields to gentle pressure on the skin.

Refrigerate; use within 2 to 3 days. Season: April and early May

Lovage: Lovage is a member of the carrot family to which parsley and celery also belong. Fresh and dried lovage leaves are used for flavor in cooking; the seeds, in a cheesecloth bag, are often simmered with stews. The root may be blanched and served like celery, or candied.

Lukewarm: At a temperature of about 95°F. Lukewarm water will feel neither warm nor cold when sprinkled on or held to the inside of the wrist.

Lunch, Luncheon: This word is used to denote a light meal in the middle of the day. A luncheon is a midday meal, too, but a more social one. Generally, the word is used when a group of people are being entertained whether at home or in a restaurant.

Lychee: The sole member of the genus Litchi in the soapberry family Sapindaceae. It is a tropical tree native to the Guangdong and Fujian provinces of China. The lychee bears a fleshy fruit that matures in 80 to 112 days depending on the climate. The thin tough skin is green when immature ripening to red or pink-red, and is smooth or covered with small sharp protuberances roughly textured. The rind is inedible but easily removed to expose a layer of translucent white flesh, with a floral scent and a fragrant sweet flavor.

Look for firm, rough and rubbery-skinned fruit with no indication of decay at stem end. Avoid blemished fruit.

Refrigerate; use within 1 or 2 days. Season: June and July

Lyonnaise: A French culinary expression meaning "in the manner of Lyons," a city renowned throughout France for the richness and excellence of its food. Food seasoned with onions, parsley.

M

Macaroni: The food paste made from a mixture of semolina and water, and dried in the form of slender tubes or fancy shapes, elbow macaroni and macaroni shells, for example. The semolina used is the purified middling's of durum and other hard wheat. Like all pasta, macaroni is healthful, nutritious and inexpensive.

Macaroon: A small round, crunchy confection made of almond paste or ground almonds, sugar and egg whites. The little cakes are called **macaron** in French and the English have adopted the name. But originally the Italians gave the delicacies their title of **maccarone**, a word of the Neapolitan dialect, which refers to dumplings, small cakes, and macaroni.

Mace: An aromatic spice made from the arillode, or false aril, which cover the seed of the nutmeg. Mace has the sweet strong flavor and odor of the nutmeg although it is considerably less pungent. It is used to flavor sauces, soups, poultry, and fish, and in creamed vegetables, custards, soufflés, cakes and desserts.

Macédoine: A French culinary term which refers to a mixture of raw or cooked fruit or vegetables. A proper French macédoine de fruits, is served in a glass or silver bowl bedded in a bucket of crushed ice to keep it chilled. The fruit in season is sprinkled with sugar or with sugar syrup, and often flavored with a few spoonfuls of kirsch or other liqueurs.

Macerate: The process of softening or breaking into pieces using liquid, often referring to fruits or vegetables in order to absorb the flavor of the liquid.

Madeleine: A small delicate cake, somewhat like a butter cookie, baked in special shell shape pans.

Madrilène: A name usually given to a clear soup which is flavored with tomato juice and served cold or chilled.

Maize: A cereal grain which is also known as Native American corn.

Malt: Malt is a substance made by sprouting or germinating grains, generally parley, but occasionally corn, rye, and oats. During the process various enzymes, among them diastase, are formed, partially converting the starch to sugar and changing proteins to amino acids.

This makes the formerly hard, raw grain into mellow, crisp, sweet-tasting malt.

Mango: Fruit of an evergreen tree taken from India to the West Indies over 200 years ago. Mangoes range from plum size varieties to those weighing 2 or 3 lbs. Usually oval in shape; the skin is smooth and yellow or yellowish green, often with s splotch of scarlet; the stone inside is long and flat. When ripe, the yellow flesh is sweet and juicy.

Look for oval or round, yellowish or orange fruit, perhaps with speckled skin. Ripe mangoes should yield slightly to gentle pressure on the skin. (Unripe mangoes have very poor flavor.) Avoid soft or shriveled fruit.

Let ripen at room temperature; refrigerate and use in 2 or 3 days. Season: April to August.

Maple: A tree native to the northern temperate zone, of the gnus Acer. There are thirteen species of maple native to the American continent, nine of them are found east of the Great Plains, two in the Rocky Mountain region, and two on the Pacific Coast. Maple syrup is made by boiling the sap down to a syrup. When the syrup is boiled to the density of stained honey, it is called maple honey. Maple cream or maple butter is syrup boiled to the soft sugar stage, cooled, and then stirred smooth. Maple sugar is syrup boiled to the hard sugar stage then stirred to prevent the individual crystals of sugar from hardening together. Maple syrup can be used on hot cereals, pancakes, waffles, and other quick breads, to sweeten milk, custards, bread pudding, and applesauce and other fruits.

Maraschino: A sweet cherry which is bleached, pitted, and steeped in syrup made of sugar, water, a touch of oil of bitter almonds, and food coloring. Sweet Royal Ann cherries are the variety most commonly used. Maraschino is also the name of a liqueur distilled from cherries.

Margarine: With 80 percent fat, is interchangeable with butter in some recipes. Soft margarine is readily spreadable even at refrigerator temperature and can be substituted for butter in cooking. Whipped margarine has air beaten in to increase volume; imitation or diet margarine has greatly reduced fat content and only half the calories of regular margarine and should not be used in certain recipes or when frying.

Marguerites: Salty crackers covered with a mixture of boiled frosting and nuts or coconuts...baked in the oven until browned.

Marinate, Marinade, And Macerate: To marinate foods is to steep them in a seasoned liquid, or "marinade", before or after cooking in order that they absorb flavor and/or become more tender. Marinades began as simple brines for preserving fish. A marinade consists of cooking oil, and acid (vinegar and/or lemon juice and/or wine), and spices. As the food stands in the mixture, the acid and the oil impart the savory flavors of the spices of the food. The acid also has a tenderizing action. Because of this action, marinating is most often associated with tougher, less expensive cuts of meat. However, since such delicious flavor is gained from marinating, foods, which need no tenderizing, may be marinated for flavor reasons only. The length of time for marinating foods varies. Two hours is a good rule of thumb for chicken, fish and seafood.

As a general rule, if the meat is cubed, steep it for three to five hours, if in one piece, overnight.

Marjoram: This culinary herb, a member of the mint family, is more exactly known as sweet marjoram. Sweet marjoram has always been a beloved herb, partly because of its delightful fragrance. It is among the "herbs for stewing" mentioned by the Elizabethan writer, Tusser, in 1577. Marjoram can be bought fresh in season. Most marjoram, however, is packaged ground or sold as dried leaves. (Uses: meats, poultry, fish, seafood, meat and poultry pies, stews, casseroles, egg dishes, vegetables, salads, breads, gravies, sauces)

Marmalade: A preserve of fruit, usually citrus fruit. The fruits are cut into thin slices with the peel, and cooked in water until tender. Sugar is then added and the mixture is cooked again until the solids are suspended in a clear jellylike mixture. The word marmalade comes from the Portuguese **marmelada**, derived from the Latin melimelum meaning "honey apple", which in its turn, can be traced to the Greek **melimelon**, from meli "honey", and melon, "apple". In addition to its use as a spread, marmalade is used in cooking for glazes, fillings, toppings and sauces.

Marron: A French word describing a species of cultivated chestnuts whose fruit contains only a single large nut. The varieties include a purée of whole nuts, in sweetened and unsweetened form, or preserved in vanilla syrup.

Marrow, (Beef): The fatty filling of beef bones, which is prized for its rich and delicate taste and which is also one of the lightest and most digestible of fats. Marrow is used to enrich dishes, or by itself as a spread, or baked or broiled in the bone.

Marrow, (Vegetable):   A squash-like edible gourd shaped like a long egg. They are peeled, cut into halves, and seeds removed from the center, they are cooked as any firm squash is cooked. Marrow is similar to squash in food and caloric value. This vegetable must be well seasoned and is usually combined with richly flavored foods. Vegetable marrows are available in specialty vegetable stores during the summer months.

Marshmallow: A confection made of sugar, unflavored gelatin, corn syrup, and flavoring. Marshmallows can be colored and flavored and rolled in colored sugar and coconut or chocolate sprinkles. Some marshmallows are made with the addition of egg whites to make them lighter and puffier. Marshmallows are also made in the form of a thick cream sold in jars (marshmallow fluff).

Marzipan: A confectionery paste made of ground blanched almonds, sugar, and egg whites. The paste should be as malleable as clay and can be colored and flavored as desired. It can be rolled into thin layers between sheets of wax paper and used to cover entire cakes; it can be cut with scissor or a sharp knife into roses and other flowers, letters, bows, and decorations, limited only the your imagination.

Maté: A beverage made from the leaves of various species of holly, chiefly Ilex paraguariensis, which is also known as yerba maté or Paraguay tea.   It is a relatively inexpensive drink and is popularly used in most South American countries.

Matzoth: Thin unleavened, cracker-like bread made of flour and water.

Mayonnaise: A cold sauce of French origin made with egg yolks, oil, and seasonings, which are blended into an emulsion. It is used as a spread, a sauce for fish, meat, and vegetables, and as a salad dressing.

Mead: An ancient drink made of water and honey, fermented with malt, yeast, and other ingredients.

Meal: The food, or foods, and drink eaten at a particular and usually fixed time to satisfy hunger or appetite. The word meal is also used to describe the ground seeds of cereal grasses or legumes, especially when coarsely ground and unbolted, i.e.; cornmeal and oatmeal.

Measure: In culinary terms "to measure" means to calculate accurate amounts of required ingredients. For consistently successful results in cooking and baking it is necessary to have standard measuring equipment and to measure ingredients for each recipe accurately. <u>Standard Measuring Cups</u>: Two standard measuring cups are necessary, one for dry ingredients, and the other for liquids. A set of graduated measuring cups is convenient for measuring and leveling part cup amounts. These hold exactly, **1, ¾, ⅔, ½, ⅓ and ¼** cup. The liquid measuring cup extends the cup level so that you can measure without spilling. These cups also have lips for pouring. <u>Standard Measuring Spoons</u>: A set includes **1 tablespoon, ½ tablespoon, 1 teaspoon, ¾ teaspoon, ½ teaspoon, ¼ teaspoon and ⅛ teaspoon**.

Meat: The flesh of domesticated animals. The most favored meat, by all odds, is the flesh of the steer or cow, called beef. Strangely enough, it has been the Anglo-Saxons who have made this meat so popular. Three king of England (Henry VIII, James I, and Charles II) are credited with knighting the loin of beef, from which comes "sirloin" and early French gastronome's who wrote about beefsteak acknowledged that England had introduced it to them. Second in popularity to beef, or possibly equal, is pork. It is the most versatile. Pork, when cured and smoked, presents the main meat supply of millions of people.

Meatballs: A dish made of ground meat, shaped into a ball before cooking. Meatballs can be made from any kind of meat, of any size, they can be fried, boiled, stewed, or cooked with other foods. They can be served by themselves or as an accompaniment, such as spaghetti and meatballs. They are often stretched and bound with other foods such as cereals, bread, eggs, cheese and vegetables.

Meatloaf: There's nothing lowly about a meatloaf it it's carefully seasoned, baked to the perfect level of doneness. They can be made ahead and baked at the last minute, served hot or cold. To give it variety bake it in a ring or other fancy molds, packing it with hidden surprises, or making it with a beautiful crust of mashed potatoes or rich flaky pastry.

Melon: The fruit of a number of annual trailing plants which grown from seed and belong to the gourd family. Some of the more popular melons are: Cantaloupe, Casaba, Crenshaw, Honeydew, and Watermelon.

Look for fully ripened fruit for best sweetness and flavor. Avoid bruised or cracked fruit. Season: May to November, depending upon variety.

Melt, (to): In culinary language "to melt" is to change a solid substance into a liquid one by heating. This is done to make it more assimilated with other foods, such as melting butter for sautéing, melting chocolate to incorporate it into a cake batter, etc. Generally speaking, it is best to melt foods slowly over low heat.

Menu: The bill of fare or list of dishes to be served at a given meal, written in the order in which they are to e served.

Meringue: A meringue is a mixture of beaten egg whites and granulated sugar. It may be served as a topping for pies, cakes, and puddings, or used as a pastry shell.

Meuniére: Sauce of butter, lemon juice and parsley.

Mignon: A meltingly tender cut of boneless beef tenderloin.

Milk: An opaque white, yellowish, or bluish liquid secreted by the mammary glands of female mammals for the nourishment of their young. Milk is a complete and adequate diet for the very young of its' owns species, although lacking, perhaps, some of the nutritive needs of adults, and some needs of the young of another species, i.e. cow's milk does not have enough vitamin C for human infants.

The major by-products of milk include **butter, sweet cream, dairy sour cream, cheese, yogurt and various frozen desserts.**

Other milk like liquids known as "milk," are plant latex, coconut juice and the contents of an unripe kernel of grain. The Native Americans, for instance, drank "milks" made from corn, chestnuts, or hickory nuts.

People of other countries drink milk from animals other than cows. The Egyptians use their water buffaloes for milk as well as for work. In Iraq the camel serves as a combination desert car and milk producer. In Peru the llamas flourish in the steep mountain crags and supplement the milk from the few Peruvian cows. Goats raised in Italy and Greece where lush pasturage for cows is scarce. Other animals which have been milked since early times are sheep, mares, asses, and zebras. **Whole Milk** – fresh whole milk is available pasteurized, homogenized, fortified and with chocolate flavoring added. **Pasteurized Milk**; milk which has been heated to kill any harmful bacteria and then cooled immediately to 50°F or lower.

Homogenized Milk; pasteurized milk in which the particles have been broken up and evenly distributed throughout the milk by a mechanical process. In homogenized milk the cream does not rise to the top of the container as it does in non-homogenized milk. Homogenized milk forms a softer curd in the stomach and is more easily digest. **Fortified Milk**; pasteurized milk containing added amounts of one or more of the essential nutrients present in milk. The most common addition is vitamin D. **Evaporated Milk**; homogenized whole milk from which about 60 percent of the water has been removed by heating. Vitamin D is added to prove 400 International Units per pint of evaporated milk. When diluted with an equal amount of water, it has about the same food value as fresh whole milk. **Condensed Milk**; milk made by evaporating a mixture of whole milk and sugar. It differs from unsweetened evaporated milk only in the addition of the sugar which accounts for 40 to 45 percent of the final produce. **Skim Milk**; fresh milk from which some fat has been removed. **Buttermilk**: milk that is left over after butter has been churned. It contains very little fat, since the fat has gone into the butter. Real buttermilk is a thin liquid with little fat globules, whereas commercial buttermilk is a smooth, homogenized product which is far more appetizing to drink than the original product. **Cultured Milk products** include; buttermilk, yogurt, sour cream, and half-and-half.

Milk Shake: A drink in which milk is shaken or blended together with such other ingredients as ice cream, fruit, or flavorings. Although a thick mixture, milk shakes are sipped, often through a straw. They should be frothy and made quickly from chilled ingredients.

Millet: Any of a large number of small seeded cereal and forage grasses, or the grain or seed of these grasses.

Mince, (to): A method of cutting food into very small pieces. When a food is minced, the pieces still retain some shape in comparison to ground food, in which all shape is lost, and to chopped food, in which the pieces are larger.

Mincemeat: A cooked mixture of minced foods and spices. Mincemeats were originally developed as an alternative to smoking or drying as a method of preserving meat, but over the years many meatless versions have evolved.

Minestrone: A thick Italian vegetable soup served with grated cheese. The word minestrone comes from minestra, which means soup and one, a suffix meaning "big". For many Italians minestrone is often the main dish at either supper or dinner. It is served with bread and followed by cheese and fruit. There are definite regional differences in the contents of minestrone. The most famous minestrone comes from Milan, and it contains rice. The minestrone from Genoa contains basil. It may or may not contain meat and frequently contains pasta or rice.

Mint (Mentha): A fragrant herb of which there are over thirty species. The Greeks and Romans named this popular herb. They believed that Pluto, the God of the underworld, had fallen in love with a beautiful nymph, Menthe. Persephone, Pluto's wife, in a fit of wifely pique changed the maiden into a plant that would grow where it could be stepped on. Fresh mint can be grown in pots or in a shady, damp patch with very little trouble. Mint is sold fresh or dried. The dried mint comes in leaves, and is never ground. Both fresh and dried mint should be crushed before using. (Uses: beef, lamb, poultry, fish, vegetables, salads and dressings, stewed fruits, marinades, sauces)

Mirepoix: A culinary term for an essence or concentration of diced carrot, onion, and celery, cooked in butter with or without ham or bacon. It is added to sauces, soups, or stews to make them more flavorful.

Mix (to): To blend several ingredients thoroughly into a homogeneous mixture. A spoon, fork, whisk, beater or blender can be used for mixing.

Mocha: The word mocha originally referred to a certain kind of coffee grown in the Yemen district of Arabia and exported from the port of Mocha on the Red Sea. Today, mocha is the accepted term for a mixture of coffee and chocolate whether it is used as a beverage or as a flavoring.

Moisten, Moist: In culinary usage moisten means to add a small amount of liquid to an ingredient or combination of ingredients, as when milk is added to flour and other dry ingredients in the making of biscuits, cakes, etc.

Molasses: The thick brown syrup that is separated from raw sugar during the various stages of refinement. The word molasses comes from the Portuguese **melaco** derived from the Latin root mel, which means "honey", and aceus, which means "resembling". To Americans the word molasses means both the syrup that is separated from the raw sugar in the first stages of production and the syrup that is taken from the raw sugar while it is being refined. The English call this second product "treacle". Molasses syrup was probably first eaten by the Chinese and the Indians. Its American history began when Columbus introduced it to the West Indies.

Mold, Mould: A utensil in which a jelly, pudding, or other preparation is shaped.

Mollusk: One of the large phylum, *Mollusca*, containing most of the animals popularly called shellfish, except the crustaceans. Edible mollusks include snails, mussels, clams, oysters, and squid. All of these shellfish have a soft un-segmented body protected by a calcareous shell.

Monosodium Glutamate: A natural produce derived from glutamic acid, one of the twenty two amino acids which are the building blocks of all protein. It is also known as MSG.

Montmorency: With cherries.

Morel: Although the morel is unquestionably a mushroom, it does not belong to the same, class of fungi (*Basidiomycetes*). Instead, it is a member of the somewhat more primitive *Ascomycetes*, along with another fungus prized by gourmets, the truffle.

Mornay: The name of a white or béchamel sauce to which cheese, an essential ingredient, has been added. A Mornay sauce may also contain eggs for further enrichment.

Mortadella: Italian style sausage composed of very finely chopped cured pork and beef with added cubes of back fat. It is delicately spiced, smoked at high temperatures, and air-dried. German style mortadella is a high grade finely chopped bologna with cubes of fatty pork and pistachio nuts added.

Moules: Mussels.

Moussaka: This is a casserole dish found through the Near East. Its origin is credited to Greece. The classic version is made with meat and eggplant in layers, but there are an infinite number of variations in the ingredients.

Mousse: A French word which, literally translated, mean "froth". In culinary language, it is used for a rich dish that is spongy or frothy: in other words, light. Mousses can be either savory or sweet, hot or cold.

Mousseline: A culinary term applied to a variety of preparations made light and airy by the addition of whipped cream or beaten egg white.

Mozzarella: A soft white cheese of Italian origin, shaped traditionally in ovals the size of a fist. Mozzarella has a mild flavor. It is eaten fresh and it is used in cooking. The original mozzarella comes from the country around Naples and was made from buffalo's milk. However, even in Italy, most mozzarella is now made from cow's milk, but the buffalo variety is superior in taste.

Muffin: Small round bread which can be leavened with baking powder, baking soda, or yeast. Muffins made without yeast, as quick breads, are typical of Native American cooking. When leavened with baking powder or baking soda, the muffin is mixed by sifting all the dry ingredients together with any nuts or fruits folded in and all the liquid ingredients added at one time. The batter, which looks lumpy and rough, is then spooned into well greased muffin pans. Raised muffins are prepared like yeast rolls and are rich in eggs and butter. Dough is first allowed to rise in bowl, then beaten well and put in greased muffin pans to rise again before baking. **English muffins** are one type of muffin leavened with yeast. The dough is prepared as is any yeast dough and cut into three inch rounds. The rounds are baked on a preheated lightly greased griddle on the top of the stove. The muffin is cooked until golden-brown on both sides.

Mulberry: Mulberries are native to the mild climate areas of Europe, Asia, and America. Mulberries resemble blackberries in shape and structure, ranging in color from white through red to black. The fruit is soft and bland in taste and can be eaten raw. Cooked, it is used in making desserts, preserves, and wine.

Mullet: The name is used to describe several families of fish. Their flesh is tender, white, and firm textured with a sweet, delicate taste.

Mulligatawny: An Indian soup whose name means "pepper water". It may be a thin clear soup or a thick one, made with meat or chicken, usually the latter and it has a curry flavor. Rice, eggs and cream are optional ingredients.

Muscat, Muscatel: Muscat is the name of several varieties of grapes. The muscat is a white or black grape with a sweet musty flavor, cultivated especially for making raisins and wine.

Mushroom: Mushrooms are fungi, members of the enormous and varied group of living things which are responsible for decay. Like most other fungi, mushrooms lack chlorophyll, which means that unlike green plants, they cannot manufacture their own food but must obtain nourishment from others, living or dead. Who can describe a mushroom? It can look like a button, an ear, a bird's nest with eggs in it, trumpet, cone, bear's head, saddle or a clump of coral. There are thousands of varieties, 3000 in this hemisphere alone, ranging in color from the tan of the little mushroom of the field to crimson, yellow, blue, and green, white, black or a combination of two or three of these. The cap can be smooth, pitted, tufted, dotted, warted, convoluted or spongy. The aroma runs the gamut from delightful to a stink like rotten fish.

Select firm, plump, cream colored mushrooms with short stems and caps that are closed around stem or slightly open, with pink or light tan gills. Buy only cultivated mushrooms.

Refrigerate, covered, use within1or 2 days. Season: all year.

Mussel: A bivalve mollusk, which includes both salt water and fresh water varieties. It is the salt water mussel, found in both the Atlantic and Pacific which is generally eaten. Mussels cling by a dark, hairy beard to rocks, wharves, and mud. It is best to pick them at low tide because the fresh, live ones are exposed at that time.

Mustard: Any of several herbs cultivated for its pungent seeds and/or leaves. The seeds are used to make the various forms of mustard seasonings; the leaves are used as a vegetable and known as mustard greens. The mustard plant belongs to the large Brassica group, a family which includes many well known, vegetables: broccoli, Brussels sprouts, Chinese cabbage, collards, kale, kohlrabi, red cabbage, rutabaga, and turnips. The word "mustard" is derived from the old French **mostrade** or **moustard**, which meant a condiment made from mustard seed. Mustard has had a long culinary history and a medical one as well. Pliny the Elder, the 1st century A.D. Roman writer, reported it to be effective in curing hysterical females, those who swoon from epilepsy or lethargy, and persons who suffer "all deep-seated pains in any part of the body". The later Middle Ages prized mustard as a cold cure. Even today mustard leaves, mustard baths, mustard poultices and mustard tisanes are often used to relieve chest congestion and break up colds. (Uses: corned beef, egg dishes, macaroni salads, sauerkraut, marinades, sauces, dips, salads dressings, pickles)

Mutton: Good mutton is a delight. True mutton, is carefully fed mature sheep that has been treated extraordinarily well, and after slaughtering has been carefully prepared for the market; hung long enough to give it tenderness and excellent flavor. The most traditional and certainly the most famous cut is the great English mutton chop. This is a thick chop, 2 to 2½ inches thick, cut across the double loin. It is often boned and rolled around a kidney.

N

Napkin: A fabric or paper square used at the table for wiping lips or fingers. The word napkin came into English from the French, which was derived from the Latin word mappa. This word also gave birth to the modern words "map", "napery", and "apron". The Romans used napkins at the banquets and the custom spread from Rome to Britain and France during the conquests of those two countries. Medieval English directions for eating instruct. "Drye they mouthe aye wele and fynd (fine). When thou shall drynke (either ale or wyne)."

Napoleon: A French pastry made with several layers of puff paste filled with pastry cream, cut into oblong slices, and sprinkled with confectioners' sugar or glazed.

Neapolitan, À la Napolitaine: The word is English, the phrase is French, and the literal meaning is "in the manner of Naples", the Italian city. However, the term has several culinary usages, most commonly, an ice cream or other dessert, salad, cookie, or other dish which is made in three contrasting layers. The usual ice cream combination is chocolate, vanilla, and strawberry.

Nectar: The word, which is of Greek origin, has two means. First, according to the poets of ancient Greece, nectar was the drink of the gods who live on Mount Olympus. The second meaning of the word refers to a sweet liquid secreted by a plant. The composition of the nectars of the different plants varies, but it is mostly water, sugar, with sugar and grape sugar and minute quantities of other carbohydrates.

Nectarine: A delicate variety of peach, smaller in size, roundish, and with a smooth skin that ranges in color from orange-yellow to red, sometimes mixed with green. The flesh is very juicy and may be red, yellow, or white in color.

Look for plump, rich-colored fruit with slight softening along the seam side. Color will be reddish to yellowish, depending on variety. Slightly firm fruit should ripen well at room temperature. Avoid hard, soft or shriveled fruit or fruit with large proportion of green skin.

Let ripen at room temperature; refrigerate and use within 3 to 5 days. To prevent browning if nectarines are not to be eaten immediately, sprinkle with a little lemon or ascorbic acid mixture for fruit. Season: June to September.

Nesselrode or **À la Nesselrode**:   A name used for a number of food preparations in the elegant French manner, including game soup, a rich barley and rice soup thickened with eggs and cream, a cold dish of thrushes stuffed with foie gras and truffles, and above all the best known of the Nesselrod preparations, a dessert pudding of candied fruit, nuts and cherries.

Newburg: The word describes a combination of heavy cream, thickened with egg yolks and flavored with wine, usually Madeira or sherry, but sometimes brandy. It is generally made into a sauce, Newburg sauce, in which seafood is served.

Noisette: An espresso with a splash of milk

Noodle: A food paste, or pasta, made of flour, water, and egg yolks. (It is the addition of the egg solids that makes the difference between noodles and spaghetti or macaroni.)

Nougat: A confection made with roasted nuts such as almonds or walnuts and sugar or honey. Sometimes egg whites are added to bind the mixture. The word comes from the Latin *nux* or "nut". Nougat of all kinds is a very old confection, possibly of Moorish origin. It has always been popular in Spain, Italy and France. There are a great many varieties of nougat; hard or soft, white or colored.

Nut: The word is used to describe a large number of dry fruits which generally consist of a single kernel enclosed in a woody shell. Acorns, filberts and hazelnuts are examples of true nuts. But not all shells of true nuts are hard. Some nuts are, botanically speaking, legumes. The peanut, for instance, is the pod of a vine of a pea family.

Nutmeg: The hard kernel of the apricot like fruit of the different varieties of the nutmeg tree. The tree, Myristica fragrans, is a tropical evergreen, native to the East Indies, but now also raised in the West Indies and in Brazil. The fruit, which is intermingled with the flowers, is gathered with long hooked poles. The fruit is carefully split in half to expose the hard seeds, which is the nutmeg proper, covered by a false aril which is carefully removed, dried, and used to make mace, sister spice of nutmeg. Nutmegs were first traded in the Middle East by the Arabs. In the 6th century they were used in the food at the court of Justinian of Constantinople. They became a favored and valuable spice in the Middle Ages. Chaucer, the greatest English poet of the Middle Ages, wrote in the 14th century, "Nutmegs, too, to put in ale; No matter whether fresh or sale." Nutmeg is sold either ground or whole. The warm sweet flavor of nutmeg improves many foods, particularly creamed dishes and fruit desserts, and is delicious sprinkled on custards and eggnogs. (Uses: egg dishes, sauces, desserts, cookies, pastries, breads, fruits).

O

Oat, Oatmeal: Oats are the grains of a cereal grass plant. Like the rest of the grains, oats consist of a soft inner part surrounded by a husk which is removed before being eaten by humans. Some varieties of oats, however, are hull-less. Most cultivated varieties of oats have a smooth surfaced hull, although some wild varieties are hairy. Cultivated oats are thoughts to be the descendants of two kinds of wild oats, the common and the red which probably originated in Western Europe. To produce rolled oats, the husked sterilized grains are flattened, by heated rolls, into the flakes familiar to the consumer. Oats are the most nutritious of cereals, containing a good amount of fat, proteins and minerals.

Oeuf: French for egg.

Oil: In cooking, this is an edible fatty or greasy substance occurring in the seeds of certain plants. The terms fat and oil are often used interchangeably, but to be accurate the term "fat" applies to substances that are solid at normal temperatures, whereas oils are liquid at these temperatures. Food oils are made from olives, cottonseed, corn, peanuts, coconuts, palm nuts, soybeans, grape seed, sesame seed, poppy seed, safflower seed, sunflower seed, walnuts, hickory nuts, almonds, beechnuts, and others. The principal uses of oils in cookery are: 1) To give richness and flavor, 2) To sauté, pan fry or deep fry foods, 3) For shortening, as in cakes, pies, muffins, biscuits, etc.

Ojen: Anise flavored 84 proof liqueur made in Spain.

Okra: A plant of the mallow family which yields an edible pod with a gooey, mucilaginous quality.   Okra should be eaten while very tender; the pods, which grow extremely fast, should be cut often.

Select young, tender green pods less than 4½ inches long.

Refrigerate; use within 2 to 3 day.

Okra, Chinese: Look for okra up to12 inches long, firm, with dark green color and deep ridges.

Refrigerate, use within 3 to 5 days.

Olive: The fruit of a subtropical evergreen tree Olea europea. Olives are among the world's oldest fruits and have been cultivated in the Mediterranean area since about 3000 B.C. The olive tree probably originated in Asia. The name is so old that its origins remain obscure. The original root is related to the Armenian word eul which means 'oil'. Olive and the olive tree have had a long and colorful history. In classic mythology the olive tree is said to have been created by Athena, the Greek goddess of wisdom. A new city in Greece was the named, and Athena and Poseidon, god of the sea, competed for the honor of giving the city a name. The one who produced the best gift for the welfare of the new city was to be the winner. Poseidon offered a war horse, Athena an olive tree. The new city was named Athens.

Olive Oil: A product obtained by crushing tree-ripened olives, then extracting the liquid by pressing the pulp or by centrifugal separators. Olive oil has a more distinctive flavor and a lower smoking point than other edible oils. It is used for salad dressing, seasoning vegetables, and sautéing over low heat where its special flavor is desired. Olive oil should not be exposed to extremes of light or temperature. Light will fade its color and cold will cause it to congeal and separate.

Omelet: A combination of eggs, milk or water, and seasonings, cooked in a skillet until firm. Omelets generally are two different types; puffy, which the yolks and whites are beaten

E. L. Woolford

separately, resulting in a fluffier omelet, and French, in which the yolks and whites are beaten together, producing a firmer, less fluffy omelet. All the omelets are variations of these basic types.

Onion: (Bermuda, Spanish) The underground bulb of the plant Allium cepa. There are many kinds of onions with different colored skins, and in size they vary from the very small bulbets of the spring or green onions, also known as scallions, to the huge round red Italian onions.

Look for clean, firm onions with dry, brittle skin. Avoid ones with sprouts.

Store in refrigerator or at cool room temperature (60°F or below) in container that allows good air circulation. Keep dry; will keep several months. Season: all year.

Orache, Orach: An annual herb, native to the Tatary region of Asia. Orache is prepared for the table in the same way spinach is.

Orange: This popular citrus fruit grown on an evergreen tree. There are many varieties of oranges; Indian River, Seville, Valencia, Temple, Navel, Tangerine and Mandarin are just some of the varieties.

Select firm oranges, heavy for their size. State regulations help assure tree-ripened fruits, slight greenish color or russeting of skin of certain varieties does not affect quality of the orange flesh. Navel and Temple oranges are easily peeled and sectioned: Valencia, Parson Brown, Pineapple, Hamlin varieties have abundant juice. Navel oranges are seedless. Hamlins and Valencia's have few, if any seeds. Avoid dry, soft or spongy fruit.

Keep at room temperature a few day; or refrigerate and use within 2 weeks. Season: all year with best supplies in winter and early spring.

Orangeade: Fresh, frozen, canned or dehydrated orange juice mixed with water and flavored with sugar to taste. Lemon juice can be added to give the drink a tart-sweet flavor.

136

Oregano: This popular herb, also call wild marjoram, is one variety of the aromatic plant *origanum* which is native to the Mediterranean region. The flavor is similar to that of sweet marjoram or thyme, all belonging to the mint family. Use the leaves only either fresh, dried or crushed. Oregano is considerably more bitter and pungent, and should be used with discretion. It is mostly used in pizzas, tomato sauce, also chili con carne. (Other uses: meats, fish, seafood, meat and poultry pies, stews, casseroles, egg dishes, vegetables, sauces).

Orgeat: A syrup used in France, Spain, Italy and Latin countries as a refreshing drink when mixed with water or as a flavoring for frostings and fillings. The syrup is made for an emulsion of almonds and sugar with a little rosewater or orange flower water added.

Osso Buco: An Italian dish made with veal shanks, skin, or knuckle; white wine; olive oil; tomato purée; chopped anchovies; etc. and served on saffron-colored rice. The literal translation is "hollow bone".

Oven: In simplest terms, an oven is a box which can be heated. It may be part of a range, built into a wall, or portable. It may use gas or electricity as its source of heat. It has one or sometimes two doors, shelf supports, and racks which are usually adjustable, varying degrees of insulation, as well as different combinations of controls, timers, thermostats, and thermometers. It may have a vent and/or hood and fan. It is used to broil, bake and roast, as well as cook (as in casseroles). A **Dutch oven** is a heavy saucepot with a tight fitting lid used for cooking pot roasts, stews, soups, or other dishes that require long cooking.

Oxford Sauce: An English sauce also known as Cumberland sauce, which is traditionally served with cold venison. It can also be used with other game and meats.

Oxtail: A beef tail. It is very flavorful when braised or used as the basis for oxtail soup, a favorite of English cooking.

Oyster: A bivalve mollusk, found mainly between the tidal levels or in shallow waters along the coasts of all continents except those bordered by polar seas. The oyster itself is found in the concave lower half of the shell, protected by a thin membrane, called a mantle, which lies against the inner side of the shell. The three chief sizes are: 'half shells', the smallest, usually preferred for eating raw; 'culls' or medium size, for eating raw and for stewing; and 'box', the largest, generally used for frying.

P

Paella: Paella is a casserole which must always be based on rice. It is named for the two-handled iron frying pan in which the rice is cooked and served. In Spain ingredients vary according to the food available locally.

Palm (Hearts of): Tender ivory colored hearts of shoots of palm obtained from the core of the crown or top of the palm tree. Used as a vegetable or salad ingredient may also be cooked, or pickled.

Panbroil: This is a dry heat method of cooking meats, poultry, or fish which can often substitute satisfactorily for broiling. Tender cuts of meat one inch or less thick, frying chicken parts, and thin pieces of fish such as fillets are particularly suitable.

Pancake: (flapjacks) Pancakes, or griddle cakes, are the oldest form of bread. The first ones were made of pounded grain, mixed with water, and spread upon a hot rock to dry.

Panfry: A method of cooking or frying in very little fat in an uncovered skillet or pan on top of the stove.

Papaw or **Pawpaw**: A fruit of the custard apple family. Because of the similarity in names it is often confused with the papaya, which is also called pawpaw. The fruit varies from two to six inches in length and is shaped like a short fat banana, dark brown to blackish in color, it with a soft creamy yellow flesh in which many seeds are embedded. It is sweet, rich, custard-like, and slightly aromatic.

Papaya: Papaya is a large fleshy fruit which grow on stalks from the trunk, just below the leaves. The fruit, which resembles a melon, has a rind and a juicy flesh that is yellow orange in color; it has a delicious, sweet-tart musky taste. The fruit contains an enzyme called papain which acts as a digestive ferment.

Look for greenish-yellow to almost yellow fruit that should yield to gentle thumb pressure. Avoid shriveled or bruised fruit.

Refrigerate, use within 3 to 4 days. Season: all year.

Pápillote, En: A French culinary term meaning "wrapped in paper". At one time parchment was used for the wrapping, but brown paper, aluminum foil or leaves are widely used.

Paprika: The Hungarian name given to a spice or condiment made by grinding the ripe dried pods of red capsicum or bell peppers. It is used as a seasoning and as a garnish on practically all non-sweet dishes.

Paraffin: A flammable waxy substance produced in distilling wood, shale, coal, etc. It is used for coating the tops of jars of jams and jellies to keep out air, thus preventing spoilage. Since it has an extremely low smoking point, it should be melted over very low heat or hot water.

Parboil: To parboil food is to plunge it into boiling water and cook it for a short period of time. Parboiling is used for such vegetables as potatoes or green peppers to cook them partially, or to shorten cooking time. Parboiling is also used to prepare vegetables for freezing.

Pare: To peel thinly with a sharp knife.

Parfait: The word for this ice cream dessert is the French word meaning "perfect". Originally, a parfait meant only a coffee cream, now it consists of ice cream served with whipped cream or fruit or other sauces.

Parsley: A hardy biennial plant, widely used for flavoring and as a garnish. The parsley family includes many herbs and spices such as anise, dill, angelica, chervil, caraway, coriander, cumin, fennel, lovage, sweet cicely, and the common vegetables celery and carrots. Parsley can be used in nearly anything, added at the last moment,, finely chopped to flavor, as a major constituent of the classic bouquet garni, fresh or deep fried in oil.

Parsnip: The edible underground root of a biennial plant, of the carrot family. The sweet flavor of the parsnip develops only after the first frost, as cold weather changes the starch to sugar.

Select smooth, firm well shaped, medium size parsnips. Avoid large, coarse roots or ones with gray or soft spots.

Refrigerate; use within 2 weeks. Season: all year; best supplies are from October to January.

Passion Fruit: The edible fruit of the passiflora or passion flower, a vine with solitary spectacular flowers which is a native of tropical Brazil. It has a sweet acid flavor, and it is used as a table fruit, as well as for making sherbets, candy, and in very refreshing beverages.

Pasta: The Italian word for "paste", which in culinary usage describes an alimentary paste made from semolina and water. There are more than 100 varieties, some large to be stuffed, others in small decorative shapes. The Italian names for these varieties are wonderfully descriptive. Among them can be found *amorini*, little cupids, *capelletti d'angelo*, angel's hair, *cappelli di prete*, priests' hats, *cappelli pagliaccio*, clowns hats, *conchigliette*, little shells, *ditalini*, little thimbles, *farfalle*, little butterflies, *farfalloni*, big butterflies, *fettuccine*, small ribbons, *fusilli*, spindles, *lancette*, little spears, *linguine*, little tongues, *lingue di passero*, sparrows tongues, *lumache*, *lumachine*, and *lumacone* or snails, little snails, and big snails, *manicotti*, small muff, *mostaccioli*, little mugs, *occhi di puo*, wolf's eyes, *ondulati*, wavy ones, *ricciolina*, little curls, *rigatoni*, little fluted ones, *stelline*, little stars, *stivaletti*, little boots, *vermicelli*, little worms, and *ziti*, bridegrooms.

Pasteles: (ayacas) Puerto Rican specialty made of a stuffing of meats with raisins, olives, capers, almonds in cornmeal or mashed plantains wrapped in a plantain leaf and steamed.

Pasteurize: The process of heating milk or other liquids to a certain temperature to kill harmful bacteria.

Pastille: The French name for a confection which we call a "drop". Pastilles are made from sugar, water, and flavorings.

Pastrami: A preserved meat of European origin, made from plate, brisket, or round of beef dry cured with salt and saltpeter. The beef is then rinsed and rubbed with a paste of garlic powder, ground cumin, red pepper, cinnamon, cloves, and allspice, smoked and cooked.

Pastry: The word has two culinary meanings. First it refers to dough made of flour, shortening, salt and water or other liquid. Pastry dough's are shorter and flakier than bread dough's, are used for pies, tarts, small sweet foods served as desserts, and non-sweet foods served as appetizer or snacks. In its second meaning, the word pastry described a baked food.

Pâté: A meat or fish paste or a pie or patty with a filling such as meat or fish paste. Pâté to most of us means pâté de foie gras, a sinfully expensive concoction made of livers from specially fattened geese, and usually studded with truffles.

Pâté de foie gras: Goose liver pate.

Pâté en Pot: Traditional dish of the French islands; a very thick soup of finely chopped lamb and innards and vegetables.

Patty: A small, round, flat mass of food: dough, cereal, potato, or other vegetable, ground meat, fish, poultry, or nuts; or a combination of meat and potato and/or other vegetables.

Patty Shell: A shell made from puff pastry to hold creamed mixtures or fruit.

Paupiette: A meat or fish roll made from thin slices of meat or fish stuffed with forcemeat, or other dressing, browned and braised.

Pavlova: A dessert of Australian origin which is very popular at special teas, birthday buffets, or other celebrations. It consists of a meringue topped with whipped cream and berries, or whipped cream, passion fruit, and bananas slices.

Peas: Garden peas are grown for their seed primarily, although one type, the sugar pea, which the French graphically called mange-tout, has soft thick edible pods. The seeds of garden peas can be classified as smooth skinned or wrinkled, the former being a hardier type, but the latter being a better quality pea.

Look for fresh, young pods, light green in color, slightly velvety to the touch and well filled with well developed peas. Pods with immature peas are usually flat, dark green, wilted, over mature pods are swollen, light, gray-flecked.

Keep peas in pods in refrigerator, use within 1 or2 days. Season: all year, best supplies from March to June.

Peas, Chinese or Snow: Select fresh green, thin pods.

Keep peas in pods in refrigerator, use within 1 or2 days. Season: all year, best supplies from May to September.

Peach: The peach is a cousin of the cherry, the apricot, the plum and the almond. All are members of the Prunus persica genus. The peach is a rounded fruit, with a fuzzy velvety skin, creamy yellow when ripe (The nectarine, a variation of the peach, has a smooth skin.) The flesh may be white or yellow, with a pitted or furrowed stone of the free or cling-type.

Look for fairly firm to slightly softened fruit with yellow or cream color and, depending on variety, a red blush. Avoid green, shriveled or bruised fruit. Freestone comes readily from the seed; cling-stone do not.

Refrigerate and use in 3 to 5 days. Season: May to October.

Peanut: The pods of the peanut vary. They may grow from one to two inches in length, which one, two, or three seeds. The pod shapes may also vary but usually they are contracted between the seeds and are thin, nettle and spongy.

Pear: The pear tree belongs to the rose family, whose varieties include a large number of such favorite fruits as apples, plums, cherries, apricots, raspberries, and strawberries. Fruit may be roundish or bell-shape, symmetrical or uneven. It may have a long or short neck. The skin ranges in color from green to yellow to red tinge to russet. Flesh is finely grained and juicy. Taste may be sweet buttery, spicy, or acid.

Look for well-shaped, fairly firm fruit, the color depending upon the variety. Ripen firm pears at room temperature; when ready to eat, they should yield readily to soft pressure in the palm of the hand. Avoid shriveled discolored, cut or bruised fruit. Select Bartlett, Anjou, Bosc pears for both eating fresh and cooking; Comice, Seckel, Nelis, Kieffer for eating fresh.

Let firm pears ripen at room temperature a few days, then refrigerate and use within 3 to 5 days. Season: all year with best supplies from August to December.

Pecan: Pecans have very thin shells and the meat has a fat content over seventy percent, which is higher than any other vegetable product. They can be salted, spiced, or sugared for eating out of hand.

Pectin: A water soluble substance present in the cell walls of citrus fruits, apples, and sugar beets. When properly combined with sugar and acid, it forms a jelly and is used in the making of jams and jellies. The commercial liquid pectin is made from apple pectin; and powdered pectin is made from citrus or apple pectin.

Peel, (to): When used as a noun, "peel" refers to the outer skin of such fruits and vegetables as apples and potatoes. As a verb "to peel" means to remove the outer peel, skin or find of food. At times the peelings can be used and cooked separately as in candied orange and grapefruit peels. Apple peelings can be added to stewed fruits for added flavor, lemon peel added to black coffee, etc.

Pemmican: Native American cake made of dried and pounded meat and mixed with melted fat and various berry and herb seasonings. Originally it was made of dried buffalo meat or venison. The paste was then shaped into cakes and carried in rawhide bags. Different Native American tribes had different recipes. All were based on some of "jerky", meat that was not jerked at all, but rather dried or smoked.

Penuche, Panocha, or **Penuchi**: This is a candy made from brown sugar which is cooked to the soft ball stage, cooled to lukewarm, and then beaten until smooth and creamy. It can be either dropped by teaspoonfuls onto a cookie sheet and allowed to harden, or poured into a pan and cut into squares like fudge. (The surface of the cookie sheet or pan should be buttered.)

Pepper Pot: In Trinidad, a highly seasoned stew made with meat, game or fowl, and thickened and flavored with cassareep. In Jamaica, a spicy soup made with meat or fowl and vegetables.

Peppers, Bell or Sweet (*Capsicum*): The many seeded fruit of a genus of herbs or shrubs which originated in tropical American. In general the members of the family can be divided into two types; the sweet, larger fruited, bell or bull nose peppers; and the smaller fruited, hotter, and more pungent chili and cayenne peppers. Most ripen from green through orange yellow to red, color does not indicate pungency, but fully ripened ones may have a more pronounced flavor. Chilies lose their flavor quickly and must be stored in the refrigerator.

Select peppers that are firm, shiny and thick-fleshed. Wilted or flabby ones, with cuts or punctures, are of poor quality. Soft spots on the sides indicate decay. Season: all year.

Pepper (*Piper nigrum*): The fruit of the pepper plant, a perennial climbing shrub indigenous to the forests of southwestern India, but now widely cultivated in warm climates throughout the world. Both black and white pepper come from the dried berry of the same vine, which can grow up to twenty feet in its wild state and climbs on tree trunks like ivy.

Black: ground from whole peppercorns
White: from peppercorns with outer skin removed

Peppergrass (*Lepidium Sativum*): Garden cress and shepherd's purse are other names for this annual spring herb. The flavor is similar to watercress and like watercress; it is used as a garnish.

Peppermint (*Mentha piperita*): An aromatic perennial herb found wild in damp lowland areas in the temperate zones of Europe, Asian and American. It has a cool refreshing flavor.

Pepperoni: This highly spiced dry sausage is of Italian origin. It is made from coarsely ground beef and pork mixed with salt, coarsely ground black pepper, cayenne, and garlic.

This mixture is cured and then stuffed in casings and linked in pieces ten to twelve inches long. The sausage is then air-dried at moderate temperatures for three to four weeks.

Perch: A widely distributed, spiny-finned fresh water food fish. Known also as the yellow, barred or ring perch, they are carnivorous, voracious and prolific. Perch is a mild fish, with firm white coarse flesh and a delicate flavor.

Pernod: Anise flavored aperitif, made in France

Persimmon: A warm weather fruit of which there are two species. One of them is the American persimmon. This species produces a small, pulpy fruit which can vary in size from a half to two inches in diameter, is yellow or orange with a reddish cheek and has large seeds embedded in its soft flesh. Select clean, plump fruit with smooth, glossy skin. The stem cap should be attached. The fruit should be soft but firm.

Look for slightly firm, plump fruit with smooth, unbroken skin and the stem cap attached. Avoid bruised or too soft fruit.

When ripe, refrigerate and use within 1 or 2 days. Season: September to January.

Petite Marmite: A meal in one soup that is a specialty of all French restaurants. The literal translation is "Small pot". The dish is so called because it is served in the small earthenware pot in which it is cooked.

Petit Fours: A French term describing fancy little cookies or small iced and decorated cakes. Four means oven, in French, and petit is small. So a petit four means a little something from the oven, or a little baked delicacy.

Peychaud Bitters: Spicy red flavoring introduced to New Orleans in the 1790's by A. A. Peychaud, an apothecary. Other bitters may be substituted for Peychaud.

Pfeffernüsse: A German word, literally translated as "pepper nut", and used to describe a spicy traditional Christmas cookie. The inclusion of black pepper among the spices used explains its name. Usually the cookie is shaped, let stand overnight, baked, and then allowed to ripen before serving.

Pheasant: The highly prized and beautiful game bird, which is closely related to the partridge and the quail. The Phasiandae family to which these birds belong numbers about 165 species. Pheasants came originally from Asia, but they are bred in a great variety of places, from semi desert steeps to dense jungles. The flesh is succulent, with a flavor somewhere between poultry and venison.

Picadillo: High seasoned hashlike meat dish made with raw ground beef or cooked beef. The Cuban version, with olives and raisins, is especially famous.

Piccalilli: A pickle relish made with chopped green tomatoes, red and green peppers, onions, sugar, vinegar pickling spices, and often cabbage. Sometimes called "Indian pickle" because of its origin in the East Indies.

Pickapeppa: Brand name of two Jamaican sauces, pickapeppa sauce, a sweet mango sauce, and picakapeppa hot pepper sauce, a hot chili sauce resembling Tabasco.

Pickles: Although any food or food mixture preserved in salt and/or an acid liquid can properly be considered a pickle, usage of the noun, "pickle" is commonly confined to the pickled cucumber.

Pickling Spice: A blend of different whole spices (allspice, bay leaf, cardamom, celery, chilies, cinnamon, cloves, coriander, dill, fenugreek, ginger, mace, mustard, and black pepper are among the most common ingredients).

Pie: Any dish of fish, flesh, fowl or fruit covered on top with a crust of some sort is a pie. In America, pies are more often than not dessert pies, baked in a shallow pan with a bottom crust. In Europe, this type of pie is known as a tart. There are many kinds of crusts used for pies; crumbs, meringues, biscuits, as well as regular pastry. "What is pie for?" asked Emerson when challenged on the custom. In 1902 the New York Times blasted an Englishman's suggestion that pie be eaten only twice a week. This, said the Times, was "utter insufficient...as anyone who knows the secret of our strength as a nation and the foundation of our industrial supremacy must admit. Pie is the American synonym of prosperity, and its varying contents the calendar of the changing seasons. Pies are the food of the heroic. No pie-eating people can ever be permanently vanquished."

Pig: The word can be used as a synonym for swine an omnivorous hoofed mammal with a stout bristle-covered body, short legs, and a long snout, however, in the United States a pig is generally considered to be a young swine, with the word "hog" used to describe the adult animal.

Pigeon Peas: (gandules, goongoo or gunga peas) Round seeds the size of a small garden pea. Young pigeon peas may be eaten green, but the seed is usually used mature and dry, when it is brownish in color with flecks of gray.

Pilaf: Rice dish basic to the cuisines of Greece and the entire Near East, and found throughout southern Asia.   The dish is usually made of well seasoned long grained rice sautéed in oil or butter, and then boiled in the stock or broth.   A pilaf can contain meats, fish, seafood, vegetables, and any herbs or spices.   There are as many kinds of pilaf as there people who make them.   Indian pilafs can be hot with curry, some Turkish pilafs are bland.

Pimento: *(See Allspice)* A large fruited, sweet, heart shape pepper.

Pinch: As used in recipes, pinch refers to a small amount of a dry ingredient such as a ground spice, about as much as can be picked up between the index finger and the thumb.

Pineapple: This hardy perennial herbaceous plant is a native of northern South America.   The English called the fruit pineapple because of its resemblance to a pinecone. In French, German, Italian and other European languages its name is ananas, from the Paraguayan Guarani Indian naná, which means excellent fruit.   From its native South America home it traveled to the West Indies where Columbus saw it in 1493.   A Spanish adventurer, Don Francisco de Paula y Marin, introduced the pineapple to Hawaii in 1790. And although today Hawaii produces most of the world's supply, for almost 100 years the pineapple was considered a weedy pest.   It was not widely cultivated until the 1880's when an English horticulturalist, Captain John Kindwell, scientifically developed the commercial growing of the fruit.   When selecting fresh pineapple select fresh pineapples that are heavy for their size, slightly soft to touch, golden yellow in color, with a piney aroma.   Avoid fruit that is too green.

Select firm fruit, heavy for its size, with distinct aroma and plump, glossy eyes. Check ease with which a leaf can be pulled from crown. Color will depend on variety, but usually dark green color indicates immaturity.

Pineapples do not ripen after harvest. Refrigerate use within 1 to 2 days. Season: all year.

Pine nut: The edible seed of several varieties of pines; the seed develops in the pine cone which is heated in order to spread its scales, and make the seed easy to dislodge. Pine nuts are the size of a small bean with a thin, light brown shell. The meat is white or cream colored. The texture is soft and the flavor mild.

Piononos: Puerto Rico's deep fried plantain rings filled with spiced ground beef.

Piperade: A combination of tomatoes, sweet peppers, and onions, or any two of them, which is cooked until very tender. To this combination eggs are added. This dish probably originated in the Basque area of France. There are numerous variations, but at least one variety is described as a frothy purée in which it is impossible to tell what is egg and what is vegetable.

Pistachio: The edible seed of a small evergreen tree. Cashew and sumac trees are members of the same family. The fruits of the pistachio tree grow in clusters. Each fruit is about the size of an olive, about one half to one inch long with a thin, hard, brownish red shell. Within it is found a seed, the pistachio nut, which is pale green to creamy white in color, a single solid piece.

Pit: To remove seed or pit from food.

Pith: Loose spongy tissues especially in the center of the stem of vascular plants. Most notably the white bitter tissue found between the rind and the flesh.

Pizza: A savory open pie of Italian origins. The word pizza in Italian means "pie", any kind of pie, and the particular pie that we have come to call pizza is a pizza alla Napoletana, a dish typical of Naples. A pizza consists of a thin layer of yeast dough, rolled or patted to fit a large cookie sheet or special pizza pan, topped with tomatoes and herbs and slices of Mozzarella cheese. The variations are endless. - Anchovies, sausages, vegetables, olives, pineapple, mushrooms, - anything goes. The style of eating is also highly individual. The wedges may be eaten from the point to the crust, it may be folded lengthwise, it may be rolled, but it is not supposed to be eaten with a knife and fork.

Plantains: The fruit of a large tree like tropical herb, *Musa paradisiaca*. The plantain belongs to the same family as the common eating banana. Plantains, however, are larger, starchier, and less sweet, they must be cooked to be palatable. When boiled, baked, fried, or made into flour they are excellent and very digestible.

Look for firm large fruit with green color and some brown spots.

Season: all year.

Plum: The tree and edible fruit of many species of the genus *Prunus*, a large family which also includes almonds, apricots, cherries and peaches. The fruit grows in clusters, have a smooth skin and a flattened pit. Plums may be round or oval, with a skin in various shades of red, purple, blue, yellow or green. The flesh is thick and juicy and it may be sweet or tart. Among the best known types of European plum are the Italian, or prune-plum, generally blue-purple in color with sweet, firm flesh, excellent for eating out of hand and for cooking, the Damson plum, a very small firm fruit, generally purple, although the well known Mirabelle is a yellow variety, and the Greengage plum, small, round, and greenish-yellow in color, with a tangy, yet sweet taste. The Japanese plums have a yellow color overlaid with various shades of red. They are pointed or heart shape, juice, sweet, and firm. Select fresh, plump, smooth plums that are firm but not hard. Color is not a reliable guide as species vary widely. Avoid cracked, shriveled, or soft fruit. Plums with a brownish color have been sunburned and are usually of poor quality.

Look for plump fruit that yields to gentle pressure on the skin and is well colored for the variety (Color varies from bright yellow-green to reddish purple to purplish-black.) Avoid hard, shriveled or soft fruit or fruit with cracks or sunburn marks.

Refrigerate; use within 3 to 5 days.

Plum Pudding: Suet pudding, which like plum cake never contains plums but is made with currants, raisins, citrus peels, and spices and is either steamed or boiled. It is served for dessert with hard sauce, foamy sauce or other preferred sauce.

Poach (to): A method of cooking used to preserve the delicate texture and prevent the toughening of such foods as fish, chicken and eggs. The food is immersed more or less completely in water or other liquid. The water may be either at or below the boiling point, depending on the type of food being cooked. It is important to maintain a low temperature to preserve the shape and texture of food. Vinegar or lemon juice can be added to the liquid for flavor and to assist in maintaining the shape. Vegetables and seasonings such as salt and herbs can be added for flavor.

Poi: A staple food of the Pacific, and particularly Hawaii, made from the edible root of the taro. The taro is a plant of the subtropics and tropics, grown for its large underground tuber which has a high starch content and is extremely digestible. It is interesting that the Kanaka, the Polynesian inhabitants of the Hawaiian Islands, who lived largely on taro, did not have a word for 'indigestion'. The taro root is too acrid to eat raw. To make poi, the root is cooked, pounded, and kneaded until smooth, then mixed with water. To the uninitiated, the grayish-white poi has a bland uninteresting flavor.

Poive: Pepper. In France, pepper is almost always freshly ground black, but occasionally is white or pink.

Polenta: The Italian word for cornmeal, for cornmeal mush, and for dishes made with cornmeal much. Polenta is a staple dish of northern Italy, where it is often eaten in place of bread. Traditionally polenta was cooked in a big copper kettle called paiuolo, which was hung over the open hearth on which the farm cooking was done, much as in our colonial days. The principle of making good polenta is still the same, the cornmeal must be constantly stirred with a wood paddle or spoon until a thin crust forms around the edge of the pan.

Pomander: An old-fashioned way of sweetening the air. A pomander ball is an orange, lemon, or lime studded with cloves and made fragrant with cinnamon and orrisroot. Its origins go back to the Middle Ages, when primitive sanitary conditions made the sweetening of the air imperative. But even in our super hygienic age pomander balls add great fragrance in closets, garment bags, and bureau drawers.

Pomegranate: The fruit of a bush or small tree with bright green leaves and orange-red flowers. Pomegranates are one of nature's most startling fruits, about the size of a large orange, with a vaguely six-sided shape, and a hard, leathery skin which can range in color from light yellow to deep purplish-red, but is most often a pinkish or brownish-yellow.

The flesh is a brilliant red, enveloping a large quantity of little seeds. In fact, pomegranates, to the eye and taste, appear to have more seeds than flesh. But what flesh there is has a delicious sweet, pleasantly acidic taste. Pomegranate is eaten as a fruit, in salads, and sprinkled over desserts. Grenadine, syrup especially popular in France, is made from pomegranates. Select pomegranates that are heavy for their size with thin skin of bright color and fresh appearance.

Select fresh looking fruit, heavy for its size. Avoid shriveled fruit or broken rinds.

Refrigerate; use within a week.

Pomerac: (Otaheite apple) Pear-shaped red fruit about 3 to 4 inches long with white flesh, eaten raw or cooked and made into jams.

Pomelo: Another name for grapefruit. The word would seem to be an early misspelling of "pummelo", a citrus fruit which is native to the East Indies and which the grapefruit greatly resembles.

Pommes: French for Apples.

Pommes frites: French Fries.

Pompano: A salt water food fish which ranges Atlantic waters from Cape Cod to Brazil. The pompano, is related to the mackerel. Its rich yet delicate flavor, make it beloved by gourmets. New Orleans is famous for its pompano, served en pápillote, in a paper bag.

Ponce: In Louisiana, a pig's stomach is filled with a spicy meat and yam mixture and steamed to produce an oversized sausage called a stuffed ponce.

Ponzu: A citrus based sauce commonly used in Japanese cuisine.

Popcorn: A variety of edible corn, with small ears about six inches long. The kernels are very hard, small, pointed or round, depending on type, with a proportionately large amount of endosperm. Popping quality depends on correct variety and proper uniform drying process. Popcorn, either whole or ground, is also consumed as a breakfast food.

Popover: A quick bread made from egg rich batter. A well made popover is large, light, puffed up on top, with firm crisp brown walls. The center cavity is moist and yellow. Since popovers are stem leavened, the thin batter must be baked in a hot oven in order to form steam rapidly. The egg protein allows the batter to expand and hold the steam and then coagulates to form the crusty walls. The walls should be firm before popovers are removed, otherwise they will collapse. Popovers should be served hot.

Poppy seed: The minute seeds of an annual species of the large Poppy family. The seeds make an excellent food flavoring and are used extensively in Austrian, and Hungarian cooking and baking. The little bluish-gray seeds look round to the eye, but they are actually kidney shape. Although small, they have a delicious crunchy texture and nutty flavor. They are especially popular sprinkled on rolls, bread, cake, cookies, and pastries. Sometimes they are crushed and sweetened and used as a filling for cakes, coffeecakes, and pastries. Added to cooked noodles and various kinds of salads they contribute both taste and texture.

Pork: The flesh of domestic swine is called pork, and it has been a vital element in the diets of many of the people of the world since the wild swine was first domesticated, reputedly by the Chinese, around 2900 B.C. *"The Gentleman that Pays the Rent"* is what Irish farmers called the pig, which gave them both food and cash to pay the land rent. For the pig, as the saying goes, is man's best friend, every part of him can be used but the squeal. Cuts of pork include: *Pork Butt; Center Rib Roast; Center Loin Roast; Sirloin Roast; Tenderloin; Baby Back Ribs; Country-Style Ribs; Blade Chops; Rib Chops; Center-Cut Chops; Sirloin Chops; Spareribs; Ham; Shoulder Arm Picnic.*

Porridge: A dish made by boiling a grain or vegetable in water or milk to make a thickened soup to be eaten with a spoon. Originally the dish was made of meat and vegetables, and often thickened with barley or other cereals.

Port: The vineyards of the Oporto district of Portugal produce a sweet wine that, when fortified, is known as port. Port, like sherry, is a fortified wine. That is to say, brandy is added to the wine at various stages of fermentation. Port has an average of seventeen to twenty five percent alcohol. There are four main varieties of port, vintage port, crusted port, ruby port, and tawny port. There are some white ports made from white grapes.

Posset: A beverage made from hot milk curdled with wine or lemon juice. It is sweetened with sugar or molasses and sometimes thickened with flour or bread.

Potage: Puréed vegetable soup.

Potato: The white potato is a starchy tuber of the nightshade family. The white potato (sweet potatoes and Yams belong to two completely different plant families) was originally cultivated in Peru and probably Ecuador, where the varied soils produce variations in the potato as well. Simply cooked potatoes, such as the Irish version, used to be the mainstay of many diets, sometimes with the addition of milk, butter, or cheese. In England the use of the potato was extended to dishes that included meat or fish. And in France, some of the most imaginative of all potato dishes were created - among them, Potatoes Anna (layers of thin slices, cooked in butter in a hot oven until crisp and brown) and Soufflé Potatoes (crisp, puffy and airy), created by mistake when, as one story has it, a chef refried potatoes for a royal feast.

Look for smooth, well shaped, firm potatoes that are free from blemishes or sprouts. Large cuts or bruises mean waste in peeling.

Store in dark, dry place at coolest room temperature; don't refrigerate. Will keep up to 2 weeks.

Pot-au-Feu: Literally translated the phrase means "pot of fire" and it is the French version of a boiled dinner. Generally it consists of one or more meat, chicken and a variety of vegetables cooked in liquid which is then served as gravy with the meat and vegetables.

Pot pie: A meat or poultry pie, usually made with vegetables and potatoes, and baked in an uncovered casserole with a single or double crust of pastry or biscuit dough.

Pot Roast: A term applied to larger cuts of meat which are then cooked slowly in a small amount of liquid or in steam. The meat may or may not be browned in a little fat before it is braised.

Poulet: French for chicken.

Poultry: A word describing all domesticated birds bred and raised for use as human food. The most common are chicken, Cornish Game hens, ducks, turkeys, geese, guinea fowls, quails and squabs.

When buying poultry, it is essential to make sure that the bird is young and tender. The bird should have pale, unblemished skin with no scars or dark spots or patches. The pale skin of ducks and geese is marked with a characteristic checked pattern. The fat should not be excessive in quantity and should be pale or clear yellow in color and evenly distributed over the body of the bird. Turkey meat is finely textured, pale and lean.

Marinating any poultry vastly improves the flavor of the meat and makes it more tender and succulent. A good all purpose marinade should contain oil and red or white wine or good quality wine vinegar, plus seasonings, spices and herbs of your choice.

The following herbs and spices enhance any poultry: parsley, chives, tarragon, rosemary, thyme, basil, marjoram, bay leaves, and sage. Nutmeg, cinnamon, cardamom, coriander, ginger, caraway, paprika, cayenne, saffron, cloves, black and white pepper, allspice, curry powder and juniper berries.

Poultry that is going to be roasted or fried and has not been marinated should be rubbed with oil and/or softened butter or sprinkled with herbs and spices of your choice before cooking to improve the flavor of the meat.

When boiling a chicken you can add herbs and spices to the water, but a bouquet garni is preferable. You may also add peppercorns, whole cloves or strips of orange or lemon peel.

Praline: Any confection made of nut kernels and sugar, although a praline was originally an almond candy, and even more specifically one made with burnt almonds. In the South the word is used to describe sugared coconut or pecan meats, especially the latter, a candy which may be described as native to Louisiana.

Prawn: A shrimp-like crustacean of the genus *Peneus setiferus*, abundant in all tropical and temperate waters, both fresh and salt. Prawns range in length from one inch to six inches, and in the tropics may grow to a length of two feet.

Preheat: As the word is applied to cooking, preheating is the process of heating a utensil, for example, a skillet or Dutch oven, an oven or broiler, or a cooking medium such as fat or water to a given temperature before putting the food into it to cook. A utensil is preheated so that food can be browned or its cut edges seared to keep juices from escaping. An oven is preheated to enable a food to start cooking as soon as it is put into it. This not only permits standardization of time and temperature in recipes, but also affects the texture, appearance, and the flavor of the cooked foods.

Preserve: Broadly speaking a preserve may be any fruit processed for future use by any method. Thus, fruit butters, conserves, jams, jellies, marmalades, and canned fruits are all preserved. Fruits suitable for preserves are cherries, peaches, pears, pineapples, quinces, raspberries, strawberries and tomatoes. The fruit is cooked with sugar and a little water until tender. Then the fruit is allowed to stand in the hot syrup so that it will absorb some of the juice and plump up. The fruit should be packed into sterilized glass jars and the syrup spooned into the jar to cover the fruit. Then it should be sealed and cooled.

Preserve, (to): To prepare perishable food so that it can be kept for long periods of time. Food can be preserved by refrigeration, canning, freezing, irradiation, freeze drying, dehydration, salting, brining, smoking, and by the addition of sugar and acids as in pickles and preserves.

Press: In culinary usage the word is used to describe an apparatus or instrument used to: 1) to *express* liquid, as in the extraction of juice from grapes; 2) to *compress* a food to make it denser or more compact, as in making pressed duck, and 3) to shape a food, as in making pressed cookies.

Pressure Cooker: A utensil, electric or non-electric, which can be either a saucepan or a canner. The distinction is chiefly one of size since both operate on the same principle and canning in small amounts can be done in a saucepan, while cooking in quantity can be done in a canner. Pressure cooking is a very quick method of cooking, dependent upon the fact that food, cooked with moisture under pressure, has a higher boiling point than food cooked at normal atmospheric pressures.

Pretzel: A long roll of dough traditionally twisted into the shape of a loose knot or the letter B. There are two kinds of pretzels, hard and soft, and either may be salted or unsalted. Hard salted pretzels are also made in the form of sticks and bite size nuggets. The soft pretzel is a round roll like pastry in pretzel shape has the longest history, dating back to the Middle Ages, while the hard pretzel is relatively new. The name, which seems as strange as the shape, may come from the Middle Latin *bracciatello*, little arms. Tradition supports this interpretation by claiming that pretzels were first baked by an Italian monk as a reward for children learning their prayers. The other explanation of the word is that it comes from *pretiola* which means "small give" in Middle Latin.

Prickly Pear: Opuntia, commonly called prickly pear, is a genus in the cactus family, Cactaceae. Once the skin is removed, you can slice up the prickly pear to eat; it has small, hard seeds, that may either be swallowed or not. Some individuals say it tastes like a cross between bubble gum and watermelon.

Look for: Thorny, tough-textured cactus pears which have had sharp spines removed. Ripe fruit should yield to careful, gentle pressure on the skin. Avoid shriveled or dried fruit.

Season: March to May, September to November

Profiterole: A miniature cream puff pastry made from puff or chou paste which can be filled with either meat, poultry, or cheese mixtures for appetizers or with sweet custard, flavored whipped cream, or jam for dessert.

Prosciutto: The Italian word for ham. The taste is slightly smoky and salty, a cross between Canadian bacon and American country cured hams.

Prune: The plum dried without fermentation. Prunes are made from several varieties of cultivated plums, most often blue-purple freestone prune-plums. The northern countries of Europe relied on prunes for winter fruit, and in Holland, Germany and the Scandinavian and Slavic countries, prunes were used as a stuffing for meats and poultry as well as an accompaniment for main dishes or as a compote.

Puchero: Also called Olla Podriada, this is a rich stew-like dish of Spanish origin, which has spread throughout the Latin American countries. It usually contains chick peas, sausage, cabbage, and several meats. Puchero is in some respects a Spanish version of a boiled dinner.

Pudding: The words is used to describe a wide variety of baked, boiled, or steamed soft foods, either savory or sweet, served hot or cold, as main dishes, side dishes or desserts. Pudding is also another name for blood sausage. The chief types of puddings are: unsweetened boiled or baked dishes, usually with a cereal base and a texture resembling custard, such as corn pudding; sweetened boiled or baked dishes of a soft, spongy or thick creamy consistency, such as chocolate pudding, and suet based or suet custard dishes, such as plum pudding, which were originally boiled in a bag, but are now often baked or steamed. Sweet dessert puddings are relatively modern. It was only when sugar became widely available in the late 18th and early 19th centuries that sweet puddings came into their own.

The sweet puddings were of such great variety that the English often use the word to mean dessert.

Puff: As applied to cooking, a puff is a light pastry frequently made hollow so that it can be filled, such as a cream puff. Sometimes the word is applied to other foods which become light and fluffy while cooking, i.e., potato puffs.

Puff Paste: A very light flaky pastry which owes its tenderness and crisp quality to the large quantity of butter rolled into the basic flour and water dough. The paste expands a great deal in baking and is made up of many flaky layers. It is used in making Napoleons, cream horns, and many other sweet and non-sweet pastries.

Pumpkin: The name of a gourd belonging to the Cucurbitaceae family which also includes melons, cucumbers, and squash. The flesh is orange colored and has a distinctive sweet flavor. The word comes from the Old French pompion, in its turn derived from the Greek word pepōn meaning 'cooked by the sun'. The pumpkin is probably native to Central America. It was being grown extensively by the Native Americans in North America when the first colonists landed. The Native Americans boiled and baked pumpkin, made it into soup, dried and ground it into meal. The meal was used much as cornmeal was to make breads and puddings. The Native Americans cut pumpkins into rings and hung them to dry so as to have them throughout the winter. In the mountains of Virginia dried pumpkin was used as a substitute for molasses. Pumpkin pie was so associated with Thanksgiving that when a 17th century Connecticut town could not get molasses it needed for the pie in time for Thanksgiving, the holiday was delayed.

Select firm, bright colored pumpkins, free of blemishes. Season: Year round; but biggest supply is in October.

Pumpkin Pie Spice: This is a blend of cinnamon, cloves and ginger ground together to meld the flavors permanently. It is used in pumpkin pie, spice cookies, gingerbread, breakfast buns, and in pumpkin, Hubbard-squash and sweet potato dishes.

Punch: An alcoholic beverage which can be made with champagne, wine, ale, or liquor, and sometimes with additions of citrus juice, spices, tea, and/or water; or a nonalcoholic beverage made with fruit juices. The beverage is served from a large punch bowl into small cups. Although an alcoholic punch may be served either hot or cold, the fruit juice punches as more often served cold. Punch was introduced to Great Britain from India. The name itself seems to have derived from the Hindi word panch, meaning 'vie', and traditionally, punch was supposed to be made with five ingredients: spirits, water, lemon, sugar and spice.

Purée: A mixture made by pressing a raw or cooked food through a sieve, or food mill, or a blender so that it is smooth and thick. The purée is used as is or can be used in sauces, soufflés, soups or as a garnish. The word is French, derived from the medieval French *purer*, 'to cleanse', which indicates that originally a purée food was meant to remove their impurities.

Q

Quail: A small gallinaceous game bird which resembles a tiny plump chicken. There are several varieties. The best known American species is often called the bobwhite. Many people use the words quail and partridge interchangeably. American quail are white meated and the flesh has a delicate flavor. Quail are cooked like all game birds. When young they can be pan-fried, pan-broiled, broiled, or roasted. Older birds should be pot roasted with a marinade.

Quenelle: A dumpling made of fish or meat, bound with eggs, and generally poached in boiling salted water or stock. The word 'quenelle" is thought to have come from the German **knödel**, 'dumpling'. (Small quenelles are used as a garnish; larger ones are served as a separate dish.)

Quiche: A savory baked custard tart thought to have originated in Lorraine, a province of eastern France bordering on Germany, although Alsace, the neighboring province, also lays claim to being the home of the true quiche. The word quiche is derived from the French-German dialect spoken in these regions and can be traced back to the German word **kuchen**, 'cake'. The best known quiche, Quiche Lorraine, is one made with eggs, bacon, cheese and cream, baked in a pastry shell.

Quince: The round to pear shape fruit of a tree of the same name. When ripe the fruit is rich yellow or greenish-yellow with a strong odor, hard flesh. Its taste is so tart and astringent that it cannot be eaten raw. Quinces are full of natural pectin and are used for making marmalade, jellies, jams, fruit paste, butters, preserves and syrups. Quinces are a native of western Asia and reached the Mediterranean countries quite early. The quince was given mythological significance by the Greeks and Romans, who considered it sacred to the Goddess of Love. If you gave a quince to someone of the opposite sex it was considered to be an engagement token, John Barlett, a 19th century bibliographer and historian, saw quinces growing in Mexico and in a report of his experiences commented: "There are to varieties of the quince here, one hard and tart like our own, the other sweet and eatable in its raw state, yet preserving the rich flavor of the former. The Mexicans gathered and ate them like apples, but I found them too hard for my digestive organs."

Select golden-yellow round or pear shaped fruit with rather fuzzy skin. Avoid small, knotty fruit or ones with bruises.

Refrigerate; use within 2 weeks.

R

Rabbit: A small furry mammal of the rodent family, the rabbit has large eyes, long ears, long strong hind legs and feet, and a short tail. It differs most significantly from its close relative the hare in its burrowing habits and in the fact that the young of rabbits are born naked, blind and helpless whereas hares are born furred and able to see. Rabbit meat is practically all white, fine gained, and mild flavored. It can be prepared in many of the ways in which chicken is prepared. Young rabbits can be pan-fried, broiled, and roasted. Older rabbits can be braised or fricasseed.

Radish: The pungent fleshy root of a hardy annual plant, Raphanus sativus, which is widely valued as a salad vegetable. Apparently it is a native to the temperate regions of Asia, and it has been cultivated in China, Japan and India for thousands of years. The name radish is derived from the Latin word for 'root', *radix*. Radishes come in many shapes and colors' round, long, or oblong, and white, pink, red, yellow, purple or black. Their taste varies from mild to peppery. Look for smooth, well formed, firm radishes. The condition of the leaves is not always an indication of quality.

Look for uniformly shaped radishes that are free of blemishes, firm and bright, deep red or white, depending on variety.

Discard tops, if any; refrigerate in crisper; use within a week.

Ragoút: A French word for a stew made from meat, poultry, or fish, with or without vegetables. It is derived from **ragoûter**, "to stimulate the taste". The word has come directly into English without the accent, and as an English word, ragout is most often used in reference to well seasoned meat and vegetable stews cooked in thick rich sauces, usually brown.

Raisin: The name given to several varieties of grapes when they are dried, either naturally in the sun, or by artificial heat. When grapes are dries, their skins wrinkle, they have higher sugar content, and a flavor quite different from that of fresh grapes. The word raisin comes from the Latin word *racemus* meaning 'a cluster of grapes or berries'. It is thought that the Egyptians were the first to notice that grapes left on the vine lost moisture and became sweeter. Thus dried, they kept better than fresh. Varieties of grapes dried to make raisins range from dark bluish-brown to golden. The two most popular varieties are Muscat's and sultanas. The golden sultanas are not dried in the sun, but dehydrated indoors and given a sulfur treatment. This preserves their golden color. In cooking raisins can be added to cereals, rice puddings, cookies, cakes, muffins, stuffing, salads and rolls. They are an indispensable part of mince pie and fruitcake.

Ramekin or **Ramequin**: A French word which originally referred to toasted cheese but has developed two different meanings: 1) A certain type of cheese tart or tartlet and 2) an individual baking dish in which food is baked and served. The word ramekin comes from the Flemish rammeken which means "a little bit of cream". In modern culinary usage, the cheese dish called a ramekin is a pastry filled with a creamy mixture of cheese, eggs, milk or cream. Ramekins are eaten hot or warm, never cold. Ramekin dishes are usually white, with straight fluted sides, resembling miniature soufflé dishes.

Rampion: A bellflower, *Campanula rapunculus*, which grows wild in Europe and is sometimes cultivated for its edible tuberous root. The root, about a foot in length, looks like a long white radish. It and the tender young leaves of the plant are used raw in salads and cooked as vegetables.

Rappini: Commonly marketed as broccoli raab or broccoli rabe. The edible parts are the leaves, buds, and stems. The buds resemble broccoli, but do not form a large head.

Rarebit: Another name for Welsh Rabbit, a popular cheese dish.

Raspberry: The fruit of a bush of the Rubus genus which is a member of the rose family. Raspberries grow wild and are also cultivated. The berry is made up of many small drupelets. Raspberries may be red, purple, black or amber in color. They are a delicately flavored fruit and can be eaten raw either plain or with cream, and can be used for jellies, jams, puddings, pies, etc. Select berries that are bright, fresh, plump, well shaped and solid in color. A stained container is an indication of overripe or damaged berries.

Ratatouille: The word is French and describes a stew or casserole which most frequently contains a well seasoned combination of eggplant, zucchini, tomato, and green pepper. Occasionally meat is added.

Ravigote: A well seasoned classic French sauce consisting of green herbs, butter and tarragon vinegar added to béchamel sauce. Ravigote sauce is served with hot or cold fish, meat, poultry, and vegetables.

Ravioli: Shells or cases of pasta dough filled with meat, chicken, cheese, or spinach. Although the word ravioli is Italian, this type of food preparation is by no means a uniquely Italian dish. It occurs under different names in the cookery of many cultures. The Chinese know ravioli as *won ton*, the Jews as *kreplach*, and the Russians as *pelmeni*.

Recipe: When applied to cooking, a recipe is a formula for preparing a dish. In old fashioned usage the words 'receipt' or 'rule' were often used to mean the same thing. A recipe is made up of two major parts; the list of ingredients and the directions for preparing the dish. In reading and interpreting recipes there are certain points to bear in mind. **1)** Read the recipe through thoroughly, making sure you understand what the ingredients are and the method to be used. **2)** Before beginning the dish, make sure you have all the ingredients. A good plan is to collect them before beginning. **3)** If you are making the dish for the first time, do not alter any ingredients or procedures. If you are an experienced cook, after you have made the dish once, you may want to alter it as far as the seasonings, method of serving, etc. are concerned. **4)** Generally speaking, it is unsafe to double or triple recipes, especially cakes and candies. The cooking time, texture, or consistency of the resulting product may be changed.

Reconstitute: To restore concentrated food to its natural state, usually by adding water.

Redfish: (red drum, channel bass) Copper or bronze colored salt water inshore commercial or game fish with a distinctive black spot at the base of the tail.

Red onions: (a.k.a. Purple onions) are sweeter than yellow, often with a flat disk like appearance. Red onions are best used raw as the flavor tends to bleed out when they've been cooked. They are great in sandwiches and soups.

Red snapper: A salt water fish of a family that includes gray snapper, mutton fish, schoolmaster, and yellowtail. All varieties are considered lean fishes, with juicy meat and a delicate flavor. They can be fried, steamed, poached, or broiled, and are particularly delicious baked.

Reduce (to): As a culinary process, the phrase means to cook a liquid until a certain amount of it is cooked away, thus concentrating the flavor, and thickening the consistency of, that which remains. Reducing is most commonly done in sauces, stews, and syrups. It is one of the simplest cooking processes; all it requires is that one watches to make sure that there is not **too** much evaporation.

Relish: As a culinary term it can be and is applied to a wide range of foods and food preparations served as accompaniments to add zest, flavor, and variety to the main dishes of a meal. Olives and such vegetables as celery, radishes, cucumbers, carrots and cauliflower, when served raw, are one major type of relish. A second major type includes such widely used condiments as ketchup and chutney, and all the other savor foods prepared from mixed chopped vegetables or fruits, either uncooked pickled, or preserved.

Remoulade: A highly seasoned classic French sauce based on a blend of mustard, flour, water, oil, and vinegar with other seasonings. It is served cold with fish and seafood, cold meats, poultry and vegetable salads.

Render (to): To melt down or dry out meat fat, especially pork, in order to separate the portions of lean or connective tissues from the clear fat. Rendering is done in a heavy pan over low heat. If the rendered fat is to be stored for later use it should be strained and refrigerated.

Rhubarb: A hardy perennial plant of the genus Rheum native to Northern Asia and is now grown chiefly for its thick succulent leaf stalks. There are many varieties of rhubarb, but the only important distinction in the edible types is between forced or hot house rhubarb and field rhubarb. The first is usually has slender pink to light red stalks with yellow green leaves and the second deep red stalks and green leaves. Only the leaf stalks of the rhubarb are edible. Leaves and root contain a substance that can sometimes be poisonous. Rhubarb is extremely popular in northern Europe and in the Scandinavian countries.

Select fresh, firm, large, crisp, straight stalks with bright red or cherry color. Avoid wilted, oversized, or very thin stalks.

Refrigerate; use within 3 to 5 days. Season: January to June (some areas may have rhubarb all year).

Rice: An annual cereal grass the seed of which provides the chief source of food for half the world's population. Brown rice is rich in vitamins of the B complex, thiamine, niacin and riboflavin, and in iron and calcium. Varieties include: **Basmati Rice**: Indian rice with very small but long grains, with a distinctive flavor. **Camargue Red Rice**: Taking its name from the region in the South of France where it is grown in comparatively small amounts, this is relatively expensive and favored for its flavor and firm texture. **Carolina Rice**: The name is no longer used to describe a particular variety; it used to be imported from the U.S. and was of a high quality. **Glutinous or Sticky Rice**: Long grain rice with very high starch content. This is suitable for Chinese dishes as rice balls or sticky rice cakes. **Thai or Jasmine Rice**: Long grain rice from Vietnam and Thailand with a distinctive taste. **Risotto Rice**: There are several types, including Arborio and Carnaroli. Risotto is characterized by high absorbency and a firm, but "clinging texture". **Surinam Rice**: Very long thin grains from Surinam, sought after by connoisseurs. **Sushi Rice**: Varieties used for Japanese sushi cling together when cooked without becoming sticky and heavy. **Wild Rice**: The seed of the aquatic grass, related to plant rice, which comes from the northern U.S. **Brown Rice**: Rice with the outer husk removed, but still retaining the bran, having a characteristic beige color, a very chewy texture and a mild nutty flavor.

Rice (to): To press a vegetable especially a potato, through a heavy sieve-like utensil this reduces it to rice like pellets.

Ricotta: An Italian curd cheese made from the whey produced as a by-produce in the manufacture of various cow's and ewe's-milk cheeses. Soft and rindless, with a granular crumbly texture and milk flavor ricotta is used mainly in cooking, to spread on canapés and sandwiches, in mixed salads, for pancake fillings, in sauces for pasta, or as an ingredient for gnocchi. It may also be served as a dessert with sugar or jam, or blended with Marsala.

Riesling: A white grape variety, also known as Weisser Riesling, Rheinriesling, Johannisberger, and Riesling Renano. It can also produce a variety of styles of wine from dry to sweet. The wines have a honey, floral and when mature petrol notes, and a crisp, citrus acidity.

Rillettes: A preparation of pork, rabbit, goose or poultry meat cooked in lard, then pounded to a smooth paste, potted and served as cold hors d'oeuvre.

Ripaille: An informal French name for a hearty feast, where the food is abundant and the wine flows freely.

Rise, (to): The culinary process of making a food light and porous by the action of yeast. Yeast dough is placed in a warm spot, thus activating the yeast and producing a gas which expands, or raises, the dough. The dough literally rises in the bowl. When the dough rises until double in volume, it is ready to be shaped. After shaping, the dough is usually allowed to rise a second time until doubled in volume, then it is ready for baking.

Rissole: A savory meat mixture enclosed in rich pastry and fried in deep fat.

Roast (to): The phrases "to roast" and "to bake" both refer to the method of cooking by exposing food to dry heat. It can be the enclosed heat of an oven or the open heat of a fire. Usage determines whether we say 'roast' or 'baked', and in general roasting is used in reference to the cooking of meats, baking to other foods. There are, however, exceptions; the commercial process of removing the excess moisture from coffee, cocoa, etc., is called 'roasting', and we speak of roasted chestnuts, peanuts and roasted corn on the cob. On the other hand, we say 'baked' ham. Whichever word is used, roasting is one of the oldest methods of cooking in the world, if not **the** oldest and most universal.

Rock Cornish Hen or **Cornish Game Hen**: A small fowl with small bones and all white meat. It was developed from the Cornish Hen, an English breed of domestic fowl with a pea comb, very close feathering, and a compact sturdy body. Rock Cornish Hens weight from one half to one and a quarter pounds and are good broiled or roasted.

Roe: Fish eggs still enclosed in the thin natural membrane in which they are found in the female fish are called roe or hard roe. Roe is taken from many species of fish. Shad roe is perhaps the most popular and best known. Sturgeon roe is so scarce that it is widely reserved for the making of caviar, which is hard roe, salted down. A large part of the salmon and whitefish roe is also used for this purpose. Soft roe or milt has a soft creamy consistency; hard roe has a grainy texture when cooked. It can be poached, broiled, or baked.

Roll: The word is derived from the Latin *rotulus*, a diminutive of *rota*, 'wheel', and its most common food usage is as a description of varieties of bread made in the form of small pointed, oval, or round cakes, and generally intended to be eaten for breakfast or dinner. The word roll is also used to describe other roll-shaped or rolled up foods, for example, jelly rolls, veal rolls, etc.

Roll, (to): The phrase is used to describe several culinary processes: **1)** The flattening of dough into a thin sheet with a rolling pin, as for cookies or pie crust, **2)** the shaping of foods such as ground meat, cookie dough, candy, etc., into round balls; **3)** the coating of foods with flour or dry crumbs, chopped nuts, parsley, paprika, etc.; **4)** the shaping of foods into long tubular shapes which are then sliced, as the dough for refrigerator cookies; **5)** the crushing of cookies for crackers into fine crumbs with a rolling pin.

Romaine: One of the principal types of lettuce, also known as Cos lettuce. Romaine has a long narrow cylindrical head with stiff leaves and a broad rib. The leaves are dark green on the outside, becoming greenish-white near the center. Romaine is a flavorful and crisp lettuce and it lends itself excellently to tossed salads of mixed greens.

Rondeau: A cooking utensil used in restaurants. It is a round shallow pan with straight sides, a lid and two covered handles (not one long handle as in a sauté pan, though used in a similar way).

Roquefort: A French ewe-milk cheese (45% fat content) made in the Rouerque district. The cheese is blue veined smooth and creamy, with a naturally formed rind, and has a strong smell and pronounced flavor.

Rose Hip: The fleshy, swollen red seed capsule of any of various roses, but especially of the wild rose. The capsules are rich in vitamin C. They are also sold dried whole, cut, and powdered. Excellent jelly and jam can be prepared from fresh rose hips.

Rosemary: (Rosemarinus officinalis): A perennial evergreen shrub which grows in Southern Europe and is cultivated through the rest of Europe and the United States. The leaves, fresh or dried are used as an herb seasoning. Rosemary can flavor many dishes. It may be added to fruit cups and various soups, almost any hearty meat and poultry, fish stuffing and creamed seafood dishes, cheese sauces and eggs, herb breads, and stuffing, many sauces and marinades, fruits salads, and vegetables such as lentils, mushrooms, peas, potatoes, spinach and squash. Rosemary, like all herbs is at its best when fresh. If brought dried, it should be crumbled before using a release the rosemary's full flavor. (Uses: meat, poultry, fish, meat pies, stews, casseroles, egg dishes, vegetables, salads, breads)

Rosette: A type of waffle or fried cake made of a thin batter or milk, eggs, and flour, fried in deep oil. Rosettes may be made in a skillet, but preferably they are prepared by dipping a specially shaped rosette iron into the batter and then immersing the iron in hot fat. After frying they are sprinkled with confectioners' sugar or granulated sugar mixed with ground cinnamon. They can also be served as a non-sweet appetizer and can be sprinkled with garlic or celery salt.

Rosewater: This is an essence distilled from rose petals, and it carries the delicious scent and flavor of the flower. Rosewater has been known for thousands of years in the countries of the Middle East. It was used for religious ceremonies, such as the purification of temples and mosques, and even for Christian baptism. In the kitchen, rosewater makes an admirable flavoring, used instead of vanilla, almond and other extracts, or sometimes in conjunction with these.

Rotisserie: There are several meanings for this French word which implies both roasting and rotating. It may be a stationary or portable appliance used to cook foods by rotating them in front of or over a source of heat. Any turning spit that was ever used by primitive man to cook the day's hunt over a campfire was a rotisserie. So were the spits that stood near or in the fireplaces of castles and inns from the Middle Ages on, where flesh and fowl were roasted for the lord and his household, and for travelers. Rotisserie roasting allows air to circulate around the food as it cooks, and it subjects the food to direct heat. Both factors make for deliciousness of flavor that cannot be duplicated.

Rouelle: A thick round slice of veal cut across the leg, it is roasted or braised, shin of veal

(veal shank) is also cut across into rounds, for example for osso bucco.

Rouille: A Provencal sauce whose name means 'rust', describes its color, due to the presence of red chilies and sometimes saffron. Rouille is served with bouillabaisse, boiled fish and octopus. Lemon juice may be added to it.

Roulade: Any of various savory or sweet preparations which are stuffed or filled and then rolled.

Roux: A French culinary term for a mixture of flour and butter (or fat) cooked together and used to thicken soups and sauces. The flour and butter are cooked before the liquid is added to them in order to give them a certain color and taste, and above all, to avoid the raw, pasty taste that insufficiently cooked flour has. There are three kinds of roux: brown, blond, and white. Brown roux is used to thicken rich brown sauces for red meats. Blonde roux is a pale gold color, and is used to thicken the sauces used in lighter dishes, such as fish, chicken, veal, etc. White roux is also only made with butter, it is used for cream and other white sauces.

Rue: The leaves of this small perennial plant have limited use as a culinary herb because they are very bitter. Great care should be taken in picking rue for the grayish-green leaves are thick and covered with a non-hairy bloom which rubs off when touched. It sometimes causes a severe rash.

Rum: Rum is an alcoholic beverage distilled from the fermented products of sugar cane. There are three chief kinds of rum. The oldest type is Jamaican rum. This was the rum known to our ancestors, heavy, dark, full bodied and usually aged in wood. Cuban rum is a relatively modern refinement of this. Dry and light bodied. Cuban type rum has only been produced since the last part of the 19th century. It is also distilled in Puerto Rico and the Virgin Islands. More aromatic rums than either the Jamaican or Cuban are produced throughout the Caribbean. Rum is used in many mixed drinks and as a flavoring in many foods. In cooked foods the alcoholic content evaporates and the flavor alone remains.

Rutabaga: A root vegetable which belongs to the mustard family and is closely related to cabbage, cauliflower, Brussels sprouts, kale, mustard and turnips. Rutabagas are larger than the turnip, has smooth yellowish skin and flesh, and smooth leaves. The flesh has a typical sweet flavor. There are white varieties of rutabaga, but the yellow is the best known. Admittedly rutabagas are not one of the more delicate vegetables. But well cooked, they add nourishment and robustness to winter meals.

Select rutabagas that have smooth skin are heavy for their size, free of decay.

Store at cool room temperature and keep dry. Use within a week or so.

Rye: A hardy annual cereal grass, Secale cereal, closely allied to wheat. The seeds are used to make flour, malt liquors, whisky, Holland gin, and a Russian drink, kvass. It is thought that rye may have grown as a weed in parts of Asia where wheat was cultivated thousands of years ago. Ancient civilizations in warm climates, such as the Egyptians who did not grow rye, but there are early traces of the grain in cold northern Europe. During Roman times it flourished in central Europe. Countries that could grow wheat easily looked down on its harsher cousin, rye. Theoparstus, a Roman naturalist who probably lived in the 3rd or 4th century B.C., thought that if wheat was planted in poor soils it would turn into rye. Rye flour can be used alone or combined with wheat flour. Rye flour makes a stickier and less elastic dough than wheat.

S

Sabayon: A dessert sauce or simple dessert made of sugar, beaten eggs or egg yolks, and wine or liqueur or orange and lemon juice and grated rind. A variation containing whipped cream is also made. Sabayon is actually the French name for the Italian **zabaglione** or Austrian **weinschaum**.

Saddle: In culinary usage the word is applied to a meat cut, more often of venison, mutton, or lamb, taken from below the last ribs to the legs on both sides and including the loins. It is a luxurious cut and may be roasted either bone-in or boned.

Safflower: An herb, Cathamus tinctorius, resembling a thistle, with large vivid red or orange flowers. Native to the East Indies, it is cultivated in southern Europe and in Egypt. The flowers are used as the basis of a dye widely used in the orient for dyeing silks and cottons. Edible oil is expressed from the white seeds which remain when the blossoms fade. Safflower oil is light, flavorless, and colorless.

Saffron: A small crocus, Crocus saturis, with purple flowers. There are three deep orange-yellow stigmas, or filaments, in the center of each tiny blossom. These are aromatic when dried, with a pungent taste, and they are used to add flavor and color to cooking. Saffron appears to have come from the Middle East. Its name would bear this out, for it is an adaptation of the Arabic word za-faran, 'yellow'. Either whole or ground, saffron should be used with discretion, not because of its spice, but because a little saffron goes a very long way. It gives distinctive color to breads and cakes, and is much in favor with rice dishes, especially those of Spain, Italy and the Middle East, and India. Saffron also enhances cream soups, sauces, potatoes, and veal and chicken dishes. As a cooking spice, saffron comes either in the shape of the dried filament shreds or it is ground. Saffron colors any food a bright yellow. (Uses: poultry, fish, seafood, stews, casseroles, rice, breads, cakes)

Sage: (Salvia officinalis) There are over 500 varieties of this popular herb growing in temperate zones throughout the world. The fresh or dried leaves are widely used in cooking for their aromatic slightly peppery flavor. Dalmatian sage grown in Yugoslavia and imported to the U.S. is one of the best varieties of the plant. Other varieties are white sage, Cyprus sage, meadow sage, pineapple sage and clary sage. Not for culinary or medicinal value is the unrelated purple sage or sagebrush, which grows profusely on the western plains of the United States. The name 'sage' comes through French from the Latin *salvus*, meaning 'safe, whole, or healthy'. Since its earliest usage as a medicinal plant it has been said to lengthen and strengthen life. Sage rates as the most popular of the seasoning herbs and is one of the most important ingredients in poultry seasoning; it is also used in stuffing, sometimes in pork sausages, marinades, meat and vegetable soups and casseroles and fish stock.

Sago: A starch extracted from the pithy trunks of various tropical palms, among them the sago palm. It is basic food in southwest Pacific where sago meal is used to making thick soups, biscuits, and puddings.

Sahina: Deep fried fritter of Indian origin made from Taro leaves and split pea meal.

Sake: National alcoholic drink of Japan; made by fermenting rice, its character lies somewhere between western beers and wines. It is yellowish white and is often drunk warm.

Salad: The first salads were edible herbs or planted dressed only with salt. The word 'salad', in fact, derives from the Latin word for salt, *sal*. Salt was the universal preservative, and vegetables could be kept year round with some sort of salt dressing. From this simple beginning, salads have expanded to include a wide variety of ingredients, fruits, vegetables, herbs, meat, cheese and fish, cooked or uncooked. There is everything from the simple lettuce salad to a chef's salad which is a main dish full of meats and cheeses. Salads are usually eaten cold but there are hot salads, such as hot potato salad. Regional and individual tastes dictate when an accompanying salad is served. Whatever the ingredients of the salad and whenever it is served, authorities agree that is should have a moist dressing, oil and vinegar, mayonnaise, or variations of these ingredients.

Salami: One of a variety of sausages of Italian origin that can be eaten without being cooked first. There are Italian, German, Hungarian, French and kosher salamis. The word is Italian and implies 'salted', meaning that the meat is preserved. The singular of the word in Italian is **salame** and in colloquial usage this word is used for a person who is not very bright and is rather gullible. Salamis differ from each other by their composition of meats, their spicing, their salting and curing, and their shape. Salamis can be divided into two major groupings, hard and soft. The soft are the less chewing varieties of salami, kosher salami for example. Italian Genoa salami is a well know example of hard salami. Salami most often contains pork and some beef, although there are pure pork and pure beef salamis.

Salmagundi(y): A culinary term derived from the French word **salmigondis**, "hodgepodge'. It is used to describe an elaborate salad laid out on a large flat dish with each ingredient minced (ground), shredded or sliced, and arranged attractively in small rings contrasting color, cold meats, fish, cooked vegetables, salads and pickles -- anything can be used.

Salsify: A root vegetable belonging to the dandelion family, salsify is also known as the oyster plant because of its oyster taste when cooked. It may look like an ugly brown stick, but don't judge salsify on its outer appearance. The root is similar in appearance to a long, thin parsnip, with creamy white flesh and a thick skin. It can be boiled, mashed, or fried like a potato, and it makes a yummy addition to soups and stews.

Salmon: Called the king of fishes, salmon has been prized as food for centuries and is probably best known of all fish. Pictures of salmon carved on bone have been found in France dating from about 12,000 B.C. Centuries after the cave man, Romans gave salmon its name. They were enthralled with the spectacle of hordes of leaping fish in the rivers of Gaul and so named them **salmon**, which comes from the verb 'to leap'. The history of salmon as food in the Western hemisphere predates the discovery of America. The coastal Native Americans used salmon as a mainstay of their diet, for winter, it was salted, smoked, kippered, dried, or beaten into pemmican. Fresh salmon is considered a great delicacy and is served broiled with Béarnaise sauce, poached, hot or cold, with a Sauce Vert. There's also a cold galantine of salmon, which is deftly sliced paper thin and served as an hors d'oeuvre. Lox, a smoked salmon is served in Jewish delicatessens.

Salsa: Spanish for sauce, either hot or cold. The term is usually applied in Spain or Mexico to spicy sauces, particularly uncooked sauces or dips.

Salt: Sodium chloride, a substance formed by the combination of one sodium atom with one atom of chloride. It occurs abundantly in nature in the sea, in other natural brines such as the Great Salt Lake, and the Dead Sea, and in crystalline form, known as rock salt. Salt is produced in different grades, the finest being table salt with the coarser grades being used for preserving and refrigeration. Salt, like water, is essential for man's good health. Iodine is sometimes added to table salt to make iodized salt, of great importance in the prevention of goiters in regions such as the Midwest where natural iodine is scarce. Salt is the world's best flavoring, bringing out the natural flavor of food.

Sambucca: A colorless anise-flavored Italian liqueur, sometimes drunk "con la mosca" (with the fly), with one or two coffee beans floating in the glass, after it has been set alight.

Sandwich: A dish made up of a filling such as sliced meat, cheese, a savory spread, etc. placed on one slice or between two or more slices of bread. Sandwich sizes can vary from the long hero to the tiny bite-size tea sandwich, they can be made with all sorts of breads and rolls, and the possibilities for filling are endless, moist creamy fillings, smooth spreadable fillings, sliced meats, fish, cheese or poultry. In fact, almost anything that spreads or slices can be made into a sandwich, as nourishing or elegant as desired. The custom of placing food between slices of bread is an old one; workers in the field have long been fed that way. But the sandwich takes its name from John Montague, fourth Earl of Sandwich, who, reluctant to leave the gaming tables long enough to dine, had cold beef sandwiches made for him so that he could eat as he played.

Sangria: The Spanish version of a cup. A mixed drink based on red or white wine with added fruit and mineral water, sometimes with a spirit as well. It is served chilled.

Sardine: The name used to describe various small salt water food fish with weak bones which can be preserved in oil. These include the pilchard, alewife, herring and sprat. It is probably the French sardine, found in abundance around the island of Sardinia, from which the overall name is derived. Fresh sardines have an excellent flavor. Sardines are fatty fish. They differ according to kind, and depending on locality.

Sashimi: A Japanese dish of raw fish, shellfish and mollusks. The fish (which must be always fresh) is trimmed, boned and cut with a long thin knife.

Sassafras: A handsome tree of the laurel family, one variety of which, *Sassafras albidum* or *varilfolium*, is a native of North America. The bark is rough and gray, and the bright green leaves are of three shapes, all on the same tree. These leaves when dried and ground are the primary ingredient of **filé**, a thickening and seasoning agent which forms the base of gumbo.

Sauce: A hot or cold liquid accompaniment to food, enhancing and complementing the dish with which it is served, or used in the cooking of a dish. The word comes from the Latin "salsus" (salted) since salt has always been the basic condiment. It must be confessed that during an earlier period in culinary history sauces were used not so much to enhance as to smother the unpleasant flavors of food resulting from lack of refrigeration. Sauces fall into several categories, being derived largely from what are known as 'les sauces mères, or "the mother sauces". These include the two basic sauces made from stock, sauce espagnole and sauce velouté, the basic white sauce, sauce béchamel, the two basic emulsified sauces, hollandaise and mayonnaise, the vinaigrette sauce, the oil and vinegar combination.

Sauerbraten: Beef prepared in a spicy, aromatic sweet-sour marinade to tenderize the meat and add flavor. The dish is of German origin and the word means "sour roast". Sauerbraten requires long cooking but, no watching. The traditional accompaniments are dumplings, boiled potatoes or noodles. **Sauerkraut**: Pickled cabbage made from cabbage which has been cut fine and allowed to ferment in a brine made of its own juice, salt, and occasionally other spices.

Sausage: A preparation of minced or ground meat, usually seasoned with salt and spices and stuffed into a casing. Sausages may be made of all pork, all beef, or a combination of two or more meats. They may be fresh or smoked, dry or semidry; and they may be uncooked partially cooked, or fully cooked. Sausage has been an important meat staple for more than 5,000 years, and just about every country has produced its own special varieties.

From Germany are brockwurst, bratwurst, blood sausage, frankfurters and liverwurst, from Austria, Vienna sausage, from Poland, kielbasa. In the warmer Mediterranean area where the summertime preservation of meat was a problem, the dried sausages predominated, the Italian cappicola, Genoa salami, mortadella, and pepperoni, the southern French Lyon sausage, the Spanish chorizo. America's contributions to the sausage world the fresh and smoked country style pork sausage, and brown and serve links and patties.

Sauté: To cook food in an uncovered shallow pan over brisk heat, using just enough fat to keep the food from sticking. The name comes from the French verb sauter, 'to jump' or 'to make jump'. Earlier the French cook turned the food in the pan by tossing it as we toss pancakes, but today it is more usual to turn the food with a fork or spatula. Sautéing is a very old cooking method designed to prepare foods quickly, using very little fuel in the process, and it is a cooking process used for the preparation of food all over the world. A sauté pan, a frying pan or skillet, should be of heavy metal with an even surface so that heat is evenly distributed and one entire surface of the piece of sliced food can be cooked at once before it is turned. Foods that are to be sautéed must be reasonably tender. The surface of the food should be dry so that it will become brown and crisp within the short cooking period.

Sauterne: A delicate sweet golden wine high in alcohol, made in the Sauternes district of France. The true sauternes are generally served as dessert wines. A drier type is usually served with fish or poultry.

Sauvignon Blanc: White grape variety widely grown in Bordeaux, the Loire Valley, Italy, New Zealand, to name a few. It has small bunches of golden yellow grapes, and flavors of gooseberries, green (bell) peppers, grass and tropical fruits.

Savarin: A raised, non-sweet baba-like cake, rich in eggs and butter, baked in a ring mold and moistened with rum syrup. Whipped cream is put in the center before serving.

Savory: An English culinary term that describes non-sweet foods served in small quantities at the end of a meal, after the dessert. The foods used for savories correspond to what we tend to serve as appetizers, hors d'oeuvre, and canapés. The reason for serving a savory was rooted in the English tradition of serving port and other fortified wines and spirits immediately after dinner, when the ladies had withdrawn from the table leaving the gentlemen alone to enjoy manly talk without interference or inhibition. The taste of the wines clashed with the taste of the sweet dessert which had just been served, and the savory was introduced to clear the palate for the enjoyment of the wine.

Savory, Summer and Winter: Two closely related herbs which belong to the mint family. Savory has a long history as both a culinary and medicinal herb. Savory is known as a bean herb because it goes so well with beans. It also added piquancy to pâté, vegetable juice, consommé, chowder and bean and lentil soups, chicken, hamburger, lamb, veal, stews and poultry stuffing, baked or broiled fish, cream cheese, scrambled eggs, herb bread and stuffing, barbecue fish, seafood or poultry sauce, artichokes, beets, cabbage, peas, rice, sauerkraut, salad, stewed pears and quinces. A native of southern Europe, it was known to the Greeks and Romans, who used it for all sorts of remedies. The aromatic leaves of both plans are widely used for seasoning. Savory is sold dried, either in whole leaves or ground.

Scald (to): In culinary usage to scald means to heat a liquid to just below the boiling point, as in scaling milk. Scalding also refers to pouring boiling water over a food, or plunging it into boiling water to facilitate peeling, or to kill surface organisms.

Scallions: This name is given without much exactitude to several plants of the onion family, the green onion, the shallot, and the leek. The word scallion, like shallot, means 'onion of Ascalon', so it is probable that this vegetable was developed in ancient times near the Mediterranean coast of Palestine and Syria. Immature yellow onions scallions are also known as green onions, or salad onions, doubtless because their mild flavor makes them an excellent choice to use raw for salads and garnishes. Use only part of the scallion that is not tired and limp.

Scallop: A group of bivalve mollusks with ribbed rounded shells. There are two varieties, the tiny bay scallop and the large sea scallop. Bay scallops have a sweeter, more delicate flavor, and are tender.

Scallop, (to): To bake in a casserole with milk or a sauce and often with crumbs, either as part of a mixture or arranged in alternate layers. The use of the word scallop to describe this type of baked food is thought to have been derived from the fact that the shells of scallops were often used as baking dishes.

Scaloppine: An Italian word, the English is escallop, for a prepared dish containing slices of meat of fish of any kind flattened slightly and fried. Usually the dish most often so called is veal, browned and cooked in a sauce of wine or tomatoes and seasonings.

Scampi: 1. Shrimp. 2. A dish of shrimp in garlic sauce.

Schnitzel: The German word for a veal cutlet which may be seasoned and garnished in a variety of ways.

Scone: Plain or sweet biscuit like tea cake cooked on a griddle or baked in the oven. Scones are usually cut into triangular or diamond shapes. They originated in Scotland where they are often made of oatmeal.

Score, (to): To slash with a knife, as when cutting the long fibers in a piece of less tender meat or the fatty surface of a piece of meat to allow fat to drain properly. Flank steak and round steak can be scored with a sharp knife to cut the long tough fibers. The fat of a ham or the fatty skin of a goose or duck can be scored decoratively to allow fat to escape and give a decorative finish to the food.

Scramble, (to): A method of preparing food by stirring it, usually applied to eggs which are beaten lightly with a fork, then sautéed in a small amount of butter. The eggs may be beaten with seasoning and a little milk, cream, or water before being poured into the pan, or may be broken into the hot butter and mixed while they are being cooked. The first method gives a creamy golden yellow scrambled egg while the second method results in scrambled eggs with a flecked white and yellow appearance.

Scrapple: A very solid mush made from the by products of hog butchering; the mush is sliced and fried for a breakfast or supper dish. Scrapple is the invention of the thrifty Pennsylvania Dutch farmers. Apart from the general ingredients, there is no set rule as to quantity and seasonings, so that scrapple is a highly individual product.

Scrod: A young cod or young haddock. Young cod is sold in steaks, filets and whole, fresh and frozen. Since it is a lean fish it can be prepared in any number of ways - baked, broiled, sautéed, fried, steamed, etc.

Sea Egg: Caribbean name for a white sea urchin, the ovaries of which are considered a delicacy.

Seafood: This word may be applied to any marine fish or shellfish used as food, but in popular usage it is apt to be confined to shellfish: the mollusks, such as clams and oysters and the crustaceans, such as lobster.

Sear, (to): A culinary method of browning the surface of meat or poultry at a very high temperature to seal in the natural juices. Pot roasts and stew meat are seared on top of the range while roasts are seared in the oven. After the meat is seared, the temperature is lowered and the food cooked slowly until desired degree of doneness is reached.

Season, (to): To make food more palatable by the addition of salt, pepper, fresh or dried herbs, whole or ground spices, and various condiments, sauces, and flavorings.

Seasoning: An ingredient such as a condiment, flavoring, or spice added to food for the primary purpose of improving its taste.

Seaweed: Seaweed is a member of a group known scientifically as algae, with a history that has been traced back to two billion year old fossils. Not all, to be sure, are edible, but there are so many wholesome varieties that almost every nation living on the sea has found ways of making seaweed palatable. During the Middle Ages monks consumed an algae jelly as a stomach remedy, it was probably effective, because one seaweed derivative is stilled used as a laxative. The Japanese, masters of the art of seaweed cooking, insist that these algae belong in any well balanced diet. Two kinds of seaweed are basic to Japanese cooking kombu or kelp, the large brown algae, and sheets of dried nori from the purple Porphyra. Kombu is a key ingredient in dashi, the soup stock that in turn is the basis of miso, the rich soup served for breakfast, lunch and dinner, as well as tempura sauce, sukiyaki sauce, and a vast number of other dishes. Rich in iodine seaweed may be eaten fresh or used in a processed from - dried, compressed into sheets or powdered, for use as a seasoning.

Seed: The fertilized ovule of a seed plant containing the embryo of the new plant and, usually, a food supply, enclosed in a seed coat. From prehistoric times seeds have been one of mankind's chief sources of food. Included among them are the cereals, such as wheat, barley and rice; legumes such as Lima beans, peas, lentils and peanuts; coffee, nuts; and the aromatic seeds used for flavoring; caraway, sesame and poppy seeds, for example.

Semolina: The purified middling's (medium size particles of ground grain) of wheat. The word is derived from the diminutive of the Italian **semola**, 'bran'. The best semolina, the type used in the manufacture of pasta is obtained in the milling of durum wheat, (a hard wheat). The French bake a wheat bread with it; the Italians combine it with other grains in making polenta and gnocchi. It is also used for puddings.

Serré: A concentrated espresso.

 **Sesame**: An annual tropical and subtropical herbaceous plant. Sesame has been grown since time immemorial for its tiny grayish-white or black seeds which has a sweet nutty flavor, and yields a bland oil, when pressed. The seed was brought to the south by the African slaves who called it 'benne' or 'bene' seed, an African name still used today in the south and elsewhere. Sesame seeds are popular in southern cooking, especially in cakes and cookies. Sesame seeds toasted are good combined with cheese or used in sweet sauces. They are especially good with butter over noodles and vegetables.

Set, (to): As a culinary term, the phrase means to become fixed, rigid, or more solid, and is applied to such foods as gelatin desserts or salads; or meats set with natural aspics. An old fashioned usage of the term was "to set bread", meaning to put the dough aside for rising.

Shad: An important food fish of the family *Clupeidae* which also includes herrings. Like the salmon, shad enters the warmer waters of rivers to spawn. The texture of the flesh is so delicate that the skin should be left on the fillets. Broiled, baked, stuffed whole or sautéed in butter, shad is superb eating.

Shallots: A mild flavored cousin of the onion, chive, garlic and leek, which belongs to the Liliaceae or Lily family. The shallot derives its name from the ancient Palestinian city, Ascalon, where it probably was first grown. The shallot has a thick outer skin shading from reddish to gray, the bulb underneath greenish at the base and violet on the upper portion. Shallots grow in pairs, or lobes, each with one flat side. The edible part of the shallot is the bulb which is used after summer maturity and dry storage, just as the garlic or onion is used. The green tops are harvested in early summer and sometimes marketed as scallions. They are traditionally used in sauces, as the classic béarnaise sauce and are excellent in vinaigrettes.

Sheep: A ruminant mammal of the genus *Ovis*, native to the upland regions of the northern hemisphere. The flesh of a sheep under one year of age is generally considered to be lamb; the flesh of an older animal, mutton.

Shellfish: These belong to two very large classes, the mollusks and the crustaceans and are found in salt and fresh waters. The mollusks have a soft structure and are partially or wholly enclosed in a one or two part shell. The former, called 'univalve' mollusk, include the abalone, conch and periwinkle. The latter called 'bivalve', include the clam, cockle, mussel, oyster and scallop. Crustaceans are covered with a crust-like shell and have segmented bodies. Among them are the crab, crayfish, lobster, prawn and shrimp.

Shepard's Pie: A British dish consisting of a minced (ground) meat sauce topped with mashed potato, baked until crisp and golden on top. Shepard's Pie differs from cottage pie in that it is made with minced lamb, unlike cottage pie, which is made with minced beef.

Sherbet: A frozen dessert made of a fruit juice or purée, a sweetener, and water to which milk, beaten egg white, gelatin, or marshmallow is added. It is the addition of milk, etc., which differentiates a sherbet from water ice. The classic French sherbet is made from fruit juices frozen with liqueurs or wines, each portion shaped by a special conical scoop and sprinkled with the same liqueur or wine.

Sherry: A world famous Spanish apéritifs or dessert wine, which comes originally from the Jerez district of southern Spain. The color varies from pale amber to dark brown the taste from very dry to very sweet. Various kinds of Sherries have different names under which they are known and sold. The best pale dry Sherries used as aperitifs, are Amontillado, Fino, Vino de Pasto, and Manzanilla. The richest dark sweet Sherries, drunk as dessert wines or like liqueurs, are called Oleroso, Amoroso, and Brown Sherry. The best sherry comes from its original home in southern Spain.

Shirr, (to): In culinary usage the phase describes a method of baking eggs. The eggs are broken into a buttered baking dish, seasoned with salt and pepper, and covered with a film of light cream. Then the tops are dotted with a little butter. The eggs are baked in a preheated 350°F oven until the egg whites are just set, but the yolks are still soft.

Shish Kebab: A dish of meat, usually lamb, broiled on skewers, it has also come to mean as well as a skewered combination of meat, fruits, and vegetables which may or may not have been marinated and seasoned with herbs and spices before broiling. The name comes from the Turkish, **shish**, meaning' skewer' and **kebap**, 'roast meat'. Alternative it is spelled **shish**

kabob.

Shiitake: Widely grown Asian mushroom whose European name is the edible "lentin". It has a brown cap and tight whitish-beige gills. They go well with meats, can be grilled, or used in rich sauces, and stir-fries.

Short: This word, applied to pastry, means very tender, flaky, and rich; usually desirable qualities, although a pastry can also be too tender or too short and fall apart. A short pastry is obtained by the use of a large amount of butter or other shortening.

Shortbread: A thick cookie made with flour, sugar, sometimes eggs, and a proportionally large amount of butter or other shortening, which accounts for its name. It is of Scottish origin.

Shortcake: Although shortcake can be a biscuit, cake, or cookie with a short flaky texture, it is more usually taken to mean a rich biscuit that forms the basis of a delicious dessert with the addition of fruit or berries and cream or whipped cream. It is best exemplified by the strawberry shortcake. The true strawberry shortcake or any other shortcake should be made with a biscuit dough.

Shortening: Any fat, liquid or solid, used in pastry, dough, or batter for the purpose of making the resulting product flakier, richer and more tender. Those most generally used are the hydrogenated shortenings (lard, butter margarine) and the edible oils.

Shoulder: A cut taken from the front section or forequarter of an animal. It is less tender than the hindquarter and requires tenderizing and longer cooking.

Shred, (to): To tear or cut into small fragments or strips.

Shrimps and **Prawns**: A ten legged (decapod) crustacean, whose comparatively small size is responsible for its name, the Middle English **shrimpe** meant 'puny person' and the name is akin to the Swedish **skrympa**, meaning 'to shrink'. Shrimps vary considerably in size, from tiny insect like species to giant varieties to almost 12 inches (30 cm.) long; the color also varies but is some pale shade, usually brownish red or grayish green. The bright pink color of the shell of cooked shrimps is due to a chemical change that takes place through exposure to heat.

Shrub: A beverage made from liquor, fruit juice, fruit rind, and sugar. The combination is mixed together and aged in crockery, glass, or wood containers and then strained. It is often served iced, diluted with plain or carbonated water. A nonalcoholic version may be made from acidulated fruit juice and iced water. Any kind of fruit may be used to make shrub. In earlier days in America it was usually combined with brandy or rum. One 1836 recipe for Currant Shrub by a Charlottesville cook declares; "The Shrub is indifferent unless the rum is good." The word shrub comes from the Arabic **sharab**, meaning 'drink' which is also the root of the word sherbet.

Shuck: An outer covering such as a husk, pod, or shell. Corn is shucked by having the husk stripped from it. Oysters are shucked by being removed from their shells.

Sichuan Pepper: Also known as anise pepper or Chinese pepper, this hot, slightly peppery spice is prepared from the dried berries of a tree of the prickly ash family.

Side: In culinary terms, a side is one half of the body of an animal, as a side of beef.

Sift, (to): To put dry ingredients such as flour, sugar, baking powder, baking soda, confectioners' sugar, or spices through a very fine sieve or sifter to aerate them. Sifting should be done before measuring since these ingredients pack down and do not measure accurately if not sifted. Confectioners' sugar is sifted to prevent lumps.

Silver dragées: Tiny, ball-shaped, silver colored candies.

Simmer, (to): To cook a food in water or other liquid at just below the boiling point. Usually this is done slowly and gently for a long period of time. It is a preferred method for many foods that would be toughened by higher heat, such as shrimps or eggs, and for delicate foods that would separate into pieces through the violent motion of rapidly boiling water, such as fish. Soups are simmered to develop the richest flavor, sauces are simmered until the desired consistency, tough meats are simmered until tender, dried fruits until plump, etc.

Singe, (to): To remove the remaining down, feathers, or pin feathers from a plucked fowl or the bristles from a pig, by exposing them to a flame, or to a hot iron, often one especially made for the purpose.

Skewer: A thin pin or rod of wood for metal. It is used for fastening meat or poultry during roasting in order to keep its shape.

Skim, (to): In culinary usage the phrase means to remove the top layer from a food or beverage. This layer may be referred to as "crust", "foam", "froth", or "scum".

Skin, (to): To strip or peel the skin from a food, either with a knife or with the hands.

Slice, (to): To cut thin flat pieces from a food with a knife.

Sliver: A long slender piece of meat, cheese, pie, etc. "To sliver" means to slice foods into small thin strips.

Sloe: The fruit of the blackthorn *Prunus spinosa*, which grows wild in the woods and hedges in most parts of the British Isles. The sloe, in French it is called *prunelle*, is edible but not usually picked to be eaten. Its chief use is to flavor sloe gin.

Smelt: Any of several small fish belonging to the family *Osmeridae*. Smelts live in both Pacific and Atlantic coastal waters. They are a migrating fish and they ascend rivers and lakes to spawn. Their flesh is delicate, rich, and oily, so much so that the Native Americans of the Pacific coast used to dry the fish and burn them for light, and called them 'candlelight fish'.

Smetana, Smitane: This culinary term refers to dishes cooked with sour cream. Smetana is a Russian word meaning 'sour cream' an ingredient much used in Slav cooking. Smitane is the French version of the word.

Smoke, (to): To preserve, or cure, by exposure to smoke. Foods smoked are meat, fish, poultry, shellfish, cheese, salt, and nuts. The artificial liquids and powders used for 'smoking' contain salt, charcoal, dextros, spices, herbs, onion and other powdered vegetables, monosodium glutamate and papain.

Smorgasbord: A word we have adopted from the Swedish **smöorgäsbord** and a food custom we have adapted to our own style of informal service. The Swedish word derives from three words, smör, 'butter', gäs, 'goose', and bord, table. The first two combined in smörgäs, means 'bread and butter', or open sandwich, so bread and butter table it was, and it did contain that, but also a few other items which were served, buffet style, as a first course, much as the Russian **zakuski** were served.

Snail: A land gastropod mollusk, greatly admired by the French and Italians as a table delicacy. Even the ancient Romans prized them and perfected the art of fattening them for the table. Snails are served in their shells. The final cooking is best done in specially grooved snail dishes which prevent them from rattling around as they would in an ordinary pan. Purists serve them with special snail forks and the pincers that bold the shell as the meat is removed.

Snap Bean: A variety of the common garden bean, which includes both round and flat green, and yellow or wax beans and the so called Italian green beans. Snap beans are also called green beans or string beans. They are native to America and both North and South American natives used them long before the white man came. Buy fresh, crisp, firm beans that snap when broken. Young tender vegetables are characterized by pale-green or golden-yellow color with very small beans inside. Most beans grown today are stringless.

Snowball: In cookery, a snowball is a round cookie, cake, or ball of ice cream. The cookie or cake may be rolled in confectioners' sugar or frosted with white frosting and rolled in coconut to give a snowball appearance. Ice cream balls are rolled in coconut and served with a chocolate or other sauce.

Soda: Chemically, soda is a sodium compound of any one of many varieties. In reference to food it is most often sodium bicarbonate or sodium acid bicarbonate, a crystalline salt used in the manufacture of baking powder, carbonated beverages and effervescent salts.

Soda Cracker: A plain white cracker, usually square and characteristically salted on top, made chiefly of flour, water, shortening, and a leavening agent.

Soda Water (Carbonated Water): A beverage charged with carbon dioxide under pressure, a process which produces a liquid which bubbles, fizzes, or sparkles when opened.

Sofrito: The term literally means lightly fried d and describes a basic sauce used in Spanish and island cooking. Always made with either onions or garlic and softened with both, a sofrito usually contains tomatoes, peppers, herbs, spices and ham. Its ingredients are chopped, then cooked in oil.

Sole: A salt water flat fish. The most important species, and the one most high prized as a food fish, is Solea vulgaris, the true common sole, which is found in European waters. Its taste and texture are incomparable. The lemon sole is another species but does not provide as fine eating as the true sole. Various related flat fishes belonging to other genera are fished in American waters and marketed as "sole".

Sommelier: Originally the monk who had charge of the crockery, linen, bread and wine in a French monastery. Nowadays, the sommelier of a large restaurant is the wine specialist, a job that requires extensive knowledge of the subject and the ability to choose the appropriate wine for a dish.

Sorghum: A genus of grasses with a large number of species, cultivated throughout the world for food, forage, and syrup. The sorghums, although less nutritious than maize, require very little water and can be grown in regions where maize will not flourish. Sorghums are among the first of the wild plants to be domesticated by man. They originated in Africa and Asia. Egyptian cultivation can be dated before 2200 B.C. and they were grown in China and India. There are four main types of sorghums: grass, grain, broomcorn, and sugar.

Sorrel or **Dock**: A hardy perennial herb which dates back to 3000 B.C. Several of its varieties, which differ in shape of leaves and strength of flavor, are cultivated. All varieties are acidic to some degree. The mildest variety is spinach. French sorrel it has an acid sour flavor, but not so sour that it cannot be used in salads. The most acidic of the three plants is garden or Belleville sorrel, also known as sour dock. Garden sorrel is used, as is French sorrel, for cream soups, for purée to accompany liver, cutlets, ham, lamb and shad, for omelets, Swedish bread, salads, and with vegetables such as cabbage, lettuce, beet tops, or spinach. It is often used in Jewish cookery to make a sorrel soup, **schav**.

Soufflé: A hot preparation that is served straight from the oven, that is well risen above the height of the mold in which it is cooked.

Soup: A liquid savory food served at the beginning of a meal or as a light meal in itself.

Soup Tureen: A wide deep bowl fitted with two handles, used for serving soup. A lid, sometimes with a notch to accommodate the ladle, keeps the soup warm.

Sour: Term expressing a sensation of acidity when it is abnormal (a sauce, milk, or wine becomes sour when it has "turned"), or when it becomes less pleasant (sour cherries, which are not edible in their natural state, become edible when they have been preserved in alcohol).

Soya Bean (Soy Bean): This staple food is known for its products rather than the bean itself. There are over a thousand varieties of soy beans, varying in size and color (white, yellow, red, green, brown and black). Extremely nutritious, the bean is low in carbohydrates and high in protein. The Chinese call it **dadou** (big bean) and the Japanese **daizu**.

Soy Sauce: A basic condiment from China, Southeast Asia and Japan (called **soyu** in Japan and **jiang yang** in China). The sauce is made from a fermented mixture of soy beans, wheat, water and salt. Tamari is a dark soy sauce made without wheat.

Spinach: A vegetable with dark green curled or smooth leaves generally cooked, but also eaten raw in salads when young and tender. (See Greens)

Sponge: 1. A high, light cake leavened with air and stem. 2. A batter made with yeast.

Squash: An edible fruit of various members of the gourd family, which are cooked and served as a vegetable.

Soft-Skinned: *Zucchini, Italian Marrow:* Look for small, young squash that are heavy for their size. The skin should be tender enough to yield easily to thumb pressure. **Hard-Shelled:**

Acorn, Butternut: Squash that is heavy for its size and has a hard skin; tender young skin indicates immaturity, poor quality.

Squid: A marine mollusk of the cephalopod family, related to the cuttlefish. Squid is found worldwide and there are numerous species. Also called calamari, squid has a spindle shaped body, which varies in size according to species.

Star Anise: The reddish-brown fruit of an evergreen shrub native to the Far East. It is shaped like an 8-pointed star and contains seeds with a slightly hot aniseed flavor.

Steak: A slice of meat. When the term is not qualified, it refers to a cut of beef; without description of a suitable cooking method, it is assumed to be a tender cut for grilling (broiling) or frying.

Steak and Kidney Pie: A British specialty consisting of a hot pie with a filling of lean beef and kidney, to which are added onions and mushrooms, or sometimes potatoes, hard boiled eggs, or oysters.

Steaming: The method of cooking whose origins are believe to predate the discovery of fire using stones of hot springs. Fish, vegetables and poultry in particular may be cooked in this way, as well as grains such as rice and couscous.

Steep: To saturate certain cakes with syrup, alcohol or liqueur to make them moist and to add flavor. Babas, savarins, plum pudding, sponge fingers (lady fingers) and Genoese sponge may be treated this way.

Stew: Term for long slow cooking in liquid. This may be carried out on the stove top or in the oven, but in either case the temperature should be kept low enough to prevent the liquid from doing any more than barely simmering.

Stir (to): To agitate ingredients with a spatula, wooded spoon, or whisk, either before or during cooking, to ensure that the mixture is smooth and free from lumps and/or that it does not stick to the pan while cooking.

Stock: A flavored liquid base for making sauce, stew or braised dishes. A white stock is prepared by placing the ingredients directly into the cooking liquid, in a brown stock; the ingredients are first browned in fat. Sauces made from white stock are always called white sauces, whether they are basic or variation sauces (i.e. allemande, poulette, aurore or suprême); all sauces made from brown stock are always called brown sauces (i.e., espagnole, bordelaise, Bercy or piquante).

Storzapreti: A Corsican specialty, particularly associated with Bastia, consisting of dumplings made of chopped green vegetables (spinach, Swiss chard or both), mixed with fresh Broccio cheese and bound with eggs, grated cheese, salt and pepper. They are poached in salted boiling water, drained and browned in the oven.

Strawberry: Red, roughly conical fruit, which has its seeds on the outside. Strawberries are cultivated in numerous varieties throughout Europe and America. The strawberry was valued in Roman times for its therapeutic properties and the alchemists of the Middle Ages considered it to be a panacea.

Select full red color, uniformly shaped berries with stem cap still attached. Avoid dull or shrunken berries or leaky ones indicated by strained containers.

Refrigerate; use within 1 or 2 days. Season: all year with best supplies from April to July.

Streusel: Crumbly topping for cakes and desserts, popular in central European cooking, the name for which comes from the German word **struesen**, 'to scatter'. Streusel comprises flour, butter and sugar with possible additional ingredients, such as ground cinnamon, vanilla extract, lemon zest and ground nuts.

Stroganov: Dish of thinly sliced beef, coated with a cream based sauce and garnished with onions and mushrooms. This traditional dish of classic Russian cookery has been known in Europe, in various forms, since the 18th century, a.k.a. as Stroganoff.

Strudel: Sheets of wafer thin pastry rolled around a sweet or savory filling (the name literally means 'whirlwind'). Strudel is one of the most famous Viennese pastries, inspired by the Turkish baklava made from the related phyllo pastry, the recipe was apparently created by an Hungarian.

Stuff, (to): To fill the interior of poultry, game birds, prepared joints of meat, fish, shellfish, hollowed out vegetables, eggs, fruit or other preparations (pancakes, croquettes) with a stuffing, a forcemeat, a salpicon, a purée or any other appropriate mixture. This is usually carried out before cooking, except in the case of certain cold dishes.

Stuffing: A mixture used as a filling for poultry, shellfish, eggs, etc.. Stuffing may be made from bread, rice or other grains, vegetables or fruit. They can be coarse or fairly fine in texture and are usually well flavored.

Sub gum: A stew of Chinese vegetables.

Suchet: Description of a method used for preparing and serving crustaceans, which are first cooked in a court bouillon. The tail shell is removed and the flesh cut into scallops (escallops) or medallions, which are gently heated in white wine with a julienne of carrots, celery and leeks. The seafood and vegetables are arranged in the half-shells and coated with a sauce made from the cooking liquid, usually enriched with white wine.

Suet: The hard fat from around the kidney and loin of beef (which tastes best) and other animals.

Sugar: Any class of sweet tasting carbohydrates, formed naturally in the leaves of numerous plants, but concentrated mainly in their roots, stems or fruits. **Granulated white sugar** is the kind used generally in cooking, and for the table. It may be labeled granulated, fine granulated or extra-fine granulated. **Superfine granulated sugar** is finer than the regular type, and is often used in beverages other foods are rapid dissolving is desirable. **Confectioners' sugar**, sometimes called powdered sugar, is granulated sugar which has been pulverized to make a very fine, soft sugar. It usually contains a small amount of cornstarch to prevent caking. Brown sugars contain some molasses, which accounts for their colors. **Dark brown sugar** contains more molasses, has a stronger flavor than **light brown sugar**. **Granulated brown sugar** is dry and pourable but should not be used as a direct substitute for regular brown sugar in baking. **Demerara** (aka Turbinado) **sugar** is a large-grained, somewhat crunchy, raw sugar with origins in Guyana (a colony formerly called Demerara). Demerara is a light brown, partially refined, sugar produced from the first crystallization during processing cane juice into sugar crystals (this process is similar to what happens with naturally evaporated cane juice). Unlike brown sugar, which has the added molasses flavor, Demerara has a natural caramel-like flavor; this lends warm, caramel notes to whatever you add the sugar to. **Raw sugar** is unrefined crystalline sugar. It consists of coarse, sticky brownish-yellow crystals.

Sugar Snap Pea: Type of pea similar but distinct from the mange-toute (Snow Pea), in that the pod is similarly wholly edible but is lumpy rather than flat because the peas inside have swollen and matured.

Sukiyaki: A typically Japanese dish, of the type described as nabemano (cooked directly on the table). Its origin goes back to the year when religion banned the consumption of meat. However, the peasants used to cut birds and game into fine strips and grill them secretly out in the fields (sukiyaki means literally "grilled on a ploughshare").

Sumac: Also known as sumach or shoomak the shrub originating in Turkey; certain varieties of which are cultivated in Southern Italy and in Sicily. Its fleshy petals and small berries are dried and reduced to purple powder, which has an acid taste and is very popular in Middle Eastern cookery.

Summer Pudding: A British pudding or dessert of mixed summer fruit molded in a pudding basin lined with overlapping slices of bread.

Sundae: A dessert that originated in the United States, consisting of ice cream and fruit coated with jam or syrup and topped with nuts, confectionery and cream. Originally, it was reserved for the family meal on Sundays; at the end of the 19th century North America was fairly puritanical and the consumption of sweets and delicacies was still frowned upon.

Sunflower: An annual plant, originally from Mexico and Peru, also known as helianthus. Nowadays, it is widely cultivated both for an ornament and for its seeds from which oil is extracted.

Supper: A light meal taken in the evening. Originally the only evening meal (now called dinner). Supper usually consisted of soup (hence the name) and was eaten relatively early.

Sushi: Japanese specialty comprising rice mixed with a dressing when freshly cooked. Round grain rice that remains whole when cooked but becomes slightly sticky is used. Additional ingredients include fresh raw or cooked fish, seafood or vegetables.

Suzette: A type of sweet pancake flavored with tangerine and coated with a tangerine flavored sauce.

Sweet: Term describing a sugary taste.

Sweet-and-Sour: The association of two contrasting flavors, acid and sweet, in the same dish is a very old culinary practice. Honey with vinegar and verjuice were among basic ingredients of the seasonings used in Roman times and in medieval cooking, with its sauces and ragoûts.

Sweetbread: The culinary term for the thymus gland (in the throat) and the pancreas (near the stomach) in calves, lambs and pigs, although the latter are not much used.

Sweeten: To reduce the sharpness, tartness, bitterness, sourness, acidity or excessive seasoning in a dish by adding a little water, milk, cream or sugar, or by prolonging the cooking time considerably.

Sweet onions: (Maui, Walla-Walla and Vidalia) are prized for just that -- their sweetness. Good in salads, on sandwiches and for onion rings, sweet onions don't store as well as other onions and should be used soon after purchasing.

Sweet Potato: An edible tuber originating in South America and gradually introduced to New Zealand, the Pacific Islands, Europe, Africa and Asia. It has a reddish-violet or gray skin and sweet floury flesh, white, orange-yellow, pink or violet in color, which is usually eaten cooked. In the United States the sweet potato is often wrongly referred to as a yam, which is a different plant.

Select firm, uniformly shaped sweet potatoes.

Store in cool, dry place; use with a week or so.

Swiss Chard: A variety of beet whose leaves and stalks are eaten as a vegetable. Swiss chard is also known as spinach beet. The leaves, which have prominent and broad tender white mid-ribs, have a slightly less pronounced flavor than spinach and are prepared in the same way. The stalks are usually boiled or steamed. (See Greens)

Swiss Roll (Jelly Roll): A thin sponge cake, spread with jam (jelly) and rolled up.

Sylvaner: A white-wine grape cultivated in many countries. It is grown in particular in Germany and Alace.

Syrah or **Shiraz:** Red grape variety producing bluish-purple grapes with soft juicy flesh. These make powerful, heady, tannic, rich fruity wines, which improve with age.

Syrup: A solution of sugar in water, which can be used hot or cold in the preparation of jams and ices and for many operations in pâtisserie and confectionery - for example soaking babas and savarins, dipping biscuits and working fondant.

T

Tabasco: A proprietary American sauce, popular in cookery the world over, that consists of chili peppers marinated in spirit vinegar with salt.

Table d' hôte: Meal of a definite number of courses, selected by the restaurant for the price indicated.

Taco: In Mexican cookery, a cornmeal pancake (tortilla) filled with a thick sauce, minced (ground) meat seasoned with chili pepper, black beans, or avocado purée with onions.

Tahini: Beige-colored, oily and thick paste of sesame seeds. Used in Middle Eastern cooking, both savory and sweet, also popular product for vegetarian dishes.

Tail: The caudal appendage of an animal, classed as a cheap cut of meat.

Tamales: Traditional Mexican dish made with a corn dough mixture that is then filled with various meats. They are wrapped in corn husks or plantain leaves and steamed.

Tamarind: The fruit of a leguminous evergreen tree, which originated in West Africa. The brown pods, 4 to 6 inches long and 3 inches wide, contain a bittersweet pulp dotted with a few hard seeds. Tamarinds are mostly used for preparing jams, sorbets, chutneys, drinks and condiments.

Tandoori: In Indian cookery, particularly in the Punjab district and Pakistan, a method of cooking chicken or other meat. The pieces of chicken are skinned, then coated in yogurt mixed with chili powder, turmeric, ginger, spices, onion and chopped garlic. A special cylindrical clay oven called a tandoor, until the flesh is tender but the outside crispy.

Tangelo: Hybrid fruit created in the 1890's by crossing a tangerine with grapefruit. It can be round or pear-shaped, with rough or smooth orange-colored skin. The flesh of some is rather acid tasting, others are sweeter.

Select firm fruit, heavy for its size, with good orange color. Tangelos peel and section easily, are juicy and have few seeds

Keep at room temperature a few days or refrigerate and use within a week. Season: October to January.

Tangerine: A citrus fruit resembling a small slightly flattened orange; also known as mandarin. There are many types of tangerine but there linking characteristics are sweet, fragrant flesh and loose skin, therefore, they are easy to peel.

Select deep yellow to deep orange fruit that is heavy for its size. Skin may be loose to the touch since tangerines peel easily.

Refrigerate; use within 1 or 2 days. Season: November to March.

Tapas: In Spain, an assortment of hors d' oeuvre or cocktail snacks, traditionally served to accompany Malaga, sherry, manzanilla or cider. The custom of nibbling tapas while drinking aperitifs, particularly in the evening, is widespread in bars and restaurants. The word comes from **tapa** (lid), since it originally meant a slice of bread which was used to cover a glass of wine to protect it from flies.

Tapenade: A condiment from Provence, made with capers (from Toulong), desalted anchovies and stoned black (pitted ripe) olives, pounded in a mortar and seasoned with olive oil, lemon juice, aromatics and possibly a drop of mare brandy. Tapenade is sometimes augmented by small pieces of tuna, mustard, garlic, thyme or a bay leaf.

Tapioca: A starchy food extracted from the roots of the manioc plant, which is hydrated, cooked, and then ground. It is used mainly for thickening soups and broths and making milk puddings and other desserts.

Taro: (dasheen, tannia, malanga, elephant's ear, yantía) A perennial plan grown in tropical regions for its large tuberous rhizomes, which have twice the caloric value of the potato. They are scrubbed and peeled, then used in the same way as the potato: boiled, fried or cooked au gratin. Taro's firm flesh can be white, green, gray or violet and has a somewhat nutty taste. . In china, balls of steamed taro are stuffed with meat, and then fried. In Japan, it is used in vegetable stews. Taro originally came from India (where it is called Katchu). It is known as chou-chine or chou caraibe in Martinique, malanga in Cuba and Haiti, songe in Reunion and madére in Guadeloupe.

Tarragon: An aromatic perennial plant originating in Central Asia. Its name is derived, via the Arabic tarkhūn, from the Greek drakontian (a serpent-eating bird) - the herb was formerly reputed to cure snake bite. French tarragon is the plant used as a culinary herb for its pronounced, yet delicate, aniseed-like flavor. Russian tarragon is lighter in color and more piquant, but does not have such a delicate taste. Tarragon vinegar is a classic ingredient for salad dressing and sauces. Tarragon leaves are used fresh or they may be preserved by drying or freezing. (Uses: meats, poultry, fish, seafood, veal, casseroles, stews, vegetables, salads and dressings, cheese spreads, gravies, spiced vinegars, spiced butter, egg dishes and with fresh chervil in a béarnaise sauce.)

Tart: A pastry case (shell) filled, before or after baking with savory or sweet ingredients. The words "tart" (tarte) and "flan" are often used interchangeably in Britain and France to designate a pastry filled with fruit, jam, custard or some other filling. In the United States the term often used to describe an "open pie".

Tartar (Tarte): A crystalline deposit left inside wine casks after racking. This by-product of wine consists mainly of crude potassium acid tartrate, which, when purified gives us cream of tartar, used in baking.

Tartare, a la: A term originally describing dishes covered with breadcrumbs, grilled (broiled) and served with a highly seasoned sauce, but now usually used for a sauce or a raw meat dish. Tartar sauce is a mayonnaise made with hard boiled egg yolks, onion and chives and is served with fish, oysters and pont-neuf potatoes. Steak tartare is made with ground beef (or horsemeat, according to purists) served raw with egg yolk and seasoning.

Tartlet: A small individual tart made in the same way as a large tart and with the same fillings.

Taste: The sense by which flavors of food are perceived, the organ used being the tongue, which is equipped with taste buds.

Tâte-vin: A small receptacle made of pewter, silver or silver plate it is used for examining and tasting wine.

Tatin: The name given to a tart of caramelized apples that is cooked under a lid of pastry and then inverted to be served with the pastry underneath, and the fruit on top.

Tavel: A rosé wine which has its own AOC and comes from the southern Rhône valley, in the vicinity of Avignon. Refreshing and always dry, the wines are best when drunk young and fresh.

Tea: The most universally consumed beverage, made by infusing the dried leaves of an Asiatic evergreen shrub, camellia sinesis. There are two main varieties of tea plant, that of China and that of India, with numerous local varieties and hybrids. There are three types of tea, depending on the treatment of the leaves; **green tea**, which is unfermented and roasted immediately after harvesting, gives a strong bitter, although quite clear infusion and; **black tea**, by far the most common, which is fermented and dried; and **oolong tea**, which is semi-fermented and intermediate between green and black tea, white tea, which uses immature leaves.

Teapot: A receptacle with a lid, a spout and handle, used to prepare and serve tea.

Tea Room: An establishment in which tea, hot chocolate, coffee, soft drinks and cakes (and sometimes savory pastries or egg dishes, salads, sandwiches, etc.) are served in the afternoon or at lunchtime.

Tea - the meal: A light meal in the afternoon, at which sandwiches, pastries and cakes are served with tea. A rather more substantial meal is "high tea" which is taken particularly in Scotland and in the north of England, where the evening meal is replaced by tea served with cold meat, fish and salads; as well as buttered rolls, toast and cakes. Afternoon tea is taken at 5 o'clock.

Tempering: Raising the temperature of a cold or room temperature ingredient by slowly adding hot or boiling liquid, often referring to eggs.

Tempura: Typically Japanese shrimp or vegetable fritter, using a light batter made with wheat flour, water and eggs. Tempura is traditionally accompanied by a lightly sweetened sauce and a white radish purée sprinkled with ginger.

Tenderizing: Even good quality meat may be tough for several hours after slaughtering. The storage or hanging of meat at low temperatures (0 - 2° C. - 32 - 36° F.) enables it to mature and become tender before it is sold. The cook can also encourage tenderizing during preparation and by using the appropriate cooking method. Lengthy marinating in acidic ingredients, such a yogurt or citrus juice, for 1 or 2 days, encourages tender results. Papain, an enzyme found in plants and fruits, papaya and pineapples are rich in papain, in particular, is useful for culinary purposes, breaking down protein effectively "digesting" it and making it tender.

Tequila: A spirit made in several Mexican states from the plant Agave tequilana. Some tequila is aged in wood, gaining color; the best is 5 years old and golden in tone.

Teriyaki: Japanese dish of grilled food glazed with a sauce of soy sauce, mirin or sake and sugar to give it excellent flavor and rich color.

Terrine: The preparations known as terrines are numerous and varied. They are usually made with mixed meats, but can also be made with fish, seafood and even vegetables. They are served cold in the container in which they are cooked (or in slices taken from the latter), accompanied by gherkins, pickled onions, and cherries or grapes as a sweet-and-sour garnish. Terrines are also prepared as desserts made with fruit set in jelly, which are severed with cream or a fruit sauce.

Tête-de-Nègre: A ball-shaped confection, consisting of two meringues sandwiched together with chocolate-flavored butter cream. The ball is then coated with more cream and covered with grated chocolate or, more rarely, grated coconut. The name is also given to a dome-shaped rice cake entirely coated with chocolate sauce and surrounded with a ring of whipped cream.

Thermidor: The name of a lobster dish created in January 1894 at Marie's, a famous restaurant on the Boulevard Saint-Denis in Paris, on the evening of the premiere Thermidor, a play by Victorian Sardou.

Thermometer: An instrument used to measure temperature. The meat thermometer has a pointed end and is graduated from 86° F. (30° C) to 248°F. (120°C) and has markings, often in colors, for well-done, medium and rare meat. It is implanted in the center of a joint of meat to measure the internal temperature.

Thicken, (to): To give a liquid, or liquid mixture more "body", making it slightly less runny and not as fine or thin in texture.

Thickening: There are several different methods, depending on the thickening agent used. Thickening may be carried out at the beginning of cooking or at the end.

Thigh: The upper fleshy part of the leg of animals. A thigh of beef provides choice pieces of meat for roasting, such as beef round, rump, bottom round and steak. A thigh of veal provides the fillet and rump, which may be roasted whole or cut into pauplettes or escalopes (for mutton or lamb, gigot, for pork, ham). In poultry, the thigh ends in the drumstick.

Thouarsais Wines: White, red and rosé wines of the Loire Valley. The whites are made from the Chenin Blanc, the reds and rosés from the Cabernet Franc.

Thyme: A perennial plant with small gray-green aromatic leaves and small purplish flowers, much used as a culinary herb and also to prepare infusions. Fresh thyme is particularly good for flavoring scrambled eggs, salads, tomato dishes and lentils, (meatloaves, poultry, meat and poultry pies, fish, seafood, stews, casseroles, egg dishes, vegetables, salads, breads, sauces, spreads). You can also make herb tea with lemon thyme, related to common thyme.

Tilapia: A name for freshwater fish, including several species. Known as a food source since biblical times, with references to them in the parting of the Red Sea, tilapia is usually a gray fish, with firm, white flesh of good flavor.

Timbale: This word is used in various senses. Originally timbale was a small metal drinking goblet. Today, however, the word is applied to a plain, round, high-sided mould and the preparation cooked in it -- a pie crust baked blind and then filled with meat of various kinds.

Tiramisu: Italian dessert invented during the 1970's, based on plain cake or yeasted sweet bread soaked in spirits or liqueur and coffee, topped with a mascarpone mixture, sometimes containing beaten egg yolks lightened with whisked egg whites.

Toad-in-the-Hole: A traditional British dish. It originally consisted of pieces of cooked meat mixed with smoked bacon, covered with batter and baked in the oven. In 1861, Mrs. Beeton gave an excellent recipe for steak and kidney pieces cooked in batter, but specified that and leftover meat could be used instead. Nowadays, it is made with fresh sausages, lightly baked in a shallow dish, covered with pancake batter and then cooked in a hot oven. The resulting crisp, well risen batter and golden sausages are served hot. Good onion gravy is often served with it.

Toast: A slice of bread broiled on both sides in a toaster or under the broiler and served hot. Buttered toast is traditionally eaten for breakfast or tea, often spread with marmalade, honey or jam. It is also an accompaniment to caviar, foie gras, smoked fish and pâtés, and is used as a base for various other savory preparations; cheese, flavored butters; poached, fried or scrambled eggs. A toast is also a proposal to drink to someone's health. This sense of the word derives from the old habit of placing a slice of toast in a glass of hot spiced wine; the glass of wine was passed round among the guests and the slice of toast was offered to the guest of honor.

Toffee: A Canadian sweet invented in the 16th century by Margurite Bourgeoys, who had come from Troyes in France to open the first school in French Canada. To attract the "little savages" she made syrup from molasses which she left to cool down with the first snow of winter. The basic sugar and butter syrup is flavored with nuts, chocolate, mint, licorice or treacle or left plain.

Tofu: Also known as bean curd. A basic foodstuff of far eastern cookery, especially Japanese, prepared from soy beans, which are soaked, reduced to a purée, then boiled, sieved and set in blocks. Originally from China, where it is said to have been prepared as early as the 2nd century B.C., Mongolian doufu was introduced into Japan during the 8th century by Buddhist priests. Relatively bland in taste and very rich in vegetable proteins, tofu is used in a wide variety of Japanese recipes. Chinese doufu is firmer than Japanese tofu.

Tokay: Also known as Tokaju. A world-famous sweet white wine produced in the Tokaji-Hegyalja region of northern Hungary.

Tomate: An aperitif made in Corsica with the local and excellent pastis (aniseed-flavored) and grenadine, which results in a drink looking exactly like tomato juice.

Tomatillo: The tomatillo (Physalis philadelphica and Physalis ixocarpa), also known as the Mexican husk tomato, is a plant of the nightshade family bearing small, spherical and green or green-purple fruit of the same name. Tomatillos originated in Mexico and were cultivated in the pre-Columbian era staple of Mexican cuisine, they are eaten raw or cooked in a variety of dishes, particularly salsa verde.

Even though the Spanish name translates to "little tomato," they are something else entirely. First things first. These little fruits (yes, they're fruits, just like tomatoes and cucumbers) are native to (and largely grown in) Mexico, but have been adopted by American farmers due to their resistance to disease. Tomatillos, sometimes called husk tomatoes, look like green, unripe tomatoes with a dry, leafy husk that wraps around the outside.

Tomatillos have a slightly more acidic, slightly less sweet flavor than ripe and unripe tomatoes. Overall, the flavor is more vegetal and bright, and the interior texture is denser and less watery. Prepping a tomatillo is pretty straight forward. The husks can be easily removed with your hands and discarded. You'll notice a sticky film on the surface, which will come off with a quick rinse under warm water.

Tomato: An annual plant cultivated for its red fruits, which are widely used, cooked or raw, as vegetables, in salads, or to make sauce or juice. Originally from Peru (the name comes from the Aztec tomatl), the tomato was imported to Spain in the 16th century. Until the 18th century it was thought to be poisonous and remained an ornamental plant (call "Peruvian apple" or acacia apple). When its properties as a vegetable-cum-fruit were discovered, the tomato became established in Spain, then in the Spanish kingdom of Naples, then in northern Italy, the south of France and Corsica. The numerous varieties of tomatoes are distinguished according to shape and size; round, ribbed and flattened, elongated or oval, huge or tiny. Some are used while still green or yellow.

Select firm, unblemished tomatoes with some red color. (This indicates that they are mature.) Size does not indicate quality.

If tomatoes are not fully ripe, leave at room temperature until they turn red. Then refrigerate; use within 2 to 3 days. Season: Year round

Tongs: A utensil comprising two arms made of metal, wood or plastic. They are either pivoted or connected by a spring and are used for grasping a variety of foods.

Tongue: Fleshy organ from the heads of slaughtered livestock, which are classed as offal (variety meat) for culinary purposes. Ox (beef) tongue, calf's tongue, pig and lamb's tongues are all used and can be prepared in many different ways; in ragoûts, stewed, boiled and served with highly seasoned sauces.

Torte: A dessert of the cake or meringue type, usually rich in eggs and nuts.

Tortellini: Italian pasta made with small pieces of thinly rolled dough, filled with a stuffing, folded and shaped into rings. They exist in different sizes and shapes and are called tortelli, tortelletti, tortelloni and tortigliani. All of these words derive from **torta** (tart), with various diminutives and augmentatives.

Tortilla (de maiz, de harina): A thin pancake made of cornmeal or flour, which forms an important part of the diet in Latin American countries. It was named by the Spanish conquistadors; in Spanish cookery, tortilla is a flat omelet, usually filled with salt cod or potatoes, which is cut into quarters like a cake (the word has the same origin as **torta**, a tart). The range of condiments and stuffing used include guacamole, chopped raw onion, red pepper; green tomato coulis, grated cheese or think strips of chicken breast. The main dishes prepared with tortillas are **tacos**, a very popular type of sandwich; **enchiladas**, tortillas rolled around their filling, then coated with a sauce and cooked in the oven; **tostadas**, small very crisp tortillas, covered with sautéed or fried red kidney beans, and sometimes embellished with chopped meat, served as hot hors d'oeuvres; **chilaquiles**, thin strips of fried tortilla covered with a highly spiced sauce and cooked in the oven; **quesadillas**, tortillas filled with meat in sauce or vegetables with cheese, folded into turnovers, then fried in lard; **gorditas** a small thick tortilla similar to a pita pocket, made with masa and stuffed with cheese, meat or other fillings; **chalupa**, fried tortilla in the shape of a boat, traditionally served with a spicy filling and topped with salsa, cheese, shredded lettuce; **chimichanga**, tortilla wrapped around a filling, typically of meat, rice, cheese, beans, machaca, folded into a rectangular package; deep fried and topped with salsa, guacamole, sour cream or cheese.

Toss: To mix foods lightly with a lifting motion, using two forks or spoons.

Tray: A large, flat, low-rimmed container, sometimes with handles, used for presenting and carrying to table various foods. It may be made of wood, wicker, glass or metal. A plateau fruits de mer (seafood platter) is an assortment of shellfish served on trays garnished with crushed ice or seaweed.

Treacle: An alternative term for heavy syrup or golden (corn) syrup but usually used in the context of black treacle, which is a dark (almost black), thick product of molasses and sugar syrup. It has a strong bitter flavor.

Trifle: A favorite English dessert - despite its meaning "of no account" - eaten on festive occasions. Also called tipsy cake, it is usually made of sherry-soaked sponge cake with custard and often jam, decorated with cream and sometimes fruit; however, recipes go back to the 16th century with many variations. Zuppa Inglese is a direct copy, created in Naples to honor Lord Nelson in 1798.

Trim, (to): To remove all inferior, unsuitable, or inedible parts from food before cooking. Some cooked items or dishes are trimmed to improve their appearance before serving. For example, poached eggs are trimmed after cooking to remove the rough edges.

Tripe: The stomach of ruminants (especially ox, calf or sheep) used as food. It is usually sold specially prepared or cleaned for cooking.

Trout: A fish of mountain streams, lakes and rivers, high sought after by fishermen. This carnivorous fish, with tasty flesh (its name comes from Greek **trokles**, meaning voracious), is also bred on a large scale in trout farms.

Truffle: 1) A subterranean fungus which lives in symbiosis with certain trees, mainly oak but also chestnut, hazel and beech. A high esteemed foodstuff, the truffle (from the Latin tuber, meaning "outgrowth" or "excrescence") is rounded, of various size and irregular shape, and black, dark brown, or sometimes gray or white in color, it is found especially in chalky soil, or clay, quite near the surface less than 12 inches deep. 2) A very rich chocolate candy.

Truss: To thread one or two prices of trussing twine through the body of poultry or game bird with trussing needle to hold the legs and wings in place during cooking. This is done after dressing the bird; if it is to be braised, poached or fried whole (rather than roasted), and legs are tucked under the skin before trussing.

Trussing Needle: A very large needle, usually of stainless steel, 6 to 12 inches long and about ⅛-inch in diameter, pointed at one end and having an eye at the other. It is used to pass one or two strings of thread through the body of a chicken or game bird in order to keep the legs and wings in place or for sewing up stuffed boned meat.

Tuile: A crisp tin biscuit (cookie), so named as it was considered to resemble the shape of a curved tile. The basic mixture consists of sugar, shredded (or slivered) or ground almonds, eggs and flour, sometimes with added butter and flavored with vanilla and orange. The tuile acquires its characteristic shape by being laid over a rolling pin while still hot, then left to set until cool and crisp. Flat round tuiles (called mignons) are stuck together in pairs with meringue then dried in the oven.

Tulip: Light cookie made with butter, confectioners' sugar, flour and egg whites. The mixture is spread on greased baking sheets, well apart, in circles, using a spoon or a spatula. The hot, soft cookies can be shaped when first removed from the oven by putting them in individual brioche molds. They are served cold and crisp, filled with Chantilly cream, fruit or ice cream.

Tuna: Thunnus thymus. A good source of omega-3 fish oils so high valued by modern nutritionists, tuna was high valued in ancient times as well. The Phoenicians used to salt and smoke it. Five species of tuna are now fished; the albacore, yellowfin, bluefin, blackfin and skipjack, which represents the third grade of canned tuna found in supermarkets.

Turbot: A flatfish living in the sandy pebbly beds of the Atlantic. It is one of the best sea fish. Highly esteemed since ancient times and nicknamed roi du carême (King of Lent) for centuries, turbot has been prepared in the most sumptuous ways. Its white firm flaky flesh, which is particularly delicate and tasty, makes turbot an expensive fish.

Turkey: A farmyard bird raised for its delicate flesh. The turkey was called "Indian chicken" by the Spanish conquerors, who thought they were still in the Indies when they discovered Mexico (hence the French name - a contradiction of poule d'Indies). It was already domesticated in Mexico by the Aztecs; prepared with a sauce containing chocolate, it constitutes the national dish, mole poblano de guajolote. In England, it eventually replaced the Christmas goose, and in the United States it is the traditional dish on Thanksgiving Day.

Good quality turkey meat is finely textured, pale and lean. Roast turkey makes excellent party food, but there are many other ways to prepare turkey. Turkeys are widely available, fresh and frozen, whole or in parts.

A turkey weighs from 5½ to 25 lbs. A small turkey will serve 4 people. While a turkey weighing 9 to 12½ lbs. serves 8 to 10 guests. Frozen turkey is best defrosted in cold water, changing the water often, will take a minimum of 12 hours; defrosting in the refrigerator takes twice as long (depending on size).

Carving a turkey: 1. Cut along breastbone and slice away meat, cutting at an angle; 2. Cut breast meat into slices ½ to ¾ inch thick. Cut away meat from the other breast; 3. Replace slices on turkey and cut off thighs. They can also be sliced down the bone.

Turkish Delight: A Middle Eastern confectionary made of sugar, honey, glucose, syrup and flour - usually cornstarch. It is flavored and colored, usually either pink or green, and often decorated with almonds, pistachio, pine nuts or hazelnuts. Turkish delight (loukoum, or rabat loukoum, meaning "rest for the throat") has a rubbery consistency and is presented as large cubes covered in confectioners' sugar.

Turmeric: A tropical herbaceous plant with an aromatic underground stem which resembles fresh ginger root in shape and form, but with a bright yellow color and dark skin. Turmeric is an ingredient in curry powder. The dried spice has a warm, earthy flavor that goes well with citrus fruit, ginger and cardamom.

Turnip: A fleshy root vegetable, yellow or white in color and often tinged with purple near the leaf bases. European in origin, the vegetable has been cultivated in India for centuries. Turnips should be firm and heavy with unblemished smooth skin. Turnips should be peeled and washed before they are cooked, otherwise they will darken; small new turnips need only be washed. An essential ingredient of pot-au-feu and hearty meat soups, turnips can also be prepared in the same way as carrots, sautéed in butter or cooked with cream.

Look for firm, turnips, heavy for their size, with fresh tops.

Remove tops; refrigerate tops and turnips in crisper. Use turnips within a week or so; use tops as soon as possible. Season: Year round.

Turnover: A pastry in the shape of a semi-circle, made from a thinly rolled round of puff pastry, folded over a filling of stewed fruit, traditionally, apples. Most are individual, but large turnovers, using a simple short crust pastry, may be prepared for several people. Turnovers can also be savory. They are usually small and served very hot, as an hors d' oeuvre or entrée.

Tutti-frutti: Mixed fruit.

Twelfth-Night-Cake: A traditional cake eaten on the day of Epiphany. A bean is inserted in the cake before cooking, and the person whose portion contains the bean is appointed "King" or "Queen" for the occasion. This ceremony probably dates back to Roman times. In Britain, Queen Victoria's Twelfth-Night-Cake of 1849 was described by The Illustrated London News as being of "regal dimensions, being about 30-inches in diameter and tall in proportion". The bean has been replaced by a china figurine of a baby or animal.

U

Ugli Fruit: A tropical plant, originally from eastern India, similar to the lemon tree and having fragrant fruit resembling medium-sized oranges. The Indians who call them bilva or mahura, cook ugli fruit in ashes because of their leatheriness, then eat them in sugar. They can also be made into jam.

Select grapefruit shaped fruit, yellow with greenish splotches and wrinkled, bumpy skin.

Refrigerate; use within 3 to 5 days. Season: March to June.

Unleavened Bread: Describing dough that is without leaven, or yeast. Unleavened bread plays an important role in Jewish ritual; Orthodox Jews consider fermented bread to be profane. According to tradition, unleavened bread symbolizes absolutely pure food, the fermentation brought about by the leavening agent marking the beginning of the process of decay.

Unmold: To turn out a cake, jelly, ice cream and the like from a tin or mould. This is often a delicate operation and should be carried out with care.

Unsweetened or **Baking Chocolate**: solidified chocolate liqueur.

V

Vacherin: A cold dessert, made of a ring of meringue or almond past filled with ice cream or whipped cream (or both). It owes its name to its shape and color, which resembles a cheese of the same name. The classic vacherin is made of rings of meringue placed on top of each other, filled with ice cream of one or more flavors, to which may be added fresh or crystallized fruit, sponge cookies soaked in liqueur, marrons glacés and so on, on a base of sweetened pastry.

Vacherin Cheeses: The name given to several cow's milk cheeses from Switzerland and France (Savoy or Franche-Comté), having a soft texture and a washed rind. It is a cheese that should be eaten quickly, as it rapidly loses its fragrance and flavor, once cut.

Vanilla: A climbing orchid native to Mexico and Central America, where it was discovered by Cortés, and now also cultivated in some islands of the Indian Ocean and the West Indies for its beans. The word derives from the Spanish **vanilla** (little sheath), referring to the long, thin shape of the pod. Vanilla is sold in various ways; in pods, in powdered form (the pods are dried and ground, giving a fine dry dark brown powder, sold pure or sugared); as an essence, or in the form of vanilla sugar.

Veal: The meat of a calf up to one year old, specially reared for slaughter when weaned. Veal is a white, tender and delicate meat, highly prized in cooking, but its quality varies considerably according to the method of rearing. Some popular cuts: *Rib Chop, Sirloin Steak, Blade Steak, Round Steak, Rib Roast, Rump Roast, Shank.*

Veganism: A strict form of vegetarianism in which the diet is based on cereals, fruits, nuts, fresh and dried vegetables and vegetable oils. It excludes all animal products, even eggs, milk and honey.

Vegetables: Herbaceous plants cultivated for food. According to the species, different parts of the vegetables are eaten. For culinary purposes, a distinction is made between fresh vegetables (including greens), dried vegetables (such as beans and pulses) and salads.

Velouté Sauce: One of the basic white sauces, made with white veal, chicken or fish stock, thickened with a white or golden roux. Numerous other sauces are derived from it, allemande, caper, poulette and mushroom sauces, etc. The basic velouté can also be the basis for making smooth, fine rich soups.

Venison: The meat of any kind of deer. In French, however, the term is used not only for deer meat but also for the meat of any large game animal (including wild boar). The word venison comes from the Latin *venatio* (hunt).

Verbena, Lemon: Also known as lemon vervain. The leaves of the evergreen shrub, *Aloysia triphylla*, have a distinct lemon flavor. Fresh verbena leaves contribute their lemony fragrance to stocks, sauces and moist dishes. Whole sprigs can be added to the cooking water for vegetables, rice or pasta, or they can be used to flavor steamed foods. Dried powdered verbena leaves can be added to meat and fish stuffing to give a delicate flavor.

Verdier: The name given to a dish of hard-boiled eggs stuffed with foie gras, placed on a bead of cooked sliced onions, coated with a Béchamel sauce containing truffles, sprinkled with Parmesan cheese and browned in the oven. The dish is attributed to the proprietor of the Maison Dorée.

Verjuice: The acid juice extracted from large unripend grapes or crabapples, which was formerly widely used as a sauce ingredient, a condiment and in deglazing until eventually superseded by the instruction to add a dash of lemon juice in recipes. In the latter years of the 20th century the use of verjuice experienced a revival. It is in general use in Middle Eastern cookery.

Vermicelli: Pasta made in the form of fine strands (name means, "small worms"), often used in soups but also served like spaghetti. "Angel Hair" is a very fine variety of vermicelli, used only in consommés and clear soups. Vermicelli is also used to make certain puddings and soufflés.

Vermouth: An aromatized wine whose name is derived from the German word **wermut** (wormwood or absinthe), this being an ingredient of many recipes for vermouth. Although vermouth, like win, will decline in quality after the bottle has been opened and the contents exposed to the air (in a few weeks for the dry version), it will remain usable for culinary purposes almost indefinitely.

Vert: In Flemish cooking the name au vert (green) is given to a dish of eels cooked with numerous herbs (up to 15), which very according to season and may include, sorrel, spinach, salad cress, white deadnettle, parsley, chervil, tarragon, mint, sage, salad burnet and lemon balm. Sauce vert (green sauce) is a mayonnaise containing a purée of herbs.

Veau: French for veal

Vichyssoise: A leek and potato soup thickened with fresh cream, and served cold, garnished with chopped chives. The name vichyssoise is also given to any cold soup based on potatoes and another vegetable, such as zucchini.

Vinaigrette: A cold sauce or dressing made from a mixture of one part vinegar, three parts oil, salt and pepper to which various flavorings may be added; shallot, onion, herbs, capers, garlic, gherkins, anchovies, hard-boiled eggs, or mustard, for example. It is considered to be a typically French sauce and is often called "French dressing" in Britain. It was the French émigré, Chevalier d'Albignac, who started the fashion in London high society for salads to be dressed in this way.

Vinegar: A sour liquid, widely used as a condiment, consisting of a dilute solution of acetic acid obtained by natural fermentation of wine or any other alcoholic solution. Vinegar, the

French word **vinaigre** mans "sour wine" has been produced and used since the Gallo-Roman era; vinegar diluted with water was a common drink of the Roman legionnaires. In 1682 Pasteur discovered the acidification was caused by a bacterium. Acidification takes place on contact with air; it produces a good vinegar if the wine - red or white - is light, acidic and thoroughly strained to get rid of any residue. Spirit and wine vinegars are mostly used in France and Britain, and the United States, malt and cider vinegar are also widely used.

Vodka: An alcoholic drink made from grain, molasses, potatoes or various other vegetables that are available for distillation. It probably originated in Poland (although countries of the former Soviet Union dispute this) and is now made in many countries. Various vodkas may be flavored with spices, or fruits. It is a neutral spirit and basically has neither taste nor smell. It is mainly appreciated for the stimulus given by the alcohol.

W

Wafer: A small, crisp, light biscuit with waffle-like marks from cooking plates used for the dough. Wafers are mainly produced industrially. They can be plain, shaped like a fan, rolled up like cigarettes or filled with jam or praline cream. Wafer dough is also used to make ice cream cones.

Waffle: A thin, light batter cooked between two buttered plates of a waffle iron. The waffle batter is made of flour, butter, sugar, eggs, and water or milk, sometimes a flavoring, such as vanilla, cinnamon, anise, brandy, or citrus fruit zest. The Greeks used to cook very flat cakes which they called **obelios**, between two hot metal plates. This method of cooking continued to be used in the Middle Ages, by the obloyeurs who made all sorts of oublies, which were flat or rolled into cones. Each area has its own recipe for waffles - they can be savory, made with ham, cheese or pumpkin. The batter can be enriched with cream or butter, or made lighter with whisked egg whites.

Waffle Iron: A hinged cast-iron mould, consisting of honeycomb-patterned plates between which waffle batter is cooked.

Waldorf (Salad): A mixed salad consisting of diced apple and celery and walnuts, dressed with a thin mayonnaise. It is named after the prestigious New York hotel, the Waldorf Astoria, where it originated as a simple apple and celery salad, dressed with mayonnaise.

Walnut: The fruit of the walnut tree, consisting of a hard-shelled nut surrounded by an outer green fleshy husk, called a shuck. The delicious kernel is shaped like the two halves of a brain, which is why the ancient Greeks and Romans believed that walnuts cured headaches. Grown originally on the shores of the Caspian Sea and in northern India, walnuts were valued for their oil. Walnuts are used chiefly in cakes and pastries, either as an ingredient or as decoration. They have a very high caloric content and are an important item in vegetarian diets.

Wasabi: A Japanese plant, wasabia japonica, found growing wild on river banks or cultivated in running water for its root. It is related to watercress, but the root has a hot flavor, similar to horseradish but not as harsh. Fresh wasabi root, which is green in color is grated and used in sushi or mixed with soy sauce and served as a condiment for sashimi.

Water Chestnut: The tuber of an aquatic plant originating in Southeast Asia under similar conditions to those for rice cultivation. The water chestnut has a dark brown skin enclosing crunchy white flesh, which is edible raw or cooked. One of the characteristics of the water chestnut is the fact that it does not become soft or tender during cooking, but retains its pleasing crunchy texture. The flavor is delicate and slightly nutty.

Look for firm, dark reddish brown water chestnuts; avoid dried or shriveled ones.

Refrigerate; use within 1 week. Season: Year round; best in October and November.

Watercress: Any of various plants of the mustard family which are cultivated for the sharp-tasting leaves, which can be eaten raw or cooked. It is believed to be native to the Middle East but is naturalized and widely cultivated in Europe. In the 14th century, it was used mainly for medicinal purposes, but gradually began to be used in soups. When watercress is to be eaten raw, it should be picked over carefully, the thicker stems and yellowing leaves removed, and the rest washed and drained carefully. It should not be left to soak in water.

Watermelon: A large spherical or oval fruit, with a dark green rind and pink flesh, which is sweet and very refreshing but slightly insipid; the pulp is studded with large, flat, black seeds. Of tropical original and known since antiquity, the watermelon is grown in many countries, particularly Spain and the United States. When it is bought, it should be heavy and not sound hollow. In some countries, it is picked when green and unripe and prepared like a vegetable marrow (squash).

Select firm, symmetrically shaped (round or oblong, depending on variety) watermelon with good color (some varieties have darker green stripes); the side of the melon grown next to the ground will be yellowish in appearance. Because ripeness of whole melon is most difficult to determine, look for melons sold in halves or quarters. Flesh should be firm and of good red color, seeds should be dark brown or black; avoid melons with hard white streaks running through flesh.

Refrigerate and use within a week. After cutting, cover cut surface with plastic wrap. Season: April to October.

Wheat: A cereal used to produce flour and semolina that can also be eaten, cooked, crushed, etc. Wheat was cultivated in Neolithic times and was used in griddle cakes and broth. The Egyptians, followed by the Greeks and Romans, used it to make bread. Each grain of wheat consists of a husk (bran) and a kernel. There are several varieties of wheat different uses with the food industry. Gluten-rich hard wheat is used for making semolina, especially for pasta and couscous. Soft wheat is ground for flour of varying degrees of whiteness, depending how much husk is removed.

Whip: To beat rapidly, with mixer, hand beater or wire whisk, so air is incorporated and volume is increased.

Whisk: A kitchen utensil made of tinned or stainless steel wire bent into loops and held together in a handle. An egg whisk, which is short and rounded with flexible wires attached by a ring to a wooden or metal handle, is used for whisking eggs. A sauce whisk, which is longer and has stiffer wires and a metal handle is used to beat custards and various mixtures so that they will not be lumpy.

Whiskey: A spirit originating from Scotland and made from malted grain. It is spelled "whiskey" in Ireland and the United States, but Irish whiskey is different from American whiskey, which is made from rye or corn. Whiskey is generally drunk as an aperitif, on ice, either neat or with plain or soda water; the Scots drink it with a glass of plain water beside it.

White Chocolate: contains no chocolate liquor and is made from cocoa butter, sugar, milk solids and flavorings.

Weiner schnitzel: Breaded, fried veal cutlet, served plain or garnished with lemon, parsley, fried egg, etc.

Wine: A drink made from the juice of the grape; the sugar in the fruit being converted into alcohol by the action of yeasts in the process of fermentation. Red, rosé or white, still or sparkling wine is enjoyed by millions and plays an important role in all kinds of celebrations. Its history is as old as that of civilization. The art of cultivating the vines and making wine was, according to mythology, taught to the Greeks by Dionysus. In fact, it was undoubtedly the Egyptians who spread the art throughout the Mediterranean, particularly in Sicily and southern Italy. In 1867 phylloxera, a plant bug that spread to Europe from North America destroyed the vines in the majority of European vineyards. Built up again later with vines grafted onto American rootstocks, which are resistant to phylloxera, European vineyards now extend over an enormous and increasing area, and wine is of major importance in the European economy.

Wok: A large pan with a rounded base. Traditionally made of cast iron, the wok is designed for cooking over a brazier or gas burner. It is widely used in Chinese cooking, mainly to prepare stir-frying dishes, but also for roasts, sautés, steamed dishes and even soups.

Won ton: A ravioli-like Chinese dish of noodles folded around a filling of meat, fish or vegetables.

Worcestershire Sauce: An English condiment whose recipe was apparently discovered in the East Indies by Sir Marcus Sandys, a native of Worcestershire. On returning home he asked the English grocers Lea & Perrins to make up a sauce that resembled his favorite condiment. It was launched commercially in 1838. It is made of malt vinegar, molasses, sugar, onions, garlic, tamarind, anchovies and other secret flavorings and spices.

Work, (to): To incorporate one or more ingredients into another using a spatula, mixing spoon until they are thoroughly mixed. This operation is particularly used in making beurre manié.

Y

Yam: The elongated edible tuber of a tropical climbing plant of the Dioscorea genus, of which several species are cultivated in Africa, Asia and America. The flesh is white, yellow or pink and the skin may be rough or smooth and white, pink, yellowish or blackish-brown in color, depending on the species. Yams can be used in the same way as white potatoes or sweet potatoes. They can be boiled, peeled of their skins, or baked. The flesh tastes similar to the potato and its texture is floury. In most Southern states, the preferred sweet potato is the orange-fleshed moist variety commonly called "yam".

Yeast: A microscopic fungus that multiplies rapidly in suitable conditions and is used as a raising (leavening) agent in various kinds of dough. In the right conditions, when yeast is mixed with flour and liquid to make dough, it ferments and converts sugar and starch into ethanol and carbon dioxide. This gas causes the dough to rise.

Yellow Onions: The most common type, they account for about three-quarters of the world onion output. Yellow onions are versatile- they are good in everything from soups to chili and stews. They start out pungent but become sweeter as they're cooked.

Yogurt: A fermented milk product with a slightly sour taste, obtained by the combined action of two species of bacteria, streptococcus thermophilus and thermobacterium bulgaricum; these were discovered in the early 20th century by the Russian biologist Ilya Metchnikoff. Made for centuries in the Balkans, Turkey and Asia, yogurt appeared briefly in France during the reign of François I; a doctor from Constantinople treated the kings intestinal trouble with yogurt, but later returned to the East with the secret of its preparation. The product really caught on after World War I, when Greek and Georgian immigrants started serving it in their restaurants or producing it on a small scale for local dairymen. Yogurt, both the product and the word is of Turkish origin, although many French dictionaries give the French yogurt as derived from the Bulgarian jaurt.

Yorkshire pudding: A British specialty from the north of England, Yorkshire pudding is made of a batter of eggs flour and milk, which is traditionally based in the fat or roast beef, for which it is the classic accompaniment. Fat from the cooked roast is poured into a shallow ovenproof dish and the pudding batter is then added; it is cooked in the oven until well-risen, crisp and brown and served with the roast, together with gravy, roast potatoes, a green vegetable, mustard and horseradish sauce.

Z

Zabaglione: A light, foamy dessert of Italian origin, made by whisking egg yolks, wine and sugar together over a gently heat. Zabaglione is served barely warm in cups or glasses; it is also poured over the dessert, poached fruit, a pastry or ice cream. The word is derived from the Neapolitan dialect word **zapiliare**, meaning "to foam".

Zest: The colored and perfumed outer rind of an orange, lemon or other citrus fruit. The zest is separated from the whitish part of the skin (pith) by using a zester or a potato peeler. The zest is used to flavor creams, cake mixtures and desserts.

Zinfandel: A black grape variety, very wide spread in the United States particularly California. Zinfandel makes light, elegant, blush wines, ranging from dry to sweet, as well as fragrant rosés and reds, which can be light and fruity to concentrated and full-bodies with excellent structure. It is thought to be related to the Italian Primitvito grape variety.

Zucchini: A variety of marrow (summer squash) usually eaten when young and immature. It has a fine shiny outer skin, which is edible and firm flesh with a delicate taste. For a long time it was used primarily in Mediterranean countries. They vary in size from baby vegetables with their flowers still intact and small, firm and fine textured examples, to large slightly woody produce. Zucchini can be steamed, braised, sweated with a little butter, fried, deep fried or cooked as fritters. They are equally delicious baked, stuffed, coated in sauce or cooked au gratin. They are also good raw - cut into wedges to be served with crudités or used in salads.

Zuppa Inglese: A dessert invented by Neapolitan pastry cooks and ice cream makers who settled in the big cities of Europe during the 19th century. Inspired by the English puddings that were fashionable at the time, zuppa inglese (English Soup) usually consists of a sponge cake soaked in kirsch, filled with pastry cream and candied fruits macerated in kirsch or maraschino, then covered with Italian meringue and browned in the oven.

Zwieback: A kind of toasted bread or rusk.

ABOUT THE AUTHOR

Raised by my maternal grandmother, I grew up just outside of Princeton, New Jersey, where my grandmother had chickens, pigs and at one time even turkeys, where every spring she planted a large vegetable garden. For years she sold eggs to select customers.

Her garden had everything that could be produced in the northeastern climate; corn, tomatoes, potatoes, lima beans, string beans, carrots, zucchini, cucumbers, sweet potatoes, collard greens, cabbage, turnips, you name it.

Everything she prepared was fresh; she canned what we didn't use. Making jellies and jams, preserves; canning string beans, peaches, apples, even green tomatoes. She used a wood burning stove to bake her bread, rolls and buns. My favorite time of year was when she made her hot cross buns at Easter. She even had an old meat grinder that clamped onto edge of the kitchen table and would make sausage.

I would sit for hours and watch her do all of these things, yet, I had no a clue how she did any of it. I never saw her measure; she used her fingers to add spices and herbs, an old mason jar to add flour or sugar.

I even took Home Economics in high school, which gave me the foundation for cooking and baking basics. It wasn't until a good ten to fifteen years later that I even attempted to cook a meal.

Over the years, through (a lot of) trial and error I managed to cook a few meals and bake a few pies and cakes; but nothing could beat grandmas' cooking.

Printed in Great Britain
by Amazon

54318377R00119